PAKISTAN DESIRES

*Omar Kasmani, editor*

# Pak*istan

QUEER FUTURES
ELSEWHERE

# Desires

DUKE UNIVERSITY PRESS
*Durham and London*
2023

© 2023 DUKE UNIVERSITY PRESS
*All rights reserved*
Printed in the United States of America on acid-free paper ∞
Project Editor: Bird Williams
Designed by A. Mattson Gallagher
Typeset in Warnock Pro by Westchester Publishing Services

Library of Congress Cataloging-in-Publication Data
Names: Kasmani, Omar, editor.
Title: Pakistan desires : queer futures elsewhere /
Omar Kasmani, editor.
Description: Durham : Duke University Press, 2023. | Includes bibliographical references and index.
Identifiers: LCCN 2023001580 (print)
LCCN 2023001581 (ebook)
ISBN 9781478025238 (paperback)
ISBN 9781478020325 (hardcover)
ISBN 9781478027317 (ebook)
Subjects: LCSH: Sexual minorities—Pakistan. | Sexual minority community—Pakistan. | Gender identity—Pakistan. | Gender identity—Religious aspects—Islam. | Gender identity—Law and legislation—Pakistan. | Sex discrimination—Law and legislation—Pakistan. | Human rights—Religious aspects—Islam. | BISAC: SOCIAL SCIENCE / Ethnic Studies / Asian Studies | SOCIAL SCIENCE / LGBTQ Studies / General
Classification: LCC HQ75.16.P18 P35 2023 (print)
LCC HQ75.16 P18 (ebook)
DDC 306.76/095491—dc23/eng/20230515
LC record available at https://lccn.loc.gov/2023001580
LC ebook record available at https://lccn.loc.gov/2023001581

Cover art: Fazal Rizvi, *Coloured Fields 13 (Typewriter Series)* (detail), 2018. Ink on newsprint, 10 × 15 in. Courtesy of the artist.

*May our desires*
—to dream with Billy-Ray Belcourt—
*unfinish us!*

*Contents*

xi  Acknowledgments

1   Introduction
    *stan
    Omar Kasmani

    MEHFIL

23  1  Of Girls, Desire, and Sacred Things
       Syeda Momina Masood

31  2  Loving Men, Loving God
       Shayan Rajani

49  3  Fixed Possibilities
       The Threat of Transmasculinity in the
       Urdu Tale of Agar
       Pasha M. Khan

| | | |
|---|---|---|
| 65 | 4 | **Spaces of Critique, Spaces of Desire**<br>Gender-Crossing in Pakistani Cinema<br>Gwendolyn S. Kirk |
| 83 | 5 | **Partitioned Listening**<br>Sonic Exercises Outside of Archival Time<br>Syma Tariq |
| 100 | 6 | **Miraji's Poetics for Queering History**<br>Geeta Patel |
| 118 | 7 | **This Is Home after All**<br>Nael Quraishi |
| 121 | | **After Heather Love, and Others**<br>Asad Alvi |

## MEHFIL

| | | |
|---|---|---|
| 125 | 8 | **Temporal Nonconformity**<br>Being There Together as *Khwajasara*<br>in a Time of One's Own<br>Vanja Hamzić |
| 146 | 9 | **On the Other Side of the Rainbow?**<br>*Khwaja Sira* Pieties, Politics, Performances,<br>and the Tablighi Jama'at<br>Claire Pamment |
| 166 | 10 | **A Queer History of Pakistani Art**<br>Anwar Saeed and Other Ways of Love<br>Abdullah Qureshi |

| 184 | 11 | Beyond Hooking Up |
| --- | --- | --- |
| | | Tales from Grindr in Pakistan |
| | | Ahmed Afzal |

| 203 | 12 | How I Like It |
| --- | --- | --- |
| | | Nida Mehboob |

| 216 | 13 | Queer *Desi* Formations |
| --- | --- | --- |
| | | Marking the Boundaries of Cultural Belonging in Chicago |
| | | Gayatri Reddy |

| 236 | 14 | Queer in a Time of Kashmir |
| --- | --- | --- |
| | | Jeffrey A. Redding |

| 251 | | Afterword |
| --- | --- | --- |
| | | Everywhere *Mehfil* |
| | | Anjali Arondekar |

| 257 | | *Contributors* |
| --- | --- | --- |
| 263 | | *Index* |

*Acknowledgments*

This book joins many an ongoing quest for queerer and kinder futures in Pakistan. How might we, who live under conditions of straightness, take desire as a critical mode of belonging and queer worldmaking? What shapes might a conversation on queerness take in present-day Pakistan? How might we act today so as to refuse the occlusion of queers in the nation's pasts and futures? It was with such ambition and similar questions that I convened a panel of presentations at the 26th European Conference of South Asian Studies in Paris in July 2018, titled "Pakistan Desires: Queer Futurities of the Urban." While the panel was a success and much fun was had, the importance of gathering in Pakistan was all the more sharply felt. Breaking path in March 2019, a three-day conference was held at the Gurmani School of Humanities and Social Sciences, LUMS University in Lahore: "Queer Futures: Politics/Aesthetics/Sexualities." The incredible Nida Kirmani hosted and helped co-organize the conference—in many ways, a first for Pakistan—and Anjali Arondekar delivered the keynote address. While both these events have served as springboards for this book project, the idea and endeavor of *Pakistan Desires* is also one that has slowly nurtured in the company of friends, many a time, informal *mehfil*s (Urdu for gathering, assembly, forum, party), which became sites of cothinking and desiring together: Asad Alvi, Marvi Mazhar, Jeff Roy, Pavithra Prasad, Rumya Putcha, Max Schnepf, and especially Kamran

Asdar Ali, Nida Kirmani, and Anjali Arondekar—to these friends and allies, a big and heartfelt thank you!

My gratitude in no less measure goes to Elizabeth Ault, our editor at Duke University Press. This project has benefited from her editorial vision and incredible cothinking from its inception, not least her unwavering support and company throughout. I also wish to thank Benjamin Kossack and Bird Williams at the press for shepherding this volume through the production process with great care. Equally remarkable is the love and support this work has received from its three anonymous readers across its various stages and iterations. I remain particularly grateful for their insightful recommendations and their continued faith; this volume is richer for their interlocution. I would also like to acknowledge the support I have received from colleagues at CRC 1171 Affective Societies at Freie Universität, Berlin. My greatest debt, however, is to the sixteen contributors of this book: scholars, artists, writers who agreed to come on board when all I had to offer was an idea; who believed in the endeavor of thinking queer across and beyond disciplines and in and from Pakistan; and who devoted their labors toward turning this dream into a book. Without these incredible companions and their thought-provoking contributions, *Pakistan Desires* would simply not be. I also wish to wholeheartedly acknowledge the synergies and contributions at the two aforementioned conferences as well as friends and allies who do not feature in the book, but have nonetheless inspired and supported this project along the way. In particular, I would like to thank Sara Suhail, Fazal Rizvi, Priya Sen, Bani Abidi, Ali Raza, Hajra Haider Karrar, Faris A. Khan, Kareem Khubchandani, Aimen Majeedullah, Mohsin Shafi, Maha Malik, and the late Madiha Aijaz. All this to say that above and beyond a collection in print, *Pakistan Desires* is a party of a book: a gathering in affectionate companies, a joint labor of love, a shared pursuit of kinder futures, a desirous worlding by way of queer cothinking. Welcome to our *mehfil*!

Omar Kasmani

# Introduction

*stan

To be a Pakistani today is to know half-languages, to always not find the word, to not understand because it had never been spoken. I couldn't come out in Urdu. I couldn't come in Urdu. Being queer, and orgasms, are experiences which I borrow. Without the word, does the thing exist at all?
—Syeda Momina Masood (2019, 176)

We embark from an unlikely place to think queer. We learn how queer thinking in such a place might reflect, refract, even refuse our analytical habits around the term *queer*. *Pakistan Desires* is a thinking in constellation and company that queries how desire emerges and transacts, turns abundant and acquires political charge through queer-affective forms in writing, art, image, sex, religious belonging, and political participation in the context of Pakistan. In a country where a great many civil liberties remain still at bay—and colonial laws criminalizing homosexuality remain unchallenged—desiring serves as a queer-affective rubric for diverse yet shared forms of acting and undermining in emergent and imagined conditions. Thinking queer in Pakistan then, even if a desiring in *half-languages* to lean on Masood (2019, 176), is fully critical so long as it serves to imagine, trail, and gather futures in ways that do not extend shapes of the present.

CONTENTIONS

Nesting in the very invocation, *Pakistan Desires,* is the book's principal and overarching claim. In asserting that a place desires, actively and continually, we declare and articulate not only the multiple ways in which a place feels queer but equally how queer feeling is tied to ideations of place. More critically, we contend that habituated conditions of the present in Pakistan, however restricting, afford a desiring. The desirer-seeker—as captured in the Sufi notion *talib*—invites us to consider the ways in which desiring is at once a commitment to, and a condition of, continual seeking. The emphasis here is not how desirous subjects come into being in a national context or how these might align with neoliberal subjectivities elsewhere, as one might locate in Lisa Rofel's *Desiring China* (2007). Here, desire stands for diverse pathways to pursue, imagine, want, speculate, act out, and realize the tenuous future narrative possibilities of queer lives and loves in Pakistan while also seeking to locally mitigate the "problematic occlusion of queerness"—and by extension of queers—in the narration of its public, national, and more-than-national histories (Henry 2020, 4). So long as queer desire, to quote Gayatri Gopinath, "does not transcend or remain peripheral" to the particular histories we hereby engage but is made "central to their telling and remembering" (2005, 2), we seek to "envision other possibilities of existence exterior to dominant systems of logic" (20). Similarly, we do not proceed from a stance of historical unthinkability or impossibility. This also is not simply a move to repair or recover, or for that matter, furnish Pakistan with a queer past. On the contrary, desire in this volume, to stay with Billy-Ray Belcourt, "is a present-tense verb whirling into the future tense" (2020, 81). It names an abundance-seeking, plurally conceived, forward-moving quest, that critical practice by which we overcome Pakistan's conceptual obstinacies, question its spatial and temporal constitutions, but also insist against the tyranny of its further straight or dominant narration (Kasmani 2023, 152). In other words, desire is that willful affect, which in this gathering of a book—a *mehfil* as Anjali Arondekar calls it in her afterword—binds us in shared purpose and queer companionship.

We proceed in the knowledge that Pakistan, by many a geopolitical measure and argument, is a minoritized form. The contributions in this volume, however, seek to rethink its epistemological value: they reconfigure its cartography in historically and spatially expansive terms and gather supplementary modes of being queer. In a sense, our quest is not one that can be satisfied by the facile statement, *look, Pakistan is also queer!* The introduction of an asterisk—Pak*stan—as part of the conceptualization of this volume has served to stretch, also trouble or make capacious, the idea of the modern nation-state to open it up to shifting conditions and plural possibilities. Composed of two parts, the latter *stan*, from Persian, denotes land or dominion. Pakistan means *land of the pure.* Its cognate in Sanskrit, *asthana*, refers as much to a geographical place, abode, or residence as to one's social location or physical disposition: more precisely, *asthana* is the act of standing. This is also what ties stan to its proto-Indo-European form, preserved in the German verb *stehen*, to stand. In fact, the English words *state* and *status* or the German word for city, *Stadt*, are also related. Its Urdu variation *astana* means home, dwelling, a place of rest or in Sufi terms, a shrine and a threshold. As suffix in place names—Uzbekistan, Afghanistan, Rajasthan—stan can furnish geographies with an encumbrance if not also a temporal backwardness, a *standing* so to speak disadvantageously ascribed to Muslim nations of Central, West, and South Asia. Rescripted, **stan*, whether as place, standing, or position, names a greater historical situatedness though no longer moored to an idea of territory: **stan* is desirous stand, an affective posture so to speak, a threshold to speak from.

And so, here comes another claim: *Pak*stan*, at once a particular place and a capacious geopolitical form, folds into its very idea historical, cultural, and political complexities and unevenness. Such line of thinking isn't entirely solitary. Writing on the trajectories, utopias, and dreams of the Left in colonial South Asia, the historian Ali Raza notes that by the 1940s, Pakistan had become "a concept on which a dizzying array of socio-political aspirations could be projected" (2021, 237). In other words, even before Pakistan existed as a physical place, it existed as a node of desire: it was a "tool," a "tactic" whose "deliberate vagueness" made it both potent and elastic, and whose strength, as Raza notes, "lay in its emotive appeal and in its flexibility to incorporate a potentially vast array of imaginations and interpretations" (2021, 237). With such affective volumes in place, *stan folds out the issue of land by way of complex historical and uneven interrogation. It also helps mobilize, queerly and malleably, the place's alternate imaginings and future-making. Our quest, more precisely, is the following: What might we accomplish if we are to read Pakistan not as a bounded nation-state, but rather an unusual gathering of affective geopolitics, or a hard-to-pin-down postcolonial and geopolitical form that by virtue of its orientation to vibrant Islamic cultures of

West and Central Asia cannot be neatly folded into a straight history of South Asia? Embracing both its singularity and plural orientatedness, we trouble the square and standard historicization of Pakistan as context and idea. With queer ancestors, we go astray; through queer histories, we seek other origin stories. Whether venturing wayward or sideways, we explore narrative pathways that for instance are not moored to the violence of its partition from India in 1947 or do not habitually return to a linear narration of Islam in South Asia (see Rajani, Patel, Tariq, this volume).[1] In exploring and articulating otherwise ways to think in and from Pakistan, we also question, for instance, "whether queer history is always only a history of queer activism (narrowly defined, gay rights and so on). Or can we desire more capaciously, a history of queerness per se, that makes space for and is made up of, differently alternate ways of being queer in the world?" (Kasmani 2022, 154). Here, queer doesn't begin with a catalytic event but nests in the everyday intricacies of life. It follows that the languages, bodies, materials, and archives that authors bring forth are not simply of value to the study of Pakistan or relevant only to discussions within South Asian studies—that too, of course—but more critically, we embrace the position that such gathering in locations of the Global South carries epistemic consequences for queer *mehfil*s elsewhere.

*Pakistan Desires* takes up local or alternate imaginaries and translates them into the idiom of queer scholarship. One of the urgent tasks then that the volume assigns itself is to bring attention to constellations, volumes, archives, and genealogies of queer that unfortunately remain underconsidered if not entirely lost to an English-speaking scholarship. Part of our proposition is that through such labors, some of that important archive refractingly finds its way in the volume through translations, citations, ethnographic detail, and wayward modes of reading, thinking and listening. We also claim that some of these contributions are groundbreaking insofar as our authors are culling and creating knowledge in a field that does not yet exist. In these and other ways, this book is embroiled in the politics of knowledge production: not only does this sharpen perhaps an already strained relationship between queer culture and scholarship; it warrants the admission that Global South scholars remain implicated in the power structures, systems, and institutions of the Global North. Furthermore, we write in the knowledge that foundational queer scholarship is but slowly recovering from an earlier and now questioned assumption that there is no geography to theory. *Pakistan Desires* situates itself in the growing body of "scholarship that strives to think conceptually and comparatively from, rather than simply to write empirically about, the region" (Zamindar and Ali 2020, 10). A more critical aim at hand is to unsettle the impression that some queer cultures are more amenable to idealization, more translatable into scholarship than others. By articulating distinct inheritances of queer and by pursuing its more-than-secular orientations, we point to further ways in which "marginalities within queerness are rendered as elsewheres geopolitically, institutionally, and temporally even in queer scholarship" (Roy et al. 2023, 3).

The individual chapters and collective figurations of this volume, on the one hand, consider, tackle, and enfold the intellectual and cultural diversity that a singular setting like Pakistan offers. There are no less than sixteen official languages spoken in the country. On the other hand, the multicoded genealogies of nonnormative desire and gender variance become present in the volume and are made to travel and translate through refractions of affect, language, and history. To the extent that the past and present expressions of queerness we explore in the expansive context we call Pak*stan "reveal the regulatory mechanisms and resistant forces foreclosed or enabled by a shifting set of geopolitical conditions and related epistemologies" (Henry 2020, 8), we seek narrative and epistemological possibilities for queer lives and loves that cannot correlate to or fall outside the purview of dominant scholarship. Thinking queer is a striving to formulate ways to think in, with, beyond but more critically, alongside the quagmire of a Western-Europe-and-North-America centering queer and affect studies. It engages Pakistani cultural and historical experiences of nonnormative desire and gender variance for a critique of queer thinking and histories of sexuality. It also moves across disciplinary lines and temporal frames so as to find and foreground ecologies of knowledges that are discredited by dominant ways of knowing or have been removed from historical view.

In a recent issue of *Words without Borders,* as part of their introduction to the anthology of *Urdu Feminist Writing* (Alvi et al. 2020), authors forgo the aim of creating a new, rival canon; rather, in gathering such writing's "many different faces, tones, concerns, and aesthetics," they "celebrate multiple, noncanonical perspectives." Through the necessary work of translation, they also orient us to new or previously disfavored idioms (Sufi or *Sufiana* in their usage) within feminist writing as a critical practice of "unmaking." Like them, we conceive this collection as *a provisional space* for diverse bodies and voices to gather, engage, learn, translate and cross-act, make and unmake in queer company. In other words, a great deal of what this volume achieves and articulates is precisely through gathering. One might also say that as a constellation of various voices, aspirations, and views, our response is not so much a singular line of argument as it is a diversely un/folding perspective. The critical work of gathering and collecting we do in this volume is also intently political insofar as we put forth our stories and histories, our lives and loves to serve as not only the object but the very ground for queer theorization. A good illustration of this claim of ours or how a place might serve as a site of critical re/gathering or un/making of queer is given in the volume's readiness to fold in religious inheritances and spiritual subtexts of queer, as several of our contributors do, especially through the region's vast reserve of Sufi-cultural idioms, archives, texts, and contexts.[2] In desiring and seeking expansively, the volume generates equivalences that do not yet exist, most pronounced in how queer traffics through poetics and hermeneutics of Islam. It follows that gathering "queer futures elsewhere" as the subtitle of the volume suggests is a regathering of queer in con/figurations that do not comfortably fit in Euro-American genealogies or that too often sit jaggedly with its secular, if not also Christian, orientations.

In a poem entitled *Nirman* (1994)—meaning neither man nor woman—the Pakistani-American literary figure and self-professed "first Urdu gay poet," Iftikhar Nasim (1946–2011), inhabits a religious template to create queer equivalences. "Here is my revelation / a woman completes another woman / man is the other half of man."[3] He evokes the particular Sufi notion of *kashf* to speak of his radical corporeal un/becoming, what for Sufis is privileged inner knowledge, acquired through mystical experience and often through a direct vision of God. In declaring the self as neither man nor woman, the poet is made free of dualisms and through yet another Sufi metaphysic, *fana'* (annihilation), declares becoming divine: "I am complete Creator." However, transgressive, queer desire thus embedded in sacred aesthetics cannot be taken as simply antagonistic to religion; rather, it is complexly conversant with it. In fact, scholars of Islam, too, have varyingly illustrated how betraying or subverting Islamic-religious code forms part of a religious ethos prevailing in Sufi con/texts at least since the eleventh century (Ahmed 2016; Ewing 1997; Karamustafa 2006). In other words, queer desire thus conceived and explored can be both an *inclination* toward the divine and a *continuation* of historically given possibilities of living an otherwise life.[4]

Queer con/texts like the poem above serve as critical openings that this volume takes up. In fact, the work of exploring other genealogies and archives demands that we read desire in a wider social and interpretive frame, which in this case includes its complex workings with sacred aesthetics and religious affect.[5] For instance, Syma Tariq's contribution in this volume articulates queer-political desire through an unstable listening of the poem *We Shall Witness* by Faiz Ahmed Faiz, which notwithstanding its overtly Islamic-religious vocabulary serves as a communist and feminist anthem of protest in both contemporary Pakistan and India. Syeda Momina Masood's reflection on queerness in this volume is entangled with female spaces of religious devotion. And Shayan Rajani takes on the idea of the beloved, creating equivalences between loving God and loving men. Whether in unequivocal terms or through implicit overtures, several of the authors question "the theoretical emphases and epistemological assumptions" through which we come to know sexuality, its objects and history (Babayan and Najmabadi 2008, vii). At the same time, such attentiveness to alternate universes and the pasts they bear and from where we might cull value in the present is attendant with the hope that such moves uncover pathways for a kind of theoretical forgetting and moving on that Arondekar and Patel have called for in their critique, "Area Impossible" (2016, 159). The multifolded response we articulate through gathering is not in service of making queer slick or more slippery than it already is; rather, following Kadji Amin (2017, 183), our intent is to figure the following: What are those different affective histories or historical affects that give body to queer elsewhere; what sticks to it, what adheres or is shed in such process; how it is developed, deployed, or what happens to it as it takes on life in new or hitherto underconsidered contexts—fields, places, settings, disciplines, geopolitical areas, conceptual and demographic locations? Potentially then, as a place desires, it queers away, so to speak, "the sedimented conditions that constitute what is in place in the first place" (Gordon 2008, 4). So long as queerness is "a doing for and toward the future" (Muñoz 2009, 1), we understand and explore desire as a queer affordance so long as desirous acts lay the ground for other ways of doing place; or to the extent that shared fields of desire help disrupt or intervene into the place's crystallizing pasts and presents; or insofar as such desires' awkward rhythms and less than ordinary refrains afford futures other than those given, prescribed, or inherited.

DEPARTURES

To embark on queer thinking in and from Pakistan, unlikely as it may first seem and sound, is in many ways timely. Recent years have witnessed the extraordinary introduction of additional gender categories in the national identity database and a state-backed landmark move toward transgender rights (locally *khwajasara, khwaja sira*). In May 2018, Pakistan's parliament passed into law the Transgender Persons (Protection of Rights) Act, regressively amended in 2023.[6] Equally significant if not widely known are more grassroot developments like the quiet emergence of a queer film festival, a steady center-staging of sexual identity in Pakistani art practice, and several transgender-led initiatives across the country's urban centers. Challenges abound and gains are fragile: anti-trans sentiment is on the rise and violence shadows the lives of queers and other minorities in Pakistan. Thinking queer in these conditions also allies with increasingly controversial mobilization of the Aurat (Women's) March and feminist-organized occupation of public space;[7] it accompanies a new abundance of on- and offline intimacies through dating apps as much as it seeks historical resonance in the country's Sufi-religious heritage. It is also tied to creative forms and artistic practices that offer diverse and affect rich modes through which the country's queer and gender-variant persons are finding ways of becoming present and public both at home and beyond it. At a time when community-based movements, queer-creative practices, HIV and health initiatives, rights-oriented activism, and transnational networking and global discourse on LGBTQIA*+ are recontouring local idioms of belonging and invigorating forms of queer political participation in the public sphere, this volume introduces a set of critical conversations that are gradually gaining ground in Pakistan.[8] Its essays gesture at the ways in which in the not-yet-here of queerness (Muñoz 2009), Pakistan, notwithstanding the repression and violence of its present, can be understood as a site of critical thinking, imagination, and inquiry.

Authors also know well that a queer conversation in and on Pakistan is new. While queer as a term of reference and claim-making is gaining salience, in particular through literary writing, social movements, and more consistently in film and the fine arts, its reception in Pakistan-centered social sciences research has been slow.[9] In this sense, the chapters evoke if not also navigate an emergent landscape while enabling a much-desired conversation across fields and disciplines. Our engagement with the term queer isn't a flat, outright, or uncritical embracing; rather, it is a response that is acutely aware how its reception in Pakistan, warranting translation, is complexly configured or that it involves shades of skepticism, mistrust, resistance, even refusals. Or that even in instances of its adoption, the term is open to being con/tested, eschewed, stretched, appropriated, and repurposed. Hence, in various ways, authors have sought to think queer broadly, to carry the term beyond the limited frame of sexual identity and lifestyle, to allow room for a critique of power, especially in cases where terms and concepts are "inadequate to the task of representing the polyglot histories that they are made to bear" (Traub 2008, 12). The fact that some of the chapters in this volume engage material and archives that are not entirely metropolitan, comfortably secular, or even gay, or are in excess to the dominant cultural-linguistic spheres of Urdu and English, makes it possible to conjure up queer from less likely, possibly alternate universes or "to think of queer futures in locations where they ostensibly have no collective pull" (Arondekar 2020, 3). Similarly, while *affect* is not a term that contributors explicitly engage with, it is present nonetheless via the register of desire. One might view it as the critical background against which an "ensemble of practices, involvements, relations, capacities, tendencies and affordances" can take shape and meaning across chapters of the volume (Anderson and Harrison 2010, 8). It is a reminder that affect, whether called out or not, is given in the ordinary gathering of elements "a gangly accrual" of forms, rhythms, and refrains in Kathleen Stewart's terms (2010, 339), and which in this volume, inhere in context and traverse texts. Proceeding thus and regardless of terms, references, and categories that might be relevant to contributors' scholarship, their fields of research, and their interlocutors, these inquiries remain broadly interested in political imagination and future-making within contexts of marginality, resistance, plurality, and intersectionality, that is to say politically charged and feeling-driven responses to normative structures in Pakistan. This enables a range of views and perspectives to find place and hold ground in the book.

GATHERINGS

Several contributions in this volume deal with desires that center around issues of time, history, and archives. Others are similarly drawn to ideas of geography, territory, boundaries, and borderlands. Attendant with encumbered geographies and retrograde temporalities, *stan reminds us that histories are after all affective mobilizations in place. Put another way, to think of what has come to pass or be is to consider how time unfolds before us now, the histories we face in place or ones we encounter and dialogue with in the present. It is thus of critical importance to this volume that time is not rendered separate from space in the organization of the chapters, which neither pursue a one-way, backward orientation to the past. Similarly, essays are not singled out on the basis of genre or form. In fact, authors engage a range of interdisciplinary modes and methods. These involve close rereading of textual sources, visual storytelling and analysis, creative nonfiction and poetry, sonic listening, ethnographic fieldwork, and archival research and historical study. In her closing reflection, Anjali Arondekar (<251>, this volume) evokes the Arabic-Persian-Urdu concept of *mehfil*—assembly, celebration, forum—to indicate how such gathering "summons publics into lives of conversation and proximity, at once a place of frenzied engagement and quiet meditation." Embracing her call to gather in affection, the chapters of this book are presented in two clusters, one big *mehfil.* That texts appear in certain company should not take away from the fact that themes, modes, and sensibilities are also shared across gatherings, or that readers will discover their own resonances, continuities, and intimacies, hopefully above and beyond those outlined in this introduction.

"Of Girls, Desire, and Sacred Things" makes for a perfect opening to this volume. Syeda Momina Masood's sharp yet meditative writing compels us to face the distinct scopes and shapes that thinking queerness in Pakistan entails and offers. Masood turns to women's sacred and intimate worlds to comment on the queers in failure and the failings of queerness: "I can't speak of desire without speaking of sacred things" (<26>, this volume), she notes, evoking affinities and equivalences between sacrality and sexuality. In what is a part-memoir, part-manifesto mode, Masood invites her readers to envision queerness in ways that remain largely unaccommodated in, if not also unimagined by, theory. Here, queer refuses as much as it is refused. Or, being queer or named such intersects with normativities of class and ethnicity; it flourishes in the space of separation, to lean on her formulation, "through strange little sacred rituals" (26) that are directed at other women, female saints as well as God. A most fitting follow-up comes in the shape of "Loving Men, Loving God." Shayan Rajani's expansive reflection engages multiple Sufi figures across historical time and space. In reading Sufi biographical accounts and dictionaries (*tazkira*s), Rajani takes to historical task overlapping notions of cross-faith and same-sex love. Without giving in to the seductions of types and identities—Hindu, Muslim, gay, straight—he identifies distinct ethics of love and intimate modes of mutual transformation, a kind of moving toward each other through the space of separation. So astute is this intellectual move in the between of categories that it also forgoes an impulse for periodization. The account that Rajani crafts is rendered aslant to time to skillfully accommodate, to quote the author's claim, "past's desire to make its own future" (31, this volume). What's more is that the account Rajani crafts serves as a historical mirror for his own desires and politics in present-day Pakistan.

In "Fixed Possibilities," Pasha M. Khan identifies both an unsettled and unsettling transness through his reading of the mid-nineteenth-century Urdu tale of Prince Agar. Here, the protagonist is a transmasculine figure assigned female at birth. And the genre, *qissah*, or what Khan contingently defines as a tale of possibilities, is in fact a queer ecology that unfolds through narration. Transgressions abound as do transformations; kinship works across species and against heteropatriarchy. Yet Khan parses a cautious telling. His careful deliberations on fixity and transness compel the reader to consider what precisely is at stake here and for whom; what temptations and obstinacies do historical forms present; how or when might we rightfully celebrate these as queer; what transancestor-making potentials and desires come attached with the tale; or, broadly speaking, how might we critically asses our own affective relations to past archives and the work of their parsing in the present? A comparable discussion of limits is differently evoked through filmic desire in "Spaces of Critique, Spaces of Desire." In a thoroughly intersectional reading of gender with class, language, and ethnicity, Gwendolyn S. Kirk analyzes three Pakistani films—two in the Punjabi language and one in Urdu. She focuses on the films' gender-crossing and gender-bending performances, their overall treatment of sexuality and instances where distinctions between homosociality and homosexuality are hard to uphold or imagine. These films, as she critically notes, are not closed texts, but complex sites of critique and play; "they open up rare spaces for subversion of gender norms, for crossing the normative limits of desire, and for critique of the heteropatriarchy" (78, this volume). And yet, she observes how these remain "productive sites for both queer and heteronormative desire" (66, this volume). Inasmuch as the undermining of norms here is not limited to gender, the space to do so also exceeds the narrative arcs of the films. Kirk additionally points the reader to the films' queer affordances, which is to think of these as affective archives, or the interpretive possibilities, agencies, and potentials that can and do arise as viewers and scholars interact with these cinematic texts.[10]

In "Partitioned Listening," Syma Tariq refigures the Partition of British India as a "sonic condition" and queers its historical narrativization from a place of unstable diasporic listening. She asks "how, as partitioned subjects, can and do we listen?" (84, this volume). Focusing on the Pakistani Communist Faiz Ahmed Faiz's poem, *Hum Dekhenge* (We Shall Witness), and folding public history, family archives, and fictive truths, she articulates a temporal continuum through listening that ties the poem's iconic rendering in the female voice of Iqbal Bano in 1986 (in Lahore) to its new life as an anthem for feminist movements in India, especially popular in the recent protests of 2019 (in Delhi). Tariq's intellectual labors of listening to the event of the Partition, a form of counter listening, not only troubles the colonial division of geography but also unsettles the straight ways in which we separate and compartmentalize the past, the present, and the future. In "Miraji's Poetics for Queering History," Geeta Patel invites her readers to tarry with an affective between-ness featuring two historically removed literary figures, or "wanderers," as she calls them. Miraji, a twentieth-century Urdu modernist poet in Lahore, and Sappho, a seventh-century Greek lyricist, are brought together in the space of *hamdardī*, literally, sharing pain. Here, translation, just as her own writing performs, is foreplay. It is not invested in returning safe and secured but is rather a transiting course that involves moments of mislaying, misplacing, forgetting, and lapsing, a "finding en route to remembering," as she calls it (102, this volume). Such intent for something else, something more than, helps the reader understand what she means when she asks, "how might we queer the desires we invest in queer archives?" (114). It is through such forgetful moves and finding through wayfaring that Patel assembles but also performs an affective theory of history, archives, and translation from the Global South.

The *mehfil* ascends with a visual essay by Nael Quraishi. "This Is Home after All" explores diasporic homemaking not through the lens of being away or beyond but through affections and intimacies of the in-between and the also-here. Here home is not a place but an affective imbrication: Quraishi juxtaposes by way of collaging that what is visually familiar across disparate geographies, Pakistan and the Netherlands. The result is a compound scenography, images layered with worded reflection, a form of remembering through picturing, or making present what is removed or left behind.

Pivoting the book's two gatherings is an interlude in verse. In the poem "After Heather Love, and Others," Asad Alvi conjures up a bilingual space of queer affect across languages, Urdu and English. Memory rises up and an affective kin-making unfolds. Not only does Alvi tie theory with poetry, two epistemic worlds sometimes seen as oppositional; verses fold ideas of *gham* (sadness) in Urdu poets Ghalib and Josh with Heather Love's notion of feeling backward.

The *mehfil* resumes with Vanja Hamzić's chapter on the distinct and shared experiences of temporality among Pakistan's gender nonconforming communities (*khwajasara*). In "Temporal Nonconformity," he reflects on how a being-there-together for *khwajasara* involves idiosyncratic, multidirectional time-making but also altogether otherworldly temporalities. Examining the processes of distemporalization and through reflections on communal experience, the chapter points to the varied ways in which a specifically Pakistani gender-nonconforming subjectivity—a space and a time of their own—is forged while sharing at the same time memories and performances from a greater South Asian and Muslim historical context. Such desirous re/turn to historical subjectivities reveals, in Hamzić's own words, "some potentially productive tensions between present-day *khwajasara* and *hijra* views of the(ir) past and those of the(ir) historians" (127). In yet another compelling portrait of local transgender communities, Claire Pamment's ethnographic study reveals the complex involvement of *khwaja sira* individuals in the Tablighi Jamaat, an Islamic missionary movement. "On the Other Side of the Rainbow?" discusses transgender performances of piety and repentance that overlap with bodied and discursive processes of "detransitioning." Pamment argues that alongside their investment in community work, civil rights initiatives, and transnational LGBTQI+ networks, such individuals explore and find "a multiplicity of pious, political and/or aesthetic possibilities" (147) through their religious affiliations though outside normative ideals of queer possibility.[11]

A desire for venturing out can also be observed in "A Queer History of Pakistani Art." Abdullah Qureshi outlines an artistic trajectory of male erotic representation through the work of the contemporary painter Anwar Saeed (b. 1955). Across a visual practice spanning four decades, Qureshi locates depictions of classed masculinity and homoerotic desire that traverse conventions of Western art and local ecologies of spirituality and sexuality. The chapter establishes how such desire and its visual representation, in the artist's terms of reference, exceed but also resist "Western" labels such as gay or queer. Such considered refusals or going beyond—"other ways of love"—reveal at best a search for genealogies that are not removed from grounded realities, or which, if and when articulated, promise to mobilize a specific historical experience of desire. Striking a similar chord in the present is "Beyond Hooking Up." Ahmed Afzal observes how digitally mediated engagements on social networking and dating apps such as Grindr are impacting constructions of sexuality and desire in urban Pakistan when it comes to intimacies and relationships among gay and bisexual men. As Afzal observes, given the absence of gay public life, online dating and networking provide critical forms of care, sociality, community, and identity-building. Weaving private reflection with ethnographic fieldwork, Afzal crafts for his readers a scenography of digital intimacies: we come to appreciate how users variously explore these networks to realize their sexual fantasies, to refashion their identities along gay cosmopolitan lines, or to simply deal with loneliness, even violence, all this while having to negotiate familial expectations or the conflicting pull to abide by religious or societal heteronorms.

A poignant parallel to male desire and men's intimate worlds of the previous two chapters is to be found in Nida Mehboob's visual essay "How I Like It." Titled after the documentary film of the same name from which the essay is also derived, it captures the extraordinary ways in which women in the film speak of, and describe, their sexual fantasies involving men and other women. Mehboob's film unsettles the silence on women's sexualities in Pakistan while also preserving it for the viewer. Women are not captured—at least not visually; instead, the camera contrastingly focuses on male bodies, intimacies, and socialities in Pakistani public space. The affective dissonance that results is intentional: women's voices and desires are juxtaposed with the film's masculine imagery. Composed of stills from the film, the short sequences—images and the spoken text assembled— afford a rare view into women's intimate lives and loves in a sexually repressive, often hostile, social and material environment.

The final duo of chapters in the volume reinscribe a beyondness of territory and geography that among other things is recorded by the asterisk in the particular conjuring that is Pak*stan. Reflecting on her fieldwork in Chicago from the early 2000s, Gayatri Reddy offers a retrospective account of *desi* gay men's desire for communal and sexual belonging in the diaspora. With a mix of ethnography and microhistory, "Queer *Desi*

Formations" tackles imaginations of community as these intersect with normativities of sexuality, ethnicity, and class in America. Revolving around the Pakistani diasporic figure of Iftikhar Nasim, or Ifti, an Urdu gay poet and Chicago socialite, Reddy observes the boundaries and expansions of cultural belonging beyond the nation while asking how racialized/brown queers "articulate and negotiate their subject position in the public arenas/ narratives of (white) gay cosmopolitanism in the U.S." (217). Closing the desirous mehfil is a spectacular meditation on the queerness of geography and gender. "Queer in a Time of Kashmir" identifies but also opens an insightful space of dialogue between the historic conflict over Kashmir and the discourse on transgender rights and politics in South Asia. Through entangled themes of self-determination and sovereignty, Jeffrey A. Redding observes how the uncertain implications of transgender rights echo a history of Pakistan's originally bifurcated, possibly also weird, imagination as a national space—across eastern and western wings, now Bangladesh and Pakistan. Insofar as queerness, as Redding observes, "is also about nonintuitive understandings and configurations of social and political power" (238), the chapter illustrates an affective resonance between territorial disputes and the historical and spatial incongruities that accompany the work of demarcating sovereignty and community in Pakistan and South Asia.

OPENINGS

*Pakistan Desires* takes up Arondekar and Patel's (2016) invitation for non-Euro-American epistemes and engages the politics of queer and area studies as coincident (152–54). As they make plain, the project is not simply adding queer to area (153). Rather, to tackle "geopolitical flattenings in queer studies" (155) and seek queer hermeneutics that refuse—through modes of forgetting—"the seductions of homing devices, of theoretical pathways that suture geopolitics to forms (refused or otherwise) of region, area, nation" (159). With cross-cutting interests in affects of language, location, and histories, this collection is a re/membering through forgetting in that it invites reflection on what meanings adhere to queer in Pakistan or what might it mean to speak from here—a *stan—where here stands in for places rendered elsewheres to queer thinking. As Anjali Arondekar (2020) notes in her returning thoughts on *Queer Futures*—one of the events from which this volume proceeds—"Pakistan is as much the minoritized and fetishized geography within South Asia as is South Asia in globalized histories of sexuality" (3). It follows that our attentiveness to left-behind, bypassed locations such as Pakistan—"places that are inherently non-recuperative, not discovered (again)" (4) ought to disturb settled habits of theorizing and politicizing sexuality. It is also to say that our investment in the question of location isn't a search for an autochthonous figure of the queer in Pakistan. Neither is it to confirm queer epistemes or idealities by merely transposing these in a different geopolitical location—historical and archival labors carried out in reparative or recuperative spirit or that seek to anachronistically restore queerness to non-Western histories and contexts (see Khan, this volume). It is in fact driven by a geopolitical pursuit whereby queerness is not located/locatable in one place any more than it is situated in another, which is to say "that it is not in any way more here than there, more now than before; that it is tied to the logic of cities and secularities in a way that it is unmappable in religious or non-metropolitan life-worlds" (Kasmani 2019, 36). Pursuing queerness in relation to place is, on the one hand, to temper, an analytical overemphasis on subject formation or queer identitarian discourse and, on the other, to privilege, how queerness worlds in the persistence of affect, rhythms, and refrains that insist against the tyranny of straight place, in this case, Pakistan. At the same time, the oversights we highlight, the blind spots we address, and the kinds of interventions we undertake by reading "other historical modes of same-sex sexuality, cross-gender identification, and nonnormative intimacies" (Henry 2020, 4) will hopefully also resonate with other locations.

Across many conjurings, Pak*stan in this volume emerges as a world in which we can locate ourselves, yet it is one that cannot be folded back to singular or exclusive frames of belonging. This, on the one hand, bolsters the view that "the nation and the nation-state are always tentative and ambiguous, one location in a complex of competing narratives of attachment and belonging" (Zamindar and Ali 2020, 10). On the other, its polyvocal routes and more-than-local shapes echo both the ambition and the methodology that Asad Ali and Kamran Asdar Ali propose in their introduction to *Towards Peoples' Histories of Pakistan* (2023): "to shift away from the singularity of the nation state" (1) and to stay attentive to forgotten pasts and othered subjects, "inaudible in the grand narratives of national history" (7). Such moves are lined with the hope that together we arrive at something different from the sticky, now weary ways in which Pakistan has come to be viewed and understood. At the same time, *Pakistan Desires* as a queer *mehfil* resists capture or intelligibility through standardized framings of discipline and area. This said, we take joy in the fact that this queer volume is a first for Pakistan. The conversation, emergent and particular as it might be, is nonetheless able to draw from fields as diverse as history, anthropology, law, literature, art, film, and performance studies. Given the volume's disciplinary range, one promise lies in reading queer from multitheoretical, intersectional perspectives while opening up the contours of queer theory itself to unlikely sites of dialogue. Beyond its regional interest, we hope this endeavor is equally critical for conversations in the field of queer studies. Finally, this gathering of ours—of scholars and scholarship—is, by many means, groundbreaking, if not also timely. Given the want of research on the subject as well as the area, such effort, as readers will appreciate, is also ambitious to begin with. Precarities loom large, institutional support is scarce for such research in Pakistan, and interviews and interlocutors are hard to find. Scholars are themselves vulnerable, at risk. Our shared aim, despite our divergent attachments, is to invigorate a conversation where there is little, to intervene in local structures and global institutions of knowledge-making, to insist on other possibilities of queer, to find new allies, to tell less-told stories of places we inhabit or come from, and, above all, to do so in familiar and queer company.

NOTES

1 For history of the Partition, see Zamindar 2010.
2 Such articulation of desire between historically disinclined analytical objects, queer and religion, is distinct from Islamizing queer or queering Islam. For more on the politics of reading religion and queer, see the coda in Kasmani 2022.
3 Author's translation from Urdu into English.
4 For an Islamic politics of religious-social deviance in a Sufi historical context, see the introduction in Kasmani 2022.
5 For same-sex desire and the erotic in Islam, see Mian 2019; on Sufi desire, intimacy, and corporeality, see Kugle 2007, Shaikh 2012, and Bashir 2011. Notable studies include Scott Kugle's monograph on saints' bodies and desire (2007), Vanja Hamzić's research on sexual diversity in the Muslim world (2016), and the volume *Islamicate Sexualities* edited by Babayan and Najmabadi (2008).
6 On the governance of sexuality, transgender rights, and activism in Pakistan, see Redding 2015, Toor 2011, Khan 2019, and Kasmani 2021. On colonial and

decolonial perspectives on transgender in South Asia, see Dutta and Roy 2014 and Hinchy 2019.

7  On the recent controversies and reactions about the Women's March in Pakistan, see Khatri 2020.

8  These lines of thought also spring from two events that have centered queer issues in relation to Pakistan: a panel at the 26th European Conference of South Asian Studies in Paris (July 2018) titled "Pakistan Desires: Queer Futurities of the Urban" and the conference "Queer Futures: Politics/ Aesthetics/ Sexualities" at the Gurmani School of Humanities and Social Sciences, LUMS University in Lahore (March 2019). To expand the scope of the edited volume beyond the proceedings of the aforementioned events, more scholars were invited with new themes in mind.

9  Research on queer women's lives and loves in Pakistan has been hard to identify and include. An emphasis on gay male life is also tempered by essays on transgender communities of Pakistan as well as by contributions that take a nonmale-centered stance.

10  For more on desire in Pakistani films, see Zamindar and Ali 2020.

11  On pious performance, religious ideas, and lexicon in transgender movement, see also Pamment 2019; on spirituality among *khwaja-sira*, see Jaffer 2017.

BIBLIOGRAPHY

Ahmed, Shahab. 2016. *What Is Islam: The Importance of Being Islamic.* Princeton, NJ: Princeton University Press.

Ali, Asad, and Asdar, Kamran A. 2023. *Towards Peoples' Histories in Pakistan: In(audible) Voices, Forgotten Pasts.* London: Bloomsbury Academic.

Ali, Kamran. 2020. "On Female Friendships and Anger." In *Love War and Other Longings: Essays on Cinema in Pakistan,* 114–30. Karachi: Oxford University Press.

Alvi, Asad, Amna Chaudhry, Khan F. Mehak, Anjali F. R. Kolb, Geeta Patel, and Haider Shahbaz. 2020. "Urdu Feminist Writing: New Approaches." *Words without Borders: The Online Journal for International Literature.* March Issue. https://www.wordswithoutborders.org/.

Amin, Kadji. 2017. *Disturbing Attachments: Genet, Modern Pederasty, and Queer History.* Durham, NC: Duke University Press.

Anderson, Ben, and Paul Harrison, eds. 2010. *Taking-Place: Non-Representational Theories and Geography.* Farnham: Ashgate.

Arondekar, Anjali. 2020. "The Sex of History, or Object/Matters." *History Workshop Journal.* doi.org/10.1093/hwj/dbz053.

Arondekar, Anjali, and Geeta Patel. 2016. "Area Impossible: Notes toward an Introduction." *GLQ: A Journal of Lesbian and Gay Studies* 22, no. 2: 151–71.

Babayan, Kathryn, and Najmabadi, Afsaneh, eds. 2008. *Islamicate Sexualities: Translations across Temporal Geographies of Desire.* Cambridge, MA: Harvard University Press.

Bashir, Shahzad. 2011. *Sufi Bodies: Religion and Society in Medieval Islam.* New York: Columbia University Press.

Belcourt, Billy-Ray. 2020. *A History of My Brief Body.* Columbus, OH: Two Dollar Radio.

Dutta, Aniruddha, and Raina Roy. 2014. "Decolonizing Transgender in India: Some Reflections." *TSQ: Transgender Studies Quarterly* 1, no. 3: 320–37.

Ewing, Katherine P. 2006. *Arguing Sainthood: Modernity, Psychoanalysis and Islam.* Durham, NC: Duke University Press.

Gopinath, Gayatri. 2005. *Impossible Desires: Queer Diasporas and South Asian Public Cultures.* Durham, NC: Duke University Press.

Gordon, Avery. 2008. *Ghostly Matters: Haunting and the Sociological Imagination.* Minneapolis: University of Minnesota Press.

Hamzić, Vanja. 2016. *Sexual and Gender Diversity in the Muslim World: History, Law, and Vernacular Language.* London: IB Taurus.

Henry, Todd. 2020. *Queer Korea.* Durham, NC: Duke University Press.

Hinchy, Jessica. 2019. *Governing Gender and Sexuality in Colonial India: The Hijra, c. 1850–1900.* Cambridge: Cambridge University Press.

Hussain, Salman. 2019. "State, Gender and the Life of Colonial Laws: The *Hijras/Khwajasaras*' History of Dispossession and Their Demand for Dignity and *Izzat* in Pakistan." *Postcolonial Studies* 22, no. 3: 325–44.

Jaffer, Amen. 2017. "Spiritualising Marginality: Sufi Concepts and the Politics of Identity in Pakistan." *Society and Culture in South Asia* 3, no. 2: 175–97.

Karamustafa, Ahmet. 2006. *God's Unruly Friends: Dervish Groups in the Islamic Later Middle Period, 1200–1550.* Oxford: Oneworld.

Kasmani, Omar. 2017. "Audible Specters: The Sticky Shia Sonics of Sehwan." *History of Emotions—Insights into Research,* October. doi 10.14280.08241.54.

Kasmani, Omar. 2019. "Thin Attachments: Writing Berlin in Scenes of Daily Loves." *Capacious: Journal for Emerging Affect Inquiry* 1, no. 3: 1–36.

Kasmani, Omar. 2021. "Futuring Trans*: Timely Reflections." *TSQ: Transgender Studies Quarterly* 8, no. 1: 96–112. doi 10.1215/23289252-8749610.

Kasmani, Omar. 2022. *Queer Companions: Religion, Public Intimacy, and Saintly Affects in Pakistan.* Durham, NC: Duke University Press.

Kasmani, Omar. 2023. "Queer in the Way of History." In *Towards Peoples' Histories in Pakistan: In(audible) Voices, Forgotten Pasts,* edited by Asad Ali and Kamran Asdar Ali, 141–54. London: Bloomsbury Academic.

Khan, Faris A. 2016. "Khwaja Sira Activism: The Politics of Gender Ambiguity in Pakistan." *TSQ: Transgender Studies Quarterly* 1, no. 3: 158–64.

Khan, Faris A. 2019. "Translucent Citizenship: *Khwaja Sira* Activism and Alternatives to Dissent in Pakistan." *South Asia Multidisciplinary Academic Journal* 20. http://journals.openedition.org/samaj/5034.

Khatri, Sadia. 2019. "Should Feminists Claim Aurat March's 'Vulgar' Posters? Yes, Absolutely." *Dawn.* March 15. https://www.dawn.com/news/1469815.

Kugle, Scott. 2007. *Sufis and Saints' Bodies: Mysticism, Corporeality, and Sacred Power in Islam.* Chapel Hill: University of North Carolina Press.

Masood, Momina. 2019. "Of Dark Rooms and Foreign Languages." In *Halal If You Hear Me*, edited by Fatimah Asghar and Safia Elhillo, 176–79. Chicago: Haymarket Books.

Mian, Ali Altaf. 2019. "Genres of Desire: The Erotic in Deobandī Islam." *History of Religions* 59, no. 2 108–45.

Muñoz, Jose Esteban. 2009. *Cruising Utopia: The Then and There of Queer Futurity*. New York: NYU Press.

Nasim, Iftikhar. 1994. *Nirman*. [E-book]. Kitaabpoint.blogspot.com.

Pamment, Claire. 2010. "Hijraism: Jostling for a Third Space in Pakistani Politics." *The Drama Review* 54, no. 2: 29–50.

Pamment, Claire. 2019. "Performing Piety in Pakistan's Transgender Movement." *TSQ: Transgender Studies Quarterly* 6, no. 3: 297–314.

Raza, Ali. 2021. *Revolutionary Pasts: Communist Nationalism in Colonial India*. Lahore: Folio Books.

Redding, Jeffrey A. 2015. "From 'She-Males' to 'Unix': Transgender Rights and the Productive Paradoxes of Pakistani Policing." In *Regimes of Legality: Ethnography of Criminal Cases in South Asia*, edited by Daniela Berti and Devika Bordia, 258–89. New Delhi: Oxford University Press.

Rofel, Lisa. 2007. *Desiring China: Experiments in Neoliberalism, Sexuality, and Public Culture*. Durham, NC: Duke University Press.

Roy, Jeff, Pavithra Prasad, Rumya Putcha, and Omar Kasmani. 2023. "Introduction: Queer Elsewheres ⇓ ◊ Un/Desirable Journeys." *Feminist Review* 133, no. 1: 1–10.

Shaikh, Saʿdiyya. 2012. *Sufi Narratives of Intimacy: Ibn ʿArabi, Gender, and Sexuality*. Chapel Hill: University of North Carolina Press.

Stewart, Kathleen. 2010. "Worlding Refrains." In *The Affect Theory Reader*, edited by Melissa Gregg and Greg Seigworth, 339–53. Durham, NC: Duke University Press.

Toor, Sadia. 2011. "Gender, Sexuality, and Islam under the Shadow of Empire." In *The Scholar and Feminist Online* 9, no. 3. http://sfonline.barnard.edu/religion/toor_01.htm.

Traub, Valerie. 2008. "The Past Is a Foreign Country? The Times and Spaces of Islamicate Sexuality Studies." In *Islamicate Sexualities: Translations across Temporal Geographies of Desire*, edited by Kathryn Babayan and Afsaneh Najmabadi, 1–40. Cambridge, MA: Harvard University Press.

Zamindar, Vazira, and Asad Ali, eds. 2020. *Love, War and Other Longings: Essays on Cinema in Pakistan*. Karachi: Oxford University Press.

Zamindar, Vazira F.-Y. 2010. *The Long Partition and the Making of Modern South Asia: Refugees, Boundaries, Histories*. New York: Columbia University Press.

Syeda Momina Masood 1

# Of Girls, Desire, and Sacred Things

IN URDU ARE WE EVER QUEER?

We have been many things before we were queer. When you don't do gender right, there is an increasing chance of being called *paindu* in certain parts of Pakistan. *Paindu* in Punjabi should technically mean someone from a village, but *paindu* has also been you when you let your body take up space, to finally let it breathe. Your unshaved legs, peeking from your trousers, the *dupatta* around your neck instead of on your chest, your masculinity as a woman, your girl-boy in-betweenness, might get you called *paindu* instead of anything else. For the longest time, I was *paindu* first, queer later. And so, I believed being queer was a class thing, a language thing, a history thing. A certain social class, a certain type of Pakistani is just always queer. The *paindu* in Punjabi is sometimes assigned when you fail gender, but failing gender sometimes means failing class and you never knew which one you're guilty of.

Urdu, unlike Punjabi, is respectable. Punjabi is for the tomboy, for the uncouth, for the small hairs above her upper lip, for the indecent, the vulgar, the working class, the rural, and sometimes, the queer. Urdu, however, is decent. Urdu, for a certain social class, is propriety and *adab* and *lehaz* and women knowing how to be women and not something less or something more. The Urdu of my mother does not have words for most of my body or the way it desires. The way it fucks. The way it bleeds every month and still carries on. Urdu doesn't know what to do with us on days when we are neither man nor woman, the days we are just flesh, the days we are abject and full of joy. Urdu demands a certain Pakistaniness, a certain costume, a drag we wear in formal settings to pass as woman, as man, as one knowable thing, as decent and respectable as knowable things come.

You were many things first before you had to use *queer* to make up for the words your mother didn't have, to conjure a language for pleasure and joy and shame. A language for the body and its in-betweenness, its failure, its excess, its lack. A language for when you failed gender, for when you simultaneously failed class, a language your country would let you live with, a country that has never really known what to do with the many languages it inherited. You have been many things in Urdu but never queer and you have been all types of queer in English but never ones that didn't feel like betrayal in your mouth. English lets you come out of the closet it put you into in the first place, English lets you become legible even as it erases you. Your desire remains illegible in Urdu, but in Urdu you have a name. In Urdu, you have a country. Or so they tell you. One you have never known what to do with, but one that hides you just as well.

FROM WHERE THE WILD THINGS ARE

You were quite young when you realized the ways in which girls loved one another despite their mothers, despite their many gods, without fully knowing what it meant to want and nurture and desire. They would let you know if you ever bled through your college uniform during your period, they would let you know what to do with the body when it became too much. They'd hand you their burqa to cover yourself then when that is not what the point ever was. What was the point exactly, you forget. No one used the veil the way it was supposed to, not as you would think. The girls you grew up loving would pass around the burqa as if it were a plaything, something to be used for indecent purposes, to hide the body when it spilled over, to keep tangled limbs unseen, and touch that lingered private. We were young when we learned to love, to use God to hold hands and braid hair, to hide in the city and be held.

To write the body in its queerness, its Muslimness, its Pakistaniness, in its utter failure to be anything at all, in the way it loves and hides, I am constantly aware of you. If I unravel, I unravel for you, to make the unknowable into something you can name, and later, own, as you do with all things, especially ones that are wild. But we have never been good with the languages we inherited and your languages have never been good with/to our bodies, so we trade legibility for incoherence for to be legible to you means losing the few words I still have. To be legible to you means losing my mother.

During my travels abroad, I'm usually asked: "What's it like over there?" I'm aware of this question even now, and yet I no longer pretend to answer. There for you is here for me, here where the wild things are that must be known and named and owned and held in glass cases hung in museums all the way over there. Here means a country, without a language of its own and yet too many poets, a country with violent inheritances, that still does not know how to keep the bodies it lays claims to, a country that feels like a revolution even on days when nothing happens, a country that is more wound, more ritual than home, a country that is a set of half-forgotten stories we pass on in languages we keep losing. To speak from here is to speak in tongues, to speak of girls in love bleeding in burqas, to speak of desire that does not translate, hands that fumble in the dark in search of something hidden and alive and impossibly wild. To speak from here is not to speak at all, not in ways you would understand anyway, not in ways we understand either.

To speak from here is to speak of Pakistan, to speak of God, to speak of mothers and the words that are never enough. It is also to speak of love, the gentle thing between girls, the violent and the desperate thing, the thing that is too much for a country sometimes and the languages it owns.

To speak from where the wild things are, to be one of those wild things, to speak from a position of wildness, to speak from here to there, I am still figuring out what that means and implies for me. Is my speech always an attempt to make myself knowable? What compels me to speak, what invisible demands are made on me that I remain unconscious of as the wild things speak of themselves to the bearers of civilization? When I speak from here, from where the wild things are, when I speak as one of the wild things, to you, what am I really doing?

This isn't an attempt toward legibility. To write the queer, racialized, colonized body, to write might very well be to unravel but not in ways that would make the wildness containable, legible. If unravel I must, I unravel toward incoherence.

## IN LOVE, WE HAVE BEEN SACRED

I can't speak of desire without speaking of sacred things. It meant something to break skin for Zaynab, it meant something to be merely flesh, just the redness of the skin. During Ashura, you once took me by the hand to a secluded corner of the *majlis* and lowered down your shirt to show off the growing bruise on your breast, beaming, proud. We grew up into intimacy with other women through strange little sacred rituals, through worship and devotion of female saints, through God. The body was queer in its very Muslimness, not in opposition to it. What other story can I tell when the very place I learned to hold your hand was where I also learned how to read the Quran?

Girls find their ways to pleasure one another in many ways. Every *majlis*, every *milaad*, every gathering of girls was holy, every secret touch, every prayer and hymn to drown out muffled sounds was sacred. Every time you wore the hijab for me instead of God, perhaps for the both of us, so we could be and exist and sit in a *dargah* among women was an act of love. Of mercy. You still fix my dupatta for me whenever we go out, and I still pretend not to know what to do with my hands. Perhaps, I'm never really pretending. My useless, trembling hands have always been the most honest parts of me. Perhaps, you have always known.

Even when our bodies no longer remembered how to fold themselves in front of God, you would still take my hands and cup them, coaxing a prayer in Arabic that would always get stuck in my throat. We have been capable of grace, even then, despite it all, even then. My mother still sits me down to read Bibi Fatimah's miracle to her every time a wish of hers comes true. My hands are clean in yours, in hers, my hands are still clean as she lets me eat what my words bless. Our words are still sacred despite the many times they still get stuck in our throats.

Girls find their ways to being girls and being boys in many sacred, tender, and violent ways as well. In college you once told me that you wished I was a boy so things could be easier. I was already too boy to be a girl for my mother, but not boy enough, not boy on days when to be a boy was to be at war with the world, when to be a girl felt like war enough. There were girls who told you that they wanted to be boys and we loved them like boys, loved them like they were ours, for us to keep secret, away from the world and the men they would eventually marry. The boys whose breasts disappeared under our hands as we shaped their bodies with dupattas they had abandoned. The boys whose fists and knuckles we let inside of ourselves, again and again, to take away the violence from their hands and make them into gentle things. The boys who let themselves be touched by girls, and boys, and all the things we ever were without words to name ourselves. In all of this, we have been ours. We have been sacred.

YOUR IMAGE IS THE LEADER
OF THE REVOLUTION

In a foreign city amid a revolution, I was once told that I was brave. Every time we have loved, we have never been brave. I'm not sure why that's even expected of me. "Thank you for your bravery," but do you not see how words still fail me and the way the handshakes, the way our mothers no longer understand us, the way you don't either? My people are not brave. My people are not martyrs for a freedom that has never been on our own terms, for languages that violate us and attempt to constantly articulate what we refuse to say. The boy I could never be, the girl I never was. My people are not brave.

It's not that they are afraid either. But bravery is such a strange thing when expected from those whose bodies are things without words, bravery is such a strange thing to be asked of sacred things. Bravery is such a strange thing because it is something that expects and demands tragedy and expects you to put on a show. We are asked to come out in languages we do not speak to fit categories that cannot contain us, we are asked to be brave and pick up flags we do not recognize, we are asked to be sellable, nameable, commodifiable by activism we do not understand. Brave little queers. Casualties of foreign revolutions, foreign words. Brave little dead queers.

My people are not brave. Bravery would mean to persevere in the way things are. But we don't. We constantly fail instead and failure is sacred. There are no brave stories I have to tell.

I see us unravel across time, without bravery, without courage, without pride, to something smaller, quieter, lonelier, restful. It isn't strength I need. But to be weak without shame, without explanation.

When the revolution comes, there will be nothing to leave behind. Our loneliness, even when I grasp your hand, our loneliness won't burden us, you won't ask me to speak just to prove that I am here.

In Beirut or Karachi, when I purposefully tried to get lost you still clambered behind me, but I came back, I always came back to you. Everything was on fire, your hands traced every bullet hole, translating every slogan, every torn pamphlet. I could see the sea and we mindlessly walked toward it, till we stopped on an empty road, never reaching, we were close enough, we could see the water just fine. It was enough. It had always been enough.

I am not sure what it is we are constantly trying to say to one another. You lift up your trousers for me to see the dark hairs that curl over your legs as if we're doing something profane, something sacred. You have always been so beautiful.

My people are not brave. No one asks them to be. I have stopped trying to work through the discomfort. It is there. I don't fight it. It reminds me of what could be instead, of what isn't, of what might be. The anxiety comes with being in a world that isn't ours, from making a world that just might be. Every girl I have loved, every boy that I have wanted to be, that I have kept and made mine, the nerves are the flutterings of the sacred and the devastating between us.

And so we find our ways to one another and to ourselves in sacred, terrible, mundane ways. When we mourn Zaynab and break skin, when we hide and are unrecognizable, when we fuck and aren't brave, if every touch must mean something, then the loneliness of girls is revolution too. The silence, the absences, the quiet solitary togetherness, the untouched skin and other kinds of love, the joy and mourning of girls is revolution too.

TO YOU, WHO DOES NOT YET EXIST

I do not perhaps exist in Urdu. A longing is a longing but Urdu doesn't know what to do with it. What to call it. It never has the words. I do not exist in Arabic either though I love to hide in it, to play with it, to love through it, despite it, against it. Arabic has never sat well on the tongue but Urdu has never felt good in the hands. Punjabi has been the body and its excess when it failed society and class. Punjabi is not mine. I betray it all the time. And yet I pretend in it just the same. We do many things to belong and imagine our people. The girls who spoke Punjabi loved me first and loved me well when my body spilled over than the English-speaking queers who aren't mine either. *You failed class first, perhaps failing what girl meant was the same.* Sometimes they pretend, and sometimes I do too. Sometimes we all pretend just a little bit. Sometimes it's easy.

English lets me come without a silence that in Urdu would only be a scream. English has words for most of my body but English is still to make space for me, it still needs to imagine me. It still needs to hurt less. English still needs to be kind to my body, to tolerate my silence, to understand why it fails me and lets me down even though it promises something else, the way it always has. English might never have the words for what it means to not know one's own country, and yet know nothing else better.

Every time I am asked my pronouns, I have never known what to say. It doesn't matter. There is no language that is fully mine and there is no language I completely belong to. To write this incoherent body, to speak of the way it desires and loves is then perhaps to speak of the land written across it. The land is her skin under my hands, it is his period blood on my burqa, the land is abandoned dupattas and carefully wrapped hijabs, the land is their dead names and our mothers, the land is sacred, the land is prison, the land is my body made of foreign words and silences. To write the body is to write the land, the body as land, the body in desire, the body cupped in the gentle, sacred hands of a girl.

In writing the body, I have always felt language slip away from my hands. To write in the language of queer time is to perhaps write toward conclusions and resolutions that always falter; to write the language of queerness for me has always been to essentially fail. What can be generated through writing that fails, that does not lead toward knowing at all, that circles and meanders, that breaks and becomes song, becomes verse, becomes an image of girls holding hands in elsewheres beyond time?

What forms of knowing can come from writing that is half song, half plea that does not merely think about incoherence, about unknowing, but that actively attempts to become that which it theorizes and imagines? What does it mean to write this very thing that constantly slips us by? There is potential in writing that fails, in forms that become the ideas they describe. There is something, after all, in this very thing in my hands that I still haven't figured out what to really do with.

In Beirut, you once asked me how we imagine the future. "What would you want"? I thought of you once sitting across the room from me, trying to make me laugh during a *Quran Khawani*. This is already the elsewhere, perhaps where I write from doesn't really exist right now for you. Perhaps, we don't either. Time moves strangely for the land that has never really known how to be a place, to be anything. The land that is less place and more desire, desire between girls when being girl is something more, something less, when being girl is the easiest thing to be for you, when being girl kills.

In being girl, in being boy, in being flesh, in love, in devastation, in joy we keep finding ways to one another, to borrowed words and incoherent languages. There is no future promised to us, perhaps because we are already here. We have always been here. Sacred, all of us, so many of us. Always here.

GLOSSARY OF TERMS

*Adab*—respect.

*Ashura*—the tenth day of Muharram that marks the annual remembrance and commemoration of the martyrdom of Husayn (the Prophet's grandson), his family, and followers during the Battle of Karbala.

*Bibi Fatimah*—daughter of the Prophet.

*Bibi Fatimah*'s miracle—A series of stories centered around the figure of Fatimah. You are supposed to have someone read the stories out loud to you and eat something sweet after if a wish has been granted and send blessings to the Prophet and his family.

*Dargah*—shrine.

*Dupatta*—a piece of cloth that can serve as a headscarf or to cover the chest similar to a shawl.

*Lehaz*—regard, can also be consideration of social norms.

*Majlis*—could be a gathering to celebrate religious festivals, anniversaries, and so forth that include collective recitations of the Quran and singing of hymns. A *majlis* can also be a religious council or meeting.

*Milaad*—a gathering usually associated with the celebration of the birth anniversary of the Prophet. Could be organized for various other purposes as well, for example, to send blessings to a departed loved one. It also includes collective prayers, recitations, and such.

*Paindu*—a word in Punjabi that means someone belonging from a village.

*Quran Khawani*—recitation of the Quran, something that could be organized in the form of a public gathering.

*Zaynab*—refers to Prophet Muhammad's granddaughter. "Break skin for Zaynab" refers to the practice of self-flagellation as part of mourning the Battle of Karbala during the Islamic month of Muharram.

Shayan Rajani

# 2

# Loving Men, Loving God

This essay engages the form and method of its historical source, the biographical dictionary, or *tazkira*.[1] Biographical dictionaries were written largely, though not exclusively, in Persian in the early modern era. They told of the lives of notable persons, kings, nobles, poets, saints, scholars, women, musicians, and so on. Historians, including myself, have used such texts to piece together chronology, historical context, and epochal change. However, biographical dictionaries themselves employed the affective power of their stories to elevate biographical accounts above their own time.

In the retellings of Sufi biographies below, I, too, orient the past and present differently. I defer analytical command over the past in favor of attending to the past's desire to make its own future. I refrain from a narrative that states an argument and proceeds through a presentation of evidences. Instead, this retelling is the grounds upon which the desires and politics of peoples past meet my own, a meeting where it is not periodization, but its dissolution that becomes the imperative.

### THE RED SAINT

Madho Lal Hussain was not a birth name. It was a name accrued over a lifetime. Hussain was born in 1538 to a family of weavers in Lahore. At the age of ten, he became a disciple of the Sufi master Shaikh Bahlul the Oceanic, who miraculously helped him memorize the Quran. Later, he served at the shrine of Syed Ali Hajviri, the Bestower of Treasures, who had lived and died in eleventh-century Lahore. In this time, Hussain practiced austerities and scrupulously observed religious practice. Later still, Hussain turned to the knowledge of books, which he learned from his teacher, Saadullah. During his studies, he came upon a Quranic verse cautioning that this worldly life is nothing but fun and games, and that the Hereafter is, in fact, life proper. In this warning, Hussain discovered a promise. He broke into dance before his astonished teacher, silencing his objections with poetry. He danced out of the mosque and flung the Quranic Commentary of Nasafi, which they had been studying, into a well. Aghast, his fellow students reproached him, whereupon Hussain retrieved the book, which upon examination, was found to be untouched by the water.[2]

In his hagiographies, this incident marks Hussain's induction into the Path of the Blameworthy (*malamati*).[3] He remained publicly drunk, sang and danced, kept company with people of the entertainment castes,[4] shaved his facial hair, and wore red. It is that red, *lal,* a color of excess, that draped not just his body, but also his name. It was the color that the Red-Ruby Falcon, Lal Shahbaz Qalandar (d. 1274), another saint of the Blameworthy Path, adorned himself in. The Red-Ruby Falcon, whose birth name was Usman of Marwand, lived three centuries before Lal Hussain, and died in Sehwan, a town around a thousand kilometers southwest of Lahore. The Red-Ruby Falcon, too, had danced in red robes.

> I have become dishonored in his love, come now oh pious one,
> I do not fear disgrace, in every market I dance.
> The whole world tells me, "Oh beggar, why do you dance so?"
> In my heart is a secret, with this secret I dance.
> I am Usman of Marwand, the friend of Khwaja Mansur [Hallaj],
> The world censures me, crucified I dance.[5]

This Persian verse, attributed to the Red-Ruby Falcon in a collection of poetry from the eighteenth century, welcomes censure, scorn, and even death in its defiant rhythms of ecstatic dance. Yet, a fourteenth-century chronicle describes a different scene: the Red-Ruby Falcon and another saint dancing to Arabic poetry, while a prince stands watching, hands respectfully clasped and tears streaming down his face.[6] Lal Hussain's life, too, would move between the poles of reproach and respect.

Sixteenth-century Lahore, which was Lal Hussain's residence, became the capital of the Timurid king Akbar in 1585. From here, Akbar sent out conquering armies north, south, and west for thirteen years, before returning in 1598 to the north Indian heartlands of his empire. In this time, Akbar evolved a new code of bodily discipline, entrenched in notions of masculinity and order.[7] These rigors, practiced upon his own body and expected of his officials, were inextricably linked to the control of the empire and to the cultivation of sacrality within himself. These experiments were partly meant to repudiate the saintly power of the Safavid kings to the west, whose distinctive red headgear had at one time been donned by Akbar's father, Humayun, and grandfather, Babur. It was this act of submission by his ancestors to their rivals in red that Akbar was determined to cast off.[8]

Lal Hussain's hagiographers report that when Akbar was told that there was a man in his city who shaved his beard, wore red, and danced drunk, Akbar had him summoned. Lal Hussain came with a bottle of wine in hand, contravening Islamic prohibitions against public drinking and arousing Akbar's censure.[9] Lal Hussain poured a cup from his bottle and offered it to Akbar. It was cold water. A second cup turned out to be milk. Akbar ordered another bottle of wine, which when served by Lal Hussain became eight different kinds of lawful beverages. Unmoved by this sign, Akbar had Lal Hussain locked away. But when he returned to his harem, Akbar found Lal Hussain sitting with his wife, making a mockery of Akbar's strict protocols of gender segregation and of his ability to maintain social and political order.[10] Astonished, Akbar checked the prison and found Lal Hussain inside occupied in meditation. Upon returning to his palace, he found Lal Hussain sitting there yet again and was compelled to accept his greatness.

MADHO

The story of Lal Hussain's first name comes last. One day, Lal Hussain saw a beautiful Brahmin on the street. This was Madho, whom Lal Hussain fell in love with. Every night, he would go to Madho's house in the suburbs of Shahdara across the River Ravi. He would spend the night circumambulating the house, while Madho lay inside with his wife. Those things that Madho whispered to his wife in bed, Lal Hussain repeated aloud outside. Lal Hussain spent years in this state of unrequited love, while Madho spurned him. Scorn and censure heaped upon Lal Hussain as he descended into lovelorn madness.

After years of unflagging devotion to an inattentive beloved, Lal Hussain's love turned Madho's heart toward him. The cruel beloved became a lover, too. Not a day went by that Madho was not in the company of Lal Hussain. On discovering this relationship, Madho's relatives feared that he would become a Muslim. They decided to catch them in bed together. Every night, Madho and Lal Hussain would share a bed, but Madho's relatives would never be able to discover the door to their abode. The secret core of their public love remained out of sight of the jealous and the curious. Finally, they attempted to take Madho on a pilgrimage to Haridwar to bathe in the Ganges River. Unable to bear separation, Lal Hussain prevented Madho from leaving. On the day of the ritual bathing, Lal Hussain had Madho stand on his feet and transported him to Haridwar in the blink of an eye, where Madho completed his ablutions with his family.

Hagiographers report that at a certain point Madho converted to Islam, but he never took a Muslim name.[11] Instead, Lal Hussain received Madho's name and became Madho Lal Hussain. The mutual transformation wrought by love upon Madho Lal Hussain and Madho eludes the concept of conversion, either religious or sexual. Madho became his devotee and lover much as he had become Madho's devotee and lover years before. To please Madho, Madho Lal Hussain celebrated the Hindu festival of colors, Holi, with him. Theirs was a story of the transformations brought about upon the self by loving another. The particularity and peculiarity of their love remained beyond identities and types.

## THE ETHICS OF LOVE

This story of mutual transformation stands in contrast to the story of the Red-Ruby Falcon's arrival in Sehwan. The Red-Ruby Falcon decided to build his dwelling on someone else's land. When the owner came to confront him, the Red-Ruby Falcon struck him with his staff, killing him instantly. When the owner's heirs came to confront him, the Red-Ruby Falcon replied, "I have only killed a dog. See, it is buried here." Upon disinterring the body, the heirs indeed discovered the body of a dog. They realized the Red-Ruby Falcon's power, became his believers, and gave him the land.[12] In this story of confrontations, the Red-Ruby Falcon supplants another person as owner of the land and leader of its people. Murder and expropriation are consecrated by a shift in the local moral order, where the erstwhile leader is transformed into a dog. We may detect in this story an allusion to religious change. Here, too, the transformation is personal and embodied. But the Red-Ruby Falcon simply replaced the old leader without transforming himself or the hierarchical relationships of local order.[13]

Manan Ahmed Asif, in his study of a thirteenth-century Persian history written at Uch, in present-day Pakistan, finds another ethics of managing difference. This relies upon acknowledging the incommensurable power of other moral orders and leaving them untouched. He finds this ethic at work when the eighth-century Arab conqueror of Sindh, Muhammad bin Qasim, encounters a Ruby-Eyed Demon, which renders him incapable of destroying and replacing the old moral order in his new land.[14] Mutual recognition and cautious distance are the guiding principles of this ethic, which he finds in the neighborhoods of twenty-first-century Uch as well. Like much of the rest of Pakistan's Punjab, Uch is largely without Hindus since the Partition of 1947. Yet, people continue to preserve abandoned Hindu temples, not appropriating them to new purposes, for fear of the unexplained and otherworldly power of these disused sites.[15]

Madho Lal Hussain points to a third ethics of relating to the stranger, neither displacement nor distancing, but mutual transformation and movement toward each other. The state that facilitates this movement is not disdain or fear, but love. This ethics found brief expression in the political philosophy of the seventeenth-century Timurid prince Dara Shukoh.[16] Dara translated Hindu philosophy into Persian and his own Persian writing into Sanskrit, mutually transforming the two traditions. His great work was titled *The Mingling of Two Oceans*. In his entourage was the naked Sufi, Sarmad, and his Brahmin beloved, Abhai Chand.[17] Here, too, the political, intellectual, affective, and embodied came together, but in a different configuration from that orchestrated by Dara's great-grandfather, Akbar. Yet, Dara was not fated to become king. He was killed by his brother Aurangzeb, who had Sarmad executed as well, both for blasphemy.

We must still reckon with the fact, that while in the other two ethics, movement is between two beings and moral orders that are formally equal, the pathos of Madho Lal Hussain and Madho's transformation lies precisely in the inversion of hierarchical difference coded in their story. Protocols of naming, with which we started our story, were meant to confirm hierarchies of power in the early modern era, as they continue to do today. Titles were conferred by those in positions of authority upon their subordinates, by the king on his subjects, and the master on his disciples.

Lal Shahbaz Qalandar's master, for example, bestowed upon him the title Falcon or Shahbaz. But Madho Lal Hussain received his name from Madho, who would have been considered inferior to him in age, status, religion, elevated above him only by virtue of his unique position as his beloved. Seen from a different vantage, it was not that the title Madho was conferred upon Lal Hussain, but rather that his love for Madho obliterated his original self and made him one, even within himself, with his beloved.

Before his death, Madho Lal Hussain had instructed Madho to leave Lahore and serve Raja Man Singh, a powerful Timurid and Rajput noble, for twelve years.[18] He had also assured his followers that, after his death, if anyone would like to see him, they would only need to look upon Madho. There was no difference between the two. Was that because Madho Lal Hussain had in his own life become Madho? After twelve years away from Lahore, when Madho returned to take custodianship of Madho Lal Hussain's shrine, his disciples were amazed to see that Madho bore the face of Madho Lal Hussain. Where Hussain became Madho in name, Madho became Hussain in his appearance. Love, catalyzed by the adversities of separation, transformed the lover's self into the beloved.

### OVERTURNING HIERARCHIES

Courting blame was a crucial element of Madho Lal Hussain's love for Madho. The inversion of status and power and the transgression of gender behavior and religious boundaries produced abjection and censure. While the disapprobation provoked by this inversion may recall the public scandal of outing inverts and homosexuals in the nineteenth and twentieth centuries, the place of loving men in this story is much more complicated than such an easy comparison might at first suggest. Disapproval in this case was not about the gender of the person whom Madho Lal Hussain loved, but rather about the way in which he loved this person. A brief comparison with the early sixteenth-century Timurid king Babur, who was also Akbar's grandfather, illustrates the point.

Babur writes in his remarkable first-person memoir that he first married at the age of seventeen, but remained shy of his wife. His mother had to force him to visit his wife once a month. Meanwhile, Babur fell in love with a boy he saw in the market named Baburi, the Little Lion, which is the diminutive of his own name. Babur confesses, with disarming honesty, which characterizes much of his memoir, that this was the first time he felt desire for anyone. If Baburi ever approached him, Babur would become tongue-tied, unable even to look at him, let alone get a word out.[19] Babur wrote his memoir in the final years of his life, when he was the king of Hindustan.[20] In this famous passage, adorned with couplets of love poetry, he describes his first love with a candor that suggests its lasting impact on his life, but also without a sense that this love was taboo or out of the ordinary. He explains his passion as "the foment of youth and madness" and confesses that he got over Baburi "with a hundred embarrassments and difficulties."[21]

Babur's explanation of his love for Baburi as a temporary state associated with his own youth fits well with Walter Andrews and Mehmet Kalpaklı's account of the stages of love in the Ottoman world of the sixteenth century, where youthful chasing of beautiful boys is eventually superseded by the mature relationships of devotion and service to one's superiors and masters, both spiritual and material. They argue that in this Age of Beloveds, the hierarchical political and social relations of an absolutist monarchical order were eroticized. Sexual desire structured by the unequal relation between the lover and the beloved charged and animated this political order.[22] Appropriate love was limited not by its direction across genders, but rather by its direction upward within hierarchical order. The king and God, at the very apex of material and spiritual orders, were the ultimate beloveds.[23]

Babur's love for Baburi bears the hallmarks of this developmental logic. Moreover, the resonance of their names, Lion and Little Lion, suggests that Babur's love was also a love of himself, his own qualities, or his past childhood. It was equally important for Babur that this love was not physical. In his memoir, he repeatedly condemns Timurid princes and nobles for keeping catamites.[24] In describing the Timurid prince Sultan Mahmud Mirza, Babur writes, "He kept a lot of catamites, and in his realm wherever there was a comely, beardless youth, he did everything he could to turn him into a catamite.... During his time this shameful vice was so widespread that there was no one at all who did not have catamites. To keep them was considered a virtue, and not to keep them a fault. His sons all died young of shameful immodesty and debauchery."[25] Sustained, physical relationships with boys attracted robust censure from Babur, who associated these activities not just with moral turpitude, but also with a form of degeneration that undoes procreation.[26] While Babur recognized that physical relationships with boys would not imperil reproductive sexual activities with women, the vice, in his mind, had fatal consequences for

Mahmud Mirza's sons and, therefore, for Mahmud Mirza's procreative mission, which was to leave male successors to continue his name.

In the Muslim tradition, circumambulation is reserved for the House of God in Mecca or for shrines of Sufi masters. It is one of the highest acts of submission and fealty. Babur performed this act at the end of his own life for his eldest son. Humayun had been stricken by an unexplained illness. Babur's daughter, Gulbadan Begum, narrates that Babur circumambulated the bed of his son for a week and prayed that his life be exchanged for that of his son. With that prayer, Humayun recovered and Babur fell ill, succumbing to death some months later.[27] Babur's act may fit the mold of selfless parental devotion and sacrifice. But it was also, in its commitment to a progenitive future, an act performed for Babur's own sake, directed toward a son, who would pass his legacy on into the future and keep his name alive. In contrast, Madho Lal Hussain circumambulated Madho's house every night, acknowledging through this ritual that Madho was the pivot of his world. His circumambulation was not misgendered but rather misdirected, toward a love that undoes the self rather than furthering its interests.

Babur's love for men, which marked his life irrefutably, was a facet of his love for himself. That love ensured the endurance of his own name. However, Madho Lal Hussain's love erased his own name in favor of his beloved. It was not simply the gossip of sex, which generated the scandal and censure of Madho Lal Hussain, but rather the spectacular undoing of the sartorial, affective, behavioral, and reproductive practices that affirmed masculinity, which centered, above all other things, upon a desire to leave a legacy.[28] Madho Lal Hussain unraveled the hierarchical logics of the Age of Beloveds through the archetypal love of the male beloved, which also sustained that order. The unraveling lay in his refusal of its temporal progression, of his refusal to reorient his devotion upon appropriate beloveds, the teacher, the master, the king. Madho Lal Hussain spurned these relationships in favor of Madho. He quarreled with his teacher Saadullah, with his first Sufi master, Bahlul the Oceanic, and went against the teachings of Syed Ali Hajviri, the Bestower of Treasures, who strictly condemned boy-love in his writings.[29] Where Babur progressed appropriately through the stages of manhood, from a youthful love of boys toward more enduring and more significant male relationships, Madho Lal Hussain rejected these mature relationships, which he had cultivated for decades, for Madho's sake.

Rather than a fleeting infatuation, Madho and Madho Lal Hussain's love endured for more than a lifetime. They spent their remaining days together. Madho became his lover and spiritual successor. In the rejection of social norms, their story resonates with folk romances of thwarted and forbidden love between men and women. Yet, forbidden love between men and women always ends in tragic death. Only in death lay the final union of Hir and Ranjha or Sassui and Punhu or Sohni and Mahiwal.[30] This resolution elevates their love, but also relegates it to the otherworldly, reaffirming social order and its restrictions in this world. But the story of Madho Lal Hussain and Madho countenances no tragedy except natural death. They lived their lives together and found numerous followers among lay persons and within Timurid royalty and nobility. Their love, transgressive though it was, did not need to await death for recognition and acceptance. It found space within the society where they lived. It was couched within numerous relationships of male love that was appropriately directed as the love due from a disciple to his master. Both Madho Lal Hussain and Madho become such masters in their own lifetime and were surrounded by devotees who kept their names alive.[31]

Madho Lal Hussain's reproachful love has been reconciled to the values of the time, both in the early modern era and in the modern, with two strategies. First, his love is described as Metaphorical Love, *Ishq-i Majazi*, which is explained as a stage toward True Love of the Divine, *Ishq-i Haqiqi*. The former is held to be but a temporary station in the journey toward the ultimate love of God, a movement from God's created beauty to God's own beauty. Stories of cross-gender love are explained similarly. Their narrative arc allows for greater congruence with this developmental model, where the love for God's creation is thwarted in this world, but also transvalued into divine love in the world hereafter.

Stories of reproachful love between men fit oddly within this progression. The lover and beloved are often united in this world: Madho Lal Hussain and Madho, Sarmad and Abhai Chand, Qadir Bakhsh Bidil, the Dejected, and his lovers. Metaphorical and True Love are not successive here, but rather simultaneous. Bidil, who lived in nineteenth-century colonial Sindh, fell madly in love with a Hindu youth, Karam Chand, in Sukkur. Every day, he sat outside Karam Chand's shop in the colonial bazaar, while Karam Chand ignored him. One day, Bidil went to see a visiting saint, who called Bidil a Hindu Faqir. Puzzled onlookers inquired with Bidil, who sheepishly admitted that it was because he was in love with a Hindu. Like Madho Lal Hussain, his love of a Hindu boy had changed his self in recognizable ways. But, my Sindhi instructor, with whom I read this story, explained that this public call was transformative because the saint freed Bidil from the snare of Metaphorical Love toward True Love.[32] Yet, curiously, Bidil continued to fall in love with other boys and men, spending his life first with Pir Ghulam Muhammad, and upon his death, with Pir Qazi Muhammad.[33] In all these cases, the boy became a man and the man became old, yet their love endured. These men loved men and loved God without contradiction. Their reproachful love is at the center of a dense network of appropriate love of disciples. It remains present in memory today, in publication projects, oral retellings, annual festivals and commemorations, with a certain unease, but without explicit reproach or a desire for its excision.

Hagiographies written afterward are at pains to save their beloved, Madho Lal Hussain, from reproach through a second strategy. They narrate stories that set up a conflict between Madho Lal Hussain's actions and Islamic law, only to reconcile them as miraculously consistent. Madho Lal Hussain pouring out nonalcoholic drinks to Akbar from his bottle of wine is a case in point. Under the inquiring gaze of the upholders of law and morality, his actions appear consistent with the law. Another example is Madho's relatives' inability to discover Madho and Madho Lal in bed together. Reliable eyewitnesses are required by Islamic law to establish carnal relations, but those evidentiary requirements could not be met. A third instance is his miraculous retrieval of the Quranic commentary from the well and finding it undamaged. His public actions constantly and purposefully risked the penalties of the law, but elude such judgment at the crucial moment.

These stories can either be read as reconciling the reproachful with the legal or as narrating the triumph of the reproachful in miraculously thwarting the requirements of evidence. This diversity of sources of evidence and protocols of judgment, which are partly a result of a time where law sought neither to be uniform nor universal, suggests an explanation for the abjection of reproachful love in Babur's memoir, but its exaltation in the hagiographies of Madho Lal Hussain. Reproachful acts were not tacitly approved across the board, but rather their righteousness was attested in contingent and risky encounters with the law. Anecdotes told in the genre of miracle stories, which are narratively predetermined to resolve in favor of the saint, no longer convey the risks and dangers of reproachful behavior, lulling moderns into a sense of a happier and permissive past now lost. Yet, these stories also reveal a dread of the law. Reproach may be welcomed, but contravening the law carried moral, political, and spiritual consequences that could not be countenanced within this genre. The gruesome executions of Mansur Hallaj and Sarmad both serve as vivid reminders of the dangers of running afoul the law. Law triumphed over the miraculous in these cases, even if it could not secure an enduring moral victory.[34]

The blameworthy and lawful remain bound up with each other. The former's contravention of the latter sets the stage for miraculous verification, which was the ultimate arbiter of moral order, capable even of leaving law's victories hollow. But what if we step back from this genre of miracle stories, and its commitment to its beloved, and return to the moment of reproach itself? Then, we find ourselves standing with the lover, who has courted public blame, without any guarantees of divine or devotional defense. We find ourselves in the company of a person who risked everything for an abject love, not yet sanctified, perhaps never to be approved as a rule, despite all the lovers who may have gone down this path before and all the lovers who may go down this path in the future. Rather than assent to the narrative arcs that defuse and contain the danger of this moment, we may instead stay with the blame that is sought out and welcomed.

BEYOND PERIODIZATION

Too often, the work of the historian has been to periodize. It is in our training. It is our disciplinary politics, our commitment to disciplining the present. Chidingly, we release the past from the clutches of political projects of our day, nationalism, imperialism, settler colonialism, misogyny, and homophobia to name a few. Carefully, we return this past to the far side of a domain that is most often called modernity. Once restored, out of the grasp of the universalizing histories of the present, we may then wistfully survey this past, now separated by the ruptures of modernity. This is a post-Foucauldian project, to tell a story of the present that reveals, but also reviles, the modern.

Alan Bray captured this spirit well in the preface to *The Friend*. He wrote, "My task as a historian is to let the past speak in its own terms, not to appropriate it to those of the contemporary world."[35] Despite accepting these historian's pieties, I have been encouraged by my own engagement with the early modern world and its relation to my present in Pakistan to wonder whether people of the past did not want to be taken up, to be part of the now, shape it, and be present in it.[36] Rather than attend to historical ruptures and disjunctures, the successive comings and goings of one period and then another, I have found myself attending to that which endures across dramatic transformations, the memories, desires, practices, and traces that persist, and more than that, insist on their presence, even in the face of our neatening periodization.

For two generations, scholars have mourned the dislocations of colonialism, and found the postcolonial present shot through with the violence of the colonial past. They have witnessed the violence of the present justified in projects of return to a hallowed past. They have fought to untangle the past from the present for the sake of a different future. For them, the evocation of the past is to be regarded with suspicion, at best a misguided desire for origins, which is another tragic legacy of colonial displacements. However, I gesture not toward the desires of moderns, but toward the wishes of the people who went before us. It is their commitment to being a part of the future, of being remembered, that molds our present.

Madho Lal Hussain may have spurned the enterprise of reproductive futurity, but he did not intend to be forgotten. Before his death, he left explicit instructions about his grave. It was first to be in Shahdara, the old neighborhood of his beloved Madho. But he had foretold that a flood would sweep away that resting place thirteen years after his death. He wanted to be reinterred in a solitary spot in Baghbanpura and had declared Madho the custodian of his grave. That line of custodians continued into the nineteenth century and beyond; so too did the visits of devotees and the curious. Rulers continued to build and endow his shrine, including even the Sikh rulers of the nineteenth century.[37] An annual festival of lights was organized from the shrine. Tens of thousands streamed into colonial Lahore for this festival.[38] Madho Lal's death anniversary continues to be commemorated today with great fanfare, music, and dancing in Lahore.[39] The verses that Madho Lal Hussain left behind inaugurated a new tradition of Punjabi poetry and continues to be sung, recited, published, studied, and remembered today.

Madho Lal Hussain may not have been able to predict the ways in which he would be remembered in the twenty-first century, but his own actions show that he hoped and desired to be remembered long after his death. Madho and Madho Lal Hussain's graves standing side by side on

FIG. 2.1. Men express their devotion at the tomb of Madho and Madho Lal Hussain, who are buried next to each other in Baghbanpura, Lahore.

a hillock under a simple roof among the constricted and crowded streets of contemporary Baghbanpura do not stand forgotten, but rather bring together people with all kinds of investments, hopes, and desires to the life works and traces of these saints (see figure 2.1). These people join their own life's labors to the works of these men. Not insignificant among them are the queer and trans persons who come to see two lovers buried together, who pore over Madho Lal's poetry for a map to their own love, *majazi, haqiqi,* or without any possibility of a name.

The problem with periodization for queer scholars is that we are left with enchanting visions of a time "before homosexuality," and the past "age of beloveds," and of the era of "women with mustaches and men without beards," but it is a past that is decidedly over and a present that is all the poorer for it.[40] It also explains the acts of past people as one with their time and tradition, rendering such acts untenable, impossible in the modern world. Yet, Madho Lal Hussain's presence in the Age of Beloveds neither fully explains his individual actions nor dulled his risks. While the closet

LOVING MEN, LOVING GOD 43

existed neither as a physical space nor as an organizing principle for queer experience, publicity came with its dangers. It also afforded unexpected opportunities for the inscription of the reproachful love of two men within a tapestry of other relations in the sixteenth century and beyond.

Madho Lal Hussain's reproachful love was neither fully of a tradition nor did it inaugurate a new one. His custodians and devotees were not systematically committed to following Madho Lal in his mode of love. Yet, other reproachful lovers made themselves public after Madho Lal and Madho, even after the early seventeenth century, when Andrews and Kalpaklı close out the Age of Beloveds in the Ottoman and European worlds. The Jewish convert to Islam, Sarmad, fell in love with a young Hindu boy, Abhai Chand, in the city of Thatta. Abhai Chand joined Sarmad and they traveled the Timurid Empire together and naked. Sarmad, buried in Delhi, is remembered till today as Sarmad the Martyr, and championed by twentieth-century political leaders and intellectuals.[41]

Two centuries later, Qadir Bakhsh Bidil, the Dejected, who was born in nineteenth-century Rohri, in upper Sindh, fell in love with a Hindu boy. He went on to love two other men over the course of his life, while cultivating a host of devotees and disciples, Hindu and Muslim, in colonial Sindh. He and his beloveds also remained householders all their lives, leaving children behind, who preserved the memories of their fathers. His son, Muhammad Muhsin Bikas, the Friendless, fell in love with a Hindu boy, Kinyo. Bidil and Bikas are buried in a shrine in Rohri, and their Sindhi poetry and Persian writings are at the heart of a sustained project of printing, research, and writing in Sindh, even as their shrine attracts devotees and disciples.

These lives and stories, remarkably similar in their contours and increasingly fascinating up close, pay heed to no neat periodizations of the past. All erupt at different historical moments, in different places. They bear no clear connection between one another, nor do they follow the conventions of the tradition of loving boys. They all make their presence felt in contemporary times, not to be reproached, but rather to be respected. The stories of their love are neither excised nor shunned as scholars have seen elsewhere with the advent of heterosexuality. Their lives, works, poetry, tombs, and spiritual power are joined to the life works and life desires of diverse peoples today, most of whom are not queer-identified. Yet, their exceptional lives live on in our presumably heteronormative present, made ordinary by their unremarked presence in contemporary life that we have somehow periodized away as inescapably hopeless.

NOTES

1. My thanks to Omar Kasmani for conversations about Lal Shahbaz Qalandar. Akber Chandio read Sindhi poetry and texts with me and shared his own research and insights into Sufism in Sindh. Nosheen Ali, Jasdeep Singh, and the Shah Hussain Sangat invited me into their passionate engagement with Madho Lal Hussain's verse.
2. My account of Madho Lal Hussain is freely adapted from *Tahqiqat-i Chishti*, which was written by Nur Ahmad Chishti in Urdu in colonial Lahore in 1867. His biographical entry, in turn, relies upon *Haqiqat al-Fuqara*, which was written by Shaikh Mahmud, a disciple of Madho, in Persian verse more than half a century after Madho Lal's death. Chishti also drew on *Kitab-i Baharia*, which was the account of Madho Lal compiled by a news reporter, Bahar Khan Munshi, appointed by Jahangir to report on Madho Lal; see Chishtī, *Taḥqīqāt-i Chishtī*, 307–60.
3. See Karamustafa, *God's Unruly Friends*.
4. Dancers and musicians comprised distinct castes that were collectively beyond the pale of elite respectability.
5. Ṭhattavī, *Tazkirah-i Maqālāt al-Shu'arā*, 435. The translation is my own.
6. Balban's son, Muhammad Sultan Khan Shaheed, invites Lal Shahbaz to Multan in 662/1263; see Baranī, *Tārīkh-i Fīrūz-Šāhī*.
7. O'Hanlon, "Manliness and Imperial Service in Mughal North India."
8. Moin, *The Millennial Sovereign*, 130–69.
9. Here, Akbar is performing the role of the king as enforcer of Islamic law, which does not correspond to what is known about historical Akbar.
10. Lal, *Domesticity and Power in the Early Mughal World*.
11. This has L. R. Krishna doubt that Madho ever converted at all; see Krishna and Luther, *Madho Lal Husain*, 14.
12. Lal Shahbaz in Ṭhattavī, *Tuhfat al-Kiram*, 429–30.
13. This story, taken from an eighteenth-century text, is enriched by the presence of a Shiva ling at Lal Shahbaz Qalandar's shrine and by his numerous Hindu and Muslim devotees. It suggests that here, too, it is not religious conversion that is necessarily at stake. On contemporary devotional practices around Lal Shahbaz, see Boivin, *Artefacts of Devotion*; and Jaffer, "A Drama of Saintly Devotion."
14. Asif, *A Book of Conquest*.
15. Asif, "A Demon with Ruby Eyes."
16. Gandhi, *The Emperor Who Never Was*.
17. Puri and Akhtar, "Sarmad, The Naked Faqir."
18. The Mughals understood themselves as descendants of Timur, or Timurids. The association with the Mongols, and the name Mughal, is a misnomer. Rajputs comprised a set of Indic martial groups, which were inducted into the Timurid

Empire in the sixteenth century, and became an important pillar of the Timurid nobility.

19 Babur, *The Baburnama*, 112–13.
20 In Babur's time, the place name denoted northern India.
21 Babur, *The Baburnama*, 112.
22 Other scholars have noted the use of the language of love and the address of the beloved to superiors in the early modern era as also to friends; see Kinra, *Writing Self, Writing Empire*, 174–200; Flatt, "Practicing Friendship"; and Ali, "The Death of a Friend."
23 Andrews and Kalpaklı, *The Age of Beloveds*.
24 Babur, *The Baburnama*, 48, 58, 60–61, 218.
25 Babur, *The Baburnama*, 60–61.
26 This condemnation was shared more broadly in society and Sufi orders; see El-Rouayheb, *Before Homosexuality in the Arab-Islamic World, 1500–1800*; and Bashir, *Sufi Bodies*, 144–48.
27 Begam, *The History of Humāyūn*, 105.
28 Andrews and Kalpaklı have argued for the importance of the semiprivate settings of love, screened from the full view and censure of the public; see *The Age of Beloveds*, 59–84.
29 Schimmel, *Mystical Dimensions of Islam*, 289–90.
30 These are folk romances told in Sindh, Punjab, and beyond. Each of them ends in the tragic death of the lovers. Significantly, stories of love across genders, while often considered historic, have tenuous links to historical figures evidenced in chronicles and other such genres.
31 On appropriately directed love between Sufi master and disciple, see Bashir, *Sufi Bodies*, 107–34.
32 My thanks to Akber Chandio for sharing his research, knowledge, and linguistic expertise.
33 For biographical accounts of Qadir Bakhsh Bidil, see Harjani, *Divan-i Bidil*, 41–127; and Soomro, *Ahval o Asar i Abdul Qadir Bidil Sufi Al-Qadri*, 33–44.
34 Mansur al-Hallaj was executed by the Abbasids in 922 for saying, "I am the Truth," which was interpreted as a claim to divinity. Sarmad was executed by the Timurid king Aurangzeb in 1660.
35 Bray, *The Friend*, 6.
36 My thinking on the present's relationship to the past has also been greatly enriched by the works of many scholars. I acknowledge some of my debts here: Arondekar, *For the Record*; Asif, *A Book of Conquest*; Zaman, "Cities, Time, and the Backward Glance"; Moffat, *India's Revolutionary Inheritance*; Kavuri-Bauer, *Monumental Matters*; and Berlant, *Cruel Optimism*.
37 Chishtī, *Taḥqīqāt-i Chishtī*, 354.
38 Chishtī, *Taḥqīqāt-i Chishtī*, 357–60.

39  See Wolf, "The Poetics of 'Sufi' Practice"; and Wolf, *The Voice in the Drum*.
40  See El-Rouayheb, *Before Homosexuality*; Andrews and Kalpaklı, *The Age of Beloveds*; and Najmabadi, *Women with Mustaches and Men without Beards*.
41  For example, the Indian Muslim and nationalist leader Abul Kalam Azad wrote an essay on Sarmad; see Troll, "Abul Kalām Āzād's 'Sarmad the Martyr.'"

BIBLIOGRAPHY

Ali, Daud. "The Death of a Friend: Companionship, Loyalty and Affiliation in Chola South India." *Studies in History* 33, no. 1 (February 2017): 36–60. https://doi.org/10.1177/0257643016677455.

Andrews, Walter G., and Mehmet Kalpaklı. *The Age of Beloveds: Love and the Beloved in Early Modern Ottoman and European Culture and Society*. Durham, NC: Duke University Press, 2005.

Arondekar, Anjali R. *For the Record: On Sexuality and the Colonial Archive in India*. Durham, NC: Duke University Press, 2009.

Asif, Manan Ahmed. *A Book of Conquest: The Chachnama and Muslim Origins in South Asia*. Cambridge, MA: Harvard University Press, 2016.

Asif, Manan Ahmed. "A Demon with Ruby Eyes." *Medieval History Journal* 16, no. 2, (2013): 335–69.

Babur. *The Baburnama: Memoirs of Babur, Prince and Emperor*. Translated by W. M. Thackston. Washington, DC: Smithsonian Institution, Freer Gallery of Art, Arthur M. Sackler Gallery, 1996.

Baranī, Ḍiyā'-ad-Dīn. *Tarīkh-i Fīrūz-Šāhī*. Edited by Syed M. Azizuddin Husain. Rampur, India: Rampur Raza Library, 2013.

Bashir, Shahzad. *Sufi Bodies: Religion and Society in Medieval Islam*. New York: Columbia University Press, 2011.

Begam, Gulbadan. *The History of Humāyūn: Humāyūn-Nāma*. Translated by Annette Susannah Beveridge. London: Royal Asiatic Society, 1902.

Berlant, Lauren Gail. *Cruel Optimism*. Durham, NC: Duke University Press, 2011.

Bray, Alan. *The Friend*. Chicago: University of Chicago Press, 2003.

Boivin, Michel. *Artefacts of Devotion: A Sufi Repertoire of the Qalandariyya in Sehwan Sharif, Sindh, Pakistan*. Karachi: Oxford University Press, 2011.

Chishtī, Nūr Aḥmad. *Taḥqīqāt-i Chishtī*. Lahore: Al-Faisal, 1993.

El-Rouayheb, Khaled. *Before Homosexuality in the Arab-Islamic World, 1500–1800*. Chicago: University of Chicago Press, 2005.

Flatt, Emma. "Practicing Friendship: Epistolary Constructions of Social Intimacy in the Bahmani Sultanate." *Studies in History* 33, no. 1 (February 2017): 61–81.

Gandhi, Supriya. *The Emperor Who Never Was: Dara Shukoh in Mughal India*. Cambridge, MA: Harvard University Press, 2020.

Harjani, Gidumal Khatanmal. *Divan-i Bidil: Bidil Ji Savanih-i Umari Ai Surudnamah*. Rohri, Pakistan: Bidil Memorial Committee, 2007.

Jaffer, Amen. "A Drama of Saintly Devotion: Performing Ecstasy and Status at the Shaam-e Qalandar Festival in Pakistan." *Drama Review* 62, no. 4 (2018): 23–40.

Karamustafa, Ahmet T. *God's Unruly Friends: Dervish Groups in the Islamic Later Middle Period, 1200–1550*. Oxford: Oneworld, 2006.

Kavuri-Bauer, Santhi. *Monumental Matters: The Power, Subjectivity, and Space of India's Mughal Architecture*. Durham, NC: Duke University Press, 2011.

Kinra, Rajeev. *Writing Self, Writing Empire: Chandar Bhan Brahman and the Cultural World of the Indo-Persian State Secretary*. Oakland: University of California Press, 2015.

Krishna, Lajwanti Rama, and A. Rauf Luther. *Madho Lal Husain: Sufi Poet of the Punjab*. Lahore: Shaikh Mubarak Ali, 1982. http://hdl.handle.net/2027/mdp.39015046409978.

Lal, Ruby. *Domesticity and Power in the Early Mughal World*. New York: Cambridge University Press, 2005.

Moffat, Chris. *India's Revolutionary Inheritance: Politics and the Promise of Bhagat Singh*. Cambridge: Cambridge University Press, 2019.

Moin, A. Azfar. *The Millennial Sovereign: Sacred Kingship and Sainthood in Islam*. New York: Columbia University Press, 2012.

Najmabadi, Afsaneh. *Women with Mustaches and Men without Beards: Gender and Sexual Anxieties of Iranian Modernity*. Berkeley: University of California Press, 2005.

O'Hanlon, Rosalind. "Manliness and Imperial Service in Mughal North India." *Journal of the Economic and Social History of the Orient* 42, no. 1 (1999): 47–93.

Puri, Rakshat, and Kuldip Akhtar. "Sarmad, the Naked Faqir." *India International Centre Quarterly* 20, no. 3 (1993): 65–78.

Schimmel, Annemarie. *Mystical Dimensions of Islam*. Chapel Hill: University of North Carolina Press, 1975.

Soomro, Abdul Ghaffar. *Ahval o Asar i Abdul Qadir Bidil Sufi Al-Qadri*. Jamshoro, Pakistan: Sindhi Adabi Board, 2012.

Ṭhattavī, Mīr 'Alī Shīr Qāni'. *Tazkirah-i Maqālāt al-Shu'arā*. Edited by Ḥusām al-Dīn Rāshidī. Karachi: Sindhi Adabi Board, 1957.

Ṭhattavī, Mīr 'Alī Shīr Qāni'. *Tuhfat al-Kiram*. Edited by Makhdum Amir Ahmed and Nabi Bakhsh Khan Baloch. Translated by Akhtar Rizvi. Karachi: Sindhi Adabi Board, 1959.

Troll, Christian W. "Abul Kalām Āzād's 'Sarmad the Martyr.'" In *Urdu and Muslim South Asia: Studies in Honour of Ralph Russell*. Edited by C. Shackle. London: School of Oriental and African Studies, 1989.

Wolf, Richard K. "The Poetics of 'Sufi' Practice: Drumming, Dancing, and Complex Agency at Madho Lāl Husain (and Beyond)." *American Ethnologist* 33, no. 2 (2006): 246–68.

Wolf, Richard K. *The Voice in the Drum: Music, Language, and Emotion in Islamicate South Asia*. Urbana: University of Illinois Press, 2014.

Zaman, Taymiya R. "Cities, Time, and the Backward Glance." *American Historical Review* 123, no. 3 (2018): 699–705.

Pasha M. Khan

# 3

# Fixed Possibilities

The Threat of Transmasculinity in the Urdu Tale of Agar

If we had to fix a definition of the *qissah*, we might call it a tale of possibilities. The kinds of possibilities that we would understand as transgender filled pre- and early modern era South Asian storytellers' accounts. In Urdu and Persian tales, men would fall into enchanted wells and emerge as women on the other side ('Izzat Allāh Bangālī 2007, 671–72), and women would dress in masculinized clothing and take to the battlefield incognito (Firdausī 1987, 2:132–37; Ghālib Lakhnawī 2011, 257–58, 444–46; 'Alī Khān 1967). The Urdu *Qissah-i Agar Gul,* or *Agar's Tale*, is ascribed to a person named 'Āsī, and was written most likely during the first half of the nineteenth century (Dā'ūdī 1967, 12–14).[1] This *qissah* is centrally concerned with the adventures of Prince Agar, who was born a girl, but transformed according to his unsettled desire for masculinity to be not necessarily a man, but most often male.

Agar's transformations were not restricted to a single change from female to male, nor did he perform any singular, fixed masculinity throughout the tale. At will he became a dragon, a demon, a woman, a prince, a physician, a magician, a trickster. Why, then, is it primarily his transmasculinity that strikes the present-day reader? Is it not our need for past exemplars, for ancestors who would render transmasculine and transgender identities transhistorical, giving them a safe firmness by rooting them in history? In the face of invalidations and denials of the very existence of any human who is not cismale or cisfemale, is it any surprise that there arises a desire for such long, firm roots?

A queer desire for a historical, celebratable past has shaped some of the most important work on pre-twentieth-century South Asian verbal art. I am thinking of the pioneering work of Ruth Vanita and Saleem Kidwai (2000), as well as Scott Kugle's (2017) engaging scholarship on Siraj Aurangabadi. On the other hand, scholars such as C. M. Naim (2004b; George et al. 2002), Tariq Rahman (1988; 1990), and Carla Petievich (2001a; 2001b; 2007), and Khaled El-Rouayheb (2005) in the Arab-Ottoman context, have drawn attention to discontinuities in the history of queered identities, the difficulty of reading history from genres of imaginative verbal art, and the noncelebratable qualities of queered texts.[2] These problems raise questions about the extent to which we could claim a text like *Agar's Tale* for ancestor-making purposes. Towle and Morgan (2002, 477–83) have argued that, for trans people in White-majority nations, depicting the "transgender native" as an ancestor living in a primordial noncisnormative utopia is simplistic, and glosses over real differences and discontinuities. The same argument might be made even for racialized elites using new terms to describe established ways of existing, such as "trans" for *hījṛās* and others, or "two-spirit" for the great variety of nonbinary gender roles recognized by Indigenous nations in Turtle Island/North America.[3] To point out the potential occlusion that such terms perform is not to delegitimize their creative appropriation, especially by non-elites, or forms of ancestor-making that recognize difference.

What if we could indeed understand Agar as a transmale ancestor? Regardless, his story is not readily celebratable. If social media is any indication, decolonial and anti-cisheteronormative activism are, in the 2020s, being glued together with the argument that to decolonize is to recover non-Euro-American traditions of queerness and transness that existed before colonialism. Trans and queer lives were valued by precolonial populations before the West brought homophobic and transphobic ideas to the societies that they colonized, so goes the recuperative argument. Certainly, in British India laws such as Section 377, aimed at homosexual acts, and the parts of the Criminal Tribes Act aimed at "eunuchs" (*hījṛās*, etc.) were unprecedented threats to the existence of marginalized people (Dudney 2018; Hinchy 2019). But the past that these laws ruptured was no queer utopia, as Kugle implicitly acknowledges when he recognizes in the male-loving male Sirāj Aurangābādī's reference to the Hanafi norm of *taʿzīr* (discretionary) punishment for sex between males (2017, 84).

When I read *Agar's Tale*, I grew prematurely excited about its representation of transmasculinity, queer desires, and kinship. Prince Agar was able to maintain his maleness throughout most of the tale, had intimate encounters with magical human and pari females, and befriended a talking horse, a jinn, and a Simurgh. His closest relationship was with his teacher, the Jogi, a quasi-kinship forged on the basis of epistemic desire. But in the final chapters of the *qissah*, King Gul managed to marry Agar, very much against his will. Agar was persuaded to change into women's clothing, and Gul raped him.

The jolt of the concluding rape made me revise my idealistic reading of the *qissah*. To appropriate Kadji Amin's words, "I grew ... disturbed by aspects of ... queer relations that would not fit this utopian narrative" (Amin 2017, 5). I went back through the narrative, and with fresh eyes I noticed the ways in which transmisogyny and the reproductive imperative had been at work from the beginning. In fact, they work not in spite of, but through queerness, in a manner that I cannot delineate here, but which would require a queer deidealizing reading à la Amin.

I owe a debt to Bee Khaleeli for making me aware of the pitfalls of an exclusive focus on survival at the cost of understanding the permanence of loss. The present reading is informed by what they have taught me.

## UNFIXED TRANSMALE/TRANS-AMRAD MASCULINITY

*Agar's Tale* brims with transformations of many kinds. Not all transformations have to do with gender as we understand it. A magic flower turns women's bodies male and vice versa. Females dress as males, men as women; while other forms of cross-dressing produce more complex layerings of binary gender. Less evident forms of gender development occur through the ingestion of food and the internalization of examples, the teaching relationship. But there are class transformations as well, through disguise and masquerade, and through kin-making acts. Trans-species metamorphoses happen. Agar becomes a dragon, Red Demon becomes a peacock, the parī Sarwāsā insists on being a pig, no matter how much her dad dances around brandishing his sword at her. People get older in the tale. They also get younger. They fall ill and they convalesce. They become invisible, and they reappear into the visible world. Flesh turns to stone, stone to flesh.

Yet gender, or the male/female binary, is foremost in my mind as a modern reader, and I believe that it would be so for many if not most of us in the present. This fixation on gender over all else is worth questioning, though I cannot perform that questioning here. We might have concentrated on other forms of transformation, but there is no doubt that masculinity and femininity are crucial to the tale, which is driven by a conflict that is between Agar's desire for his fluid masculinity and the desires of others to fix his gender as female.

Born a girl, Prince Agar insisted that he was male. He wanted masculinity. But it was not a fixed manliness that Agar wanted. If a person wished to attempt to take Prince Agar in their grip as an ancestor, they would have to describe him as a transmale; not quite as a transman. Agar did not always describe himself as a man (*mard*). At least twice, he referred to himself as an *amrad* or *sādah*: a beardless young male desired by older men ('Āsī 1967, 59, 152). The *amrad* identity or gender, forged at the confluence of maleness and bodily youth, is not the same as the manly identity that looms in the *amrad*'s future, even though such a future manliness may already haunt the *amrad*. *Amrad*ness might not be tied to the passage of time as much as to a body style associated with a certain time of life, in such a manner that a male in his twenties might remain an *amrad* (El-Rouayheb 2005, 30–31). Agar was a trans*amrad* who would never "grow up" into a man at all, but was nevertheless inhabited by the manliness expected of him in the future.

Agar became physically recognizable as male through changes of bodily extensions such as clothing, and also via fleshly changes such as chest-flattening, the latter brought about by means of magical devices (94). But his *amrad*ness and maleness were never fixed. He dressed as a woman when the necessity of doing so accorded with his desire to gain a renowned falcon (88). He married the female *parī* Sarwāsā after describing himself to her as a woman. "Sarwāsā," he said, "like you, I am a woman. Only on the outside am I a man. … Swear by Prophet Sulaimān you won't blab about my state to anybody!" (103). Though Agar told her of his internal state (*ḥāl*) of womanliness to win her consent to marriage, when the two had slept together and Sarwāsā suggested that Agar bathe in her magic pool and turn bodily into a man, Agar passed up the opportunity. He explained, "God has gifted me with a manly power [*himmat-i mardānagī*]. Because of it, so many of my labours have been successful" (104). After the two had revealed their bodies to each other, "the oyster facing the oyster," Agar indicated that though a body read as womanly lay beneath the masculine clothes, manliness flowed within that body. What other layers, currents, and forms there might be to Prince Agar, who knows?

Agar's lover and eventual rapist King Gul desired to fix Agar's femininity in his knowledge and in his home. His curiosity about Agar preceded his conviction that Agar was a woman (74). One might argue that his was an *amrad-parast* attraction, an attraction for Agar as an *amrad*. But the *qissah* mirrors the strictures of the world with regard to sex between males. For example, Red Demon's *amrad-parastī*, or preference for *amrad*s, was well within the limits of the contemporaneous understanding of Islamic law: desire and devotion, and even some cuddling, were all licit. But there was no sex between Red Demon and Prince Ruby as far as we know. When Agar visited the lovesick Gul in the habit of a physician, he guilefully admonished him for being attached to an *amrad*, demonstrating that the potential of *amrad-parastī* to exceed legal bounds is at play in the *qissah*. Gul immediately replied that Agar was a woman and not an *amrad* (152). However legitimate non- and presexual play may have been between a man and an *amrad*, it was necessary for Agar to be female for him to be a legitimate sexual partner for Gul.

And Gul was certain that Agar was a woman. He had mounted his flying throne, and hovered above Agar in secret, an astonished voyeur watching Agar turn into a demon breathing fire to show his friends his metamorphic possibilities. At seeing his transformations, an astonished Gul recited this verse: "Is he a flame, or lightning, or the air? Nothing has been fixed/proven—what is he?" "*Kuchh sābit nah hū'ā kyā hai yeh*" (86–87). The term *sābit* means fixed or stable, like a woman in her identity or in her home, but also proven, as an object of inquiry.

Merguerian and Najmabadi have argued that a *qissah*'s patriarchal or heteronormative ending need not determine our reading of the entire tale. They put forward the notion of fragmentary reading, in which the audience is at liberty to read fragments of a tale out of context (1997, 501). This strategy fits the paratactic structure of *qissah*s. As Shamsur Rahman Faruqi has shown, a *qissah* is made up of a series of episodes juxtaposed with one another, in contrast to the modern ideal of a plot with a throughline from beginning to finish. *Qissah*s would have been experienced by a storyteller's audience in this fragmentary manner. Storytelling enthusiasts might have arrived late to the performance, or they might have needed to leave early. Some evenings, they might not have been able to attend at all. They would have entered the tale at various points, and left it without hearing the end, the tale structured in such a manner that it would whet the hearer's appetite to hear more, but would not be incomplete simply by virtue of not coming to a final *telos*.

Therefore, the idea of fragmentary reading is entirely consistent with the form and performance of the *qissah*. But the kind of antiteleological reading that Merguerian and Najmabadi suggests runs into complications when we are presented with a written *qissah*, with a violently cispatriarchal ending that purports to be complete. A simple elision of the violence of this ending would be a form of complicity with its cispatriarchy, a kind of idealization. Fragmentary reading must therefore follow a thorough examination of what is disturbing about the *qissah*.

## FEMININITY, FIXED

At the nexus of reproduction, family, and political stability, dynastic continuity was the reason that Agar became male in the first place. Though he subsequently chose the maleness into which he had been rendered, it is important to recall the circumstances behind his turning from female to male. These circumstances haunted Agar's maleness, undoing it in the end.

Like many *qissah*s, *Agar's Tale* begins with the king of a patrilineal city-state that is without a male heir. The king of Poppyseed City Mansūr Shāh and his similarly childless Vizier Khushhāl each obtained an apple that proved to be the seed of their progeny. The chief wife of Mansūr Shāh gave birth to Prince Ruby, while Khushhāl's wife bore the twins Agar and Mahmūd (31–36). When the *amrad-parast* Red Demon kidnapped Prince Ruby (39), the king, though disconsolate, resorted to making the twelve-year-old Agar into the new prince, changing her into a male:

> It transpired at last that the King adopted the Vizier's daughter Agar as his son, and placed her on the royal throne as his heir. It was whispered about everywhere, amongst all the citizens of the kingdom, that the King's son, never beheld even by the eye of the Sun, was to be exhibited upon the seat of state. When they heard the news, the people of Poppyseed City took heart, and made pilgrimages to peep at the heir to the throne. ... It was said among the folk that he was a prince with a countenance like Yūsuf's, justice equal to Nausherwān's, generosity like Hātim's, and courage like that of Rustam. (58)

Neither Agar's femaleness nor his maleness was chosen by him in the first place. Like all gendered beings to a certain degree, he became gendered "for others" (Butler 2004, 25). His gender and his familial ties were changed at the king's wish, through a claim and a public spectacle on the part of the state, and on the part of the populace, through recognition, the dissemination of news, eye-witnessing, and the attribution to Agar of the virtues of the conventional male exemplars of beauty, justice, and courage. He was invested with signs of maleness at the same time as his femaleness was made invisible and effaced.

Agar set about owning his maleness *futafut*. When he attracted the Jogi, hoping to gain occult powers and knowledge from this older man, the Jogi misgendered him at first: "For a daughter like yourself I would sacrifice a thousand sons." Agar corrected him, "I am no daughter. You've mistaken me, maybe because of my *sādagī*." Agar asserted not that he was a man, but that he was *sādah*, clean-shaven, that is, an *amrad*. The Jogi laughed in response, "Oh true! Haha! You are better than any son!" (59). His laughter echoed with unfixed and ungraspable meanings. It is only for the sake of this analysis that I attempt to congeal its vibrations into an explanatory story.

What if the Jogi's laughter was conspiratorial, signaling that he was willing to play along with and play at the truth of Agar's being a male? What if it indicated his agreement to evade the interdiction on heterosociality between a man and an elite woman who ought to be in *pardah*? In this case his statement may have been a way of doubling down on the truth that the Jogi had already stated himself: *I would sacrifice a thousand sons for a daughter like you, for you are better than any son*. This statement is one of the many unanswered innuendos or suggestions (*ramz o kināyah*) in the tale (compare the reference to *ramz o kināyah* at 118). We are left to imagine on what basis the genderfluid Agar was better than a son, but I suspect it was because of his possibilities in excess of kinship, in excess of sexual relations, and in excess of maleness. Perhaps his superiority was due to the mechanism by which his excesses were possible: the play, guile, *makr*, that he shared in common with women, and with tricky men like the Jogi.

Subsequently Agar presented himself matter-of-factly as the Jogi's son to the Jogi's servants (60) and his incredulous wives (78–79), and to Gul, who fumed at the refusal of "that son of a jogi [*jogī bachchah*]" to come to the wedding he had specially arranged between Prince Ruby and Māh Parwar Parī (74). In attaching himself to the Jogi as a teacher and father, Agar claimed a subnormative masculine lineage. In doing so, he did not altogether abandon kingship or blood relations. But because kingship both empowered and threatened to constrain Agar, his kinship-play with the Jogi offered him a means of escape into a form of monastic governmentality (Chatterjee 2012; 2015), in which escape the Jogi aided him. For instance, when King Gul sent an emissary to ask the Jogi for permission to play polo with Agar, the Jogi replied, "Gul is the son of a king. Agar is the son of a jogi. What connection could there be between a king and a beggar?" (96). Although Agar participated in the state power of Poppyseed City, Agar's connection with the Jogi gave him a way to escape Gul's homosocial class desire to rub elbows with him as a fellow member of the ruling class.

The Jogi's shielding of Agar in this manner continued even after Agar's biological father, the Vizier Khushhāl, promised King Gul that he would marry Agar to Gul. Khushhāl's reply indicated four factors blocking Gul's path to making Agar his wife, of which two related to Agar's relationship with the Jogi:

> Second, there is great fondness between her and the Jogi. She keeps herself busy pleasing him, so much so that the Jogi's view must be taken into account for this matter to be accomplished. Third, the Jogi possesses occult powers over all of the jinns and paris. Even Red Demon can do nothing against him.... But, if you say so, we will have the wedding. Whenever I find her willing, I'll have them tie the knot.

Khushhāl averred further that Agar, whatever his gender, had reached the age of majority and could not be coerced into marriage. But additionally, Khushhāl recognized the Jogi's fatherhood and guardianship of Agar over his own sanguinary fatherhood (114–15). Therefore, the Jogi's authority and occult powers also stood in Gul's way, unless the Jogi could be persuaded. When Gul confronted Agar with the information that Khushhāl had promised his daughter to him, Agar retorted, "Yes, I too have heard that you're engaged to the Vizier's daughter. But I'm the Jogi's son, so why the hell are you trying to prove you have some kind of right over me, huh?" (128).

Agar's monastic kinship with the Jogi not only provided him with a subnormative male exemplar; it also gave him time and a space away from the biological kinship that cast him as the Vizier's daughter, and the patrilineal dynastic role that he did not choose, but by which was made male. The latter role was in any case threatened and finally nullified by the return of Prince Ruby to Poppyseed City. If his power in the Jogi's domain was so great, then why did he at last consent to marry Gul?

Prince Agar at last chose to make of himself a sacrifice to the same national (state-familial) regime that had made him prince. Once Gul and others suspected Agar of being female, and that he was the daughter of

Khushhāl the Vizier instead of the Jogi, the fluidity of his gender became a threat to the familial and social order. The men of Poppyseed City and neighboring states viewed him as feminine or *amrad*; the one thing that Agar never became was a bearded man. As long as he was suspected of being of a gender desirable by men, his appearance in the male homosocial sphere would cause trouble.

It was Prince Agar's misfortune to be harassed by two male lovers: King Gul and ʿAskarī Pahlwān. ʿAskarī was a hypermasculine figure, excessively male, his maleness overflowing into bestiality.[4] He laid siege to Poppyseed City and terrorized the populace. He insisted to all of the Poppyseedians that Agar was a woman. He wanted to make her his own, to sing to him. At last, however, ʿAskarī happened to read of Agar's exploits, and he realized, "How would anyone who has performed such youngmanly feats [*jis ne aisī jawānmardī kī hai*] accept to have someone rule over them?" He slunk away to the wasteland he called home, making the excuse that he had to pee (161–63).

Gul seized this opportunity to represent Agar's situation to him as one filled with perils for society:

> Today this evil happened to miss your head, ... but it has been proven [*sābit*] to everyone that you are a woman in reality. Because of your cheeks' roses, everybody is going insane and disorderly [*maftūn*]. It is better for you to settle down somewhere, and wash your hands of all this. (163)

Gul, who had previously been unsettled by Agar's unfixedness, or the unprovenness of his gender, now represented to Agar that he had been "fixed" as or "proven" (*sābit*) to be a woman by his very public showdown with ʿAskarī Pahlwān. As long as he asserted his prerogative as a man to move about unfixedly in male homosocial space, his perceived womanliness would cause disorder. The term *maftūn* is cognate with *fitnah*, "sedition," a term with sociopolitical resonances. *Fitnah* is often the upshot of the malady of desire, but it is especially connected with women, owing to a *hadīth* attributed to the Prophet Muhammad (Geissinger 2015, 147, fn. 154). Gul did not perceive *fitnah* as the fault of the *maftūn*. It was the fault of the woman who made herself an object of desire by being in the wrong place. Agar, according to Gul, must accept the fixing of his femininity as well as his spatial fixity, for the sake of social order.

The threat of social disorder was not enough to convince Agar. He immediately resisted, denying that he was anything like the *fitnah*-tastic female beloveds Shīrīn and Lailá (164). Red Demon (120–21), Mansūr

Shāh (114), and ʿAskarī Pahlwān (163) had all remarked, at various points in the tale, upon the youngmanly acts (*jawānmardī*) that made Prince Agar ungovernable. *Jawānmardī* or *futuwwat*, the knightly ethical code that I am translating as "youngmanliness," is masculine-gendered, deriving from the Persian *jawān mard* or the Arabic *fatá*, both of which mean a young man. The performance of youngmanliness is therefore a manly performance. Therefore, Agar was relatively successful at banking on his well-recognized *jawānmardī* to avoid becoming fixed as a woman. With knightly bravado, he promised to subdue any man who attempted to become his husband in future.

At last Gul suavely pressured the Jogi, pointing out the discrepancy between, on the one hand, the Jogi's claim that Agar was his son, and, on the other hand, Khushhāl Vizier's willingness to affiance Agar to Gul, which indicated that Agar was the daughter of the Vizier. Gul also brings his own kinship with the Jogi to bear in his arguments, and here the tale reminds us that the Jogi is Gul's maternal uncle. Therefore, the Jogi's persuasion would make Agar a member of his family in a more normative manner, and his obstinacy might cause familial dissension. When the Jogi's senior-most wife Māh-i Tābān represented the situation to Prince Agar in this manner, the prince bowed down before his duty. "As disgusting as this proposal is to me," he replied, "the thought of the destruction [*barbādī*] of this family [*khānah*] leads me to accept it" (178–79). The family, or "house," must not be cast to the winds (*bar-bād*), destroyed, its fragments on the move. Agar must be settled in order to settle the family. Women are sometimes figured, including in *Agar's Tale,* precisely as residences—elite wives are *mahallāt*, or mansions, and are often found after marriage in the interior and secret space of the *zanānah* (35, 48, 78). The fixing of Agar's gender as female will also establish her as a wifely fixture for the family, figured by the house.

Despite Agar's attempt to commit suicide as the wedding festivities began, Gul married him (180–83). Agar made several stipulations meant to preserve his masculinity and freedom of movement. He insisted on his right to continue wearing masculine clothing, and to continue meeting with the Jogi (179). He even continued his military exploits, leading an army against the Jogi's foes in his last battle. Though victorious in war, Prince Agar sustained several grievous sword wounds. And when King Gul saw how his spouse had been penetrated (swords and sticks, oysters and pearls are consistently allusive throughout the *qissah*), he became distraught, complaining with drama. At last, Agar agreed to stay settled indoors (184–85).

By degrees, Agar was fixed and made intelligible as a woman: by his betrothal, his marriage, his confinement to the space of the house, and by his being persuaded to wear bridal clothing followed by his rape (186–89). As much as I am stressing discontinuity, at this juncture misogynist violence looks remarkably as it does in the present, in which the clothing of the feminized person becomes an excuse for rape; and in which, as the Delhi High Court ruled in the 2017 recent rape case against Mahmood Farooqui, "a feeble no" does not signify the absence of consent to a sexual act ("Citing Doubts on Denial of Consent, High Court Acquits Farooqui in Rape Case," 2017; Marrewa-Karwoski 2018). Gul is not responsible for his "diamond boring the pearl," for he is "intoxicated with longing" (188–89). The *qissah* stresses that he has been waiting many a day; he has abstained from sex with him despite their marriage, but today, upon seeing Agar fully fixed in femininity, he takes the opportunity, as is his right, and as was to be expected—so the tale suggests.

CONCLUSION? IF . . .

*Agar's Tale* is the story of a gender-fluid *amrad* or young male who becomes a prince, though he is born a girl, due to the exigencies of a patrilineal dynasty and the state and society that it governs. Despite taking ownership of his youngmanliness, and escaping into his kinship with a monastic, subnormative male figure, Jogi, the prince was at last feminized, married, and fixed. The *qissah* of Agar narrates the proving of Agar's womanliness. It tells of his becoming fixed and settled, both in femininity and in space, to avoid the disturbance or *fitnah* that women (and *amrad*s) cause in male homosocial space. For the sake of society and of the family of King Gul and the Jogi, he must fix himself, and Gul fixes him ultimately by raping him, weighing him down to settle at the foundation of Gul's house/family (*khānah*).

No doubt it is possible to read Gul's desire for Agar as homosexual or as an *amrad-parastī* made licit by Gul's conviction that Agar can be proven to be a woman. But especially in such a case, not only do possibilities of gender transformation come to a violent end in the rape of Agar, but Gul's male-male desire becomes disturbing, unwanted as it is by Agar. It is imperative to read such a tale first in an unhappy manner (see Ahmed 2010, Amin's queer deidealization, as well as more generally pessimistic approaches to past narrative such as Saidiya Hartman's reading of the history of the trans-Atlantic slave trade [2008]). The foregoing analysis has by no means indicated all of the disturbing, cisheteropatriarchal, and reproductive futurist aspects of *Agar's Tale*.

Can queer or trans folks in the Westernized present reach out nevertheless and touch ancestors in *Agar's Tale*? Elizabeth Freeman has argued that the past touches us, and in touching the past our historiographical bodies tingle with sensation. This emphasis on the historian's desire as they read the past, which Freeman calls erotohistoriography, arises out of her reading of literary texts and films, including Mary Shelley's *Frankenstein*, and the way that they represent desires for the past (2010, 95–105). What if we seek ancestry in a text whose dominant genre is not that of *tarīkh* (history), in a text in which historical temporality is not a main player?

I have argued elsewhere that all texts are multigeneric. Histories were sometimes traversed by *qissah* elements and vice versa. The dominant genre of certain texts might be contested. In *Agar's Tale*, however, the presence of historical reference is difficult to discern. While the genre of history was characterized by the sincerity (*sidq*) of the transmitter of the account, *Agar's Tale* is framed in terms of possibility. But not all possibilities are of the same order.

The *qissah* of Agar is prefaced by praise of God (*hamd*) and of the Prophet Muhammad (*na't*). Because so many works of verbal art begin with *hamd* and *na't*, few analyses take such prefatory paratexts into account, ignoring them as obligatory bores. Yet the panegyric preface to *Agar's Tale* provides an important clue to its reading. In its narration of Agar's birth, the story makes it clear that his name refers to agarwood (36), making no mention of the most obvious meaning of "*agar*" for any Urdu-knower: "if." Yet the reader who is attentive to the preface will notice that it subtly and pleasurably alludes to "if."

Near its beginning, the preface suggests, "If the rose [*agar gul*] did not tear apart its collar in the frenzy of its love for God, then, in the eyes of the bulbul, it would be nothing but a thorn" (29). The passage's allusion to the story's title is made unmistakable by the title's omission of the "and" (*o*). A Persian reader would, strictly speaking, expect the title to be *Qissah-i Agar o Gul* (*The Tale of Agar and Gul*), whereas it is *Qissah-i Agar Gul* (*The Tale of Agar/Gul*). "*Agar gul*" or "If the rose" in the preface echoes the "*Agar Gul*" of the title. If we think of this rhetorical play in terms of Persianate poetics and grammar, the way in which the words unfold over time makes "*agar gul*" legible as a bivalence, *īhām*, disclosing a *talmīh*, allusion. The semantic figure *īhām* requires that a word or phrase have two meanings: one immediately evident or "close" (*qarīb*), while the other is "distant" (*baʿīd*), evident only following reflection. According to the manuals of poetics, it is the distant meaning that the author intends, and ostensibly it cancels and supersedes the first meaning (Ṣahbāʾī 2009, 127). However, Shamsur Rahman Faruqi has noted the possibility of *īhām-i musāwāt*: a bivalence in which the first meaning is not sacrificed for the second (1996, 15).

In this *īhām*, "if" is the only meaning of *agar* that makes sense once the sentence has unfolded. But readers' knowledge of the title or the subject of the tale signals the additional connection between this word and the main character, especially side-by-side with the similarly bivalent "*gul*." Especially at the stage in reading prior to the disclosure of the full sentence, "*agar*" flashes out as an allusion to Prince Agar. The reader who has paid attention to the rhetoric of the tale's preface carries with her, therefore, the excess meaning of Agar's name: If.

How well this name fits him. Prince If, Agar Shāh. A protean being. A creature of possibility.

A poetic device that occurs in *qissah*s with special frequency is *barāʾat-i istihlāl*, in which the opening words of a tale prefigure the content of that tale (Najm al-Ghanī Khān Rāmpūrī 2011, 90). The preface to *Agar's Tale*, and especially the excess meaning of *agar* that it signals, is a *barāʾat-i istihlāl* that tells us how to read the *qissah* that follows (Dāʾūdī 1967, 17), most obviously in terms of the possibilities that proliferate throughout the tale. What does it tell us about time?

The "if" introduces a sentence describing a past possibility that never became a reality: a counterfactual. The apodosis (*jazā*) does not describe a past or a history that happened. It only describes what would have happened in the past had a certain condition (*shart*) been fulfilled. It happens that the outcome of this negative counterfactual sentence is a happy one for the rose, whose divine love frenzy wins it the bulbul's approbation and prevents it from being a thorn. But when we come to the character of King Gul, his mother Qarīsh affirmed that he was indeed a thorn (48). Mother knows best. And Gul was certainly a thorn in Agar's side throughout the tale. The unfulfilled possibility that the sentence proffers and sacrifices in the protasis corresponds to the sacrifice, but also the possibility, of the narrative itself.

Surely ancestors belong to pasts that have happened, or that are believed to have happened. Who takes their ancestors from a nonpast, a narrated past that explicitly did not occur? From a past that is a lie, to put it in the stark terms of some of the *qissah* genre's detractors (Khan 2019, chap. 5)? Yet in a fragmentary reading of the tale that comes before the final sacrifice, heedless of its final dissolution into heteroreproductive futurity, we find exemplars for otherwise unprecedented lives. The "what if?" enables past fantasies whose polysemy is not fixed by having-happened, and whose not having happened does not hold back future happenings. It makes available exemplars—not ancestors whose legacies are effortlessly inherited, but teachers whose lessons one must labor to claim out of a nonpast.

NOTES

1   The first known copy of the Urdu version of the *qissah* edited by Dā'ūdī was published in 1846. The *qissah*'s title is properly *The Tale of Agar and Gul*, but I am at present writing a translation under the title *Agar's Tale*, and therefore use this English title.

2   El-Rouayheb argues convincingly that men who desired other males in the Ottoman world were not simply "homosexuals" (2005, 5–8). Naim (2004a, 40) and Rahman (1988, 126–28) emphasize the mandatory chronophilia that characterized *amrad-parastī*, so that those who indulged in it were not merely gay ancestors either.

   In a roundtable discussion on their book of translations, Naim finds it "problematic" that Vanita and Kidwai "seem to present these literary representations as indicative of how same-sex love was experienced by individuals in South Asia at different moments in history" (George et al. 2002, 14).

   Naim (2004b, 64–66) and Petievich (2001b, 242, 245) argue that *rekhtī* poetry depicting erotic relations between women is indicative of heterosexual male knowledge claims rather than being historical. I would emphasize that this argument seems to hold true for certain poets and not necessarily for others.

3   See, for instance, Ankush Gupta's brief remark on ambivalence and pragmatism regarding *hījṛās*' adoption of the "trans" label (2019). For the history, criticism, and qualification of "two-spirit," see O'Brien (2009) and De Groot (2019).

4   For important reflections on what I am calling hypermasculinity in Islamicate societies, see Zahra Ayubi's writing on "hegemonic masculinity" (2019) and Sonia Wigh's remarkable study of erotological texts' unfavorable comparison of hypersexual men to various beasts (forthcoming).

REFERENCES

Ahmed, Sara. 2010. *The Promise of Happiness*. Durham, NC: Duke University Press.
'Alī, Khān. 1967. "Qissah Zaitūn o Muhammad Hanīf." In *Urdū kī qadīm manẓūm dāstāneṅ*, edited by Khalīl al-Rahmān Dā'ūdī, 1:367–498. Lahore: Majlis-i Taraqqī-i adab.

Amin, Kadji. 2017. *Disturbing Attachments: Genet, Modern Pederasty, and Queer History*. Durham, NC: Duke University Press.

'Āsī. 1967. *Qiṣṣah-i Agar Gul*. Edited by Khalīl al-Raḥmān Dā'ūdī. Lahore: Majlis-i Taraqqī-i adab.

Ayubi, Zahra. 2019. *Gendered Morality: Classical Islamic Ethics of the Self, Family, and Society*. New York: Columbia University Press.

Butler, Judith. 2004. *Undoing Gender*. New York: Routledge.

Chatterjee, Indrani. 2012. "When 'Sexuality' Floated Free of Histories in South Asia." *Journal of Asian Studies* 71, no. 4: 945–62.

Chatterjee, Indrani. 2015. "Monastic 'Governmentality' Revisiting 'Community' and 'Communalism' in South Asia." *History Compass* 13, no. 10: 497–511.

"Citing Doubts on Denial of Consent, High Court Acquits Farooqui in Rape Case." 2017. *The Wire*. September 25, 2017. https://thewire.in/gender/hc-acquits-peepli-live-director-in-rape-case.

Dā'ūdī, Khalīl al-Rahmān. 1967. "Muqaddamah." In *Qissah-i Agar Gul*, by 'Āsī, 3–28. Lahore: Majlis-i Taraqqī-i adab.

De Groot, Scott. 2019. "Two-Spirit." In *Global Encyclopedia of Lesbian, Gay, Bisexual, Transgender, and Queer (LGBTQ) History*, edited by Howard Chiang, Anjali Arondekar, Marc Epprecht, Jennifer Evans, Ross G. Forman, Hanadi Al-Samman, Emily Skidmore, and Zeb Tortorici, 3:1669–76. Farmington Hills, MI: Scribner's.

Dudney, Arthur. 2018. "In Affirming LGBTQ Rights, the India Supreme Court Struck a Blow Against Colonialism." *Slate Magazine*. September 10. https://slate.com/human interest/2018/09/india-supreme-court-sodomy-colonialism.html.

Faruqi, Shamsur Rahman. 1996. *Urdū ġhazal ke ahamm moṛ: Īhām, ri'āyat, munāsibat*. New Delhi: Ghālib Academy.

Firdausī, Abū al-Qāsim. 1987. *Shāhnāmah*. Edited by Jalāl Khāliqī-Muṭlaq, Mahmūd Umīdsālār, and Abū al-Faẓl Khaṭībī, vol. 2. New York: Bibliotheca Persica.

Freeman, Elizabeth. 2010. *Time Binds: Queer Temporalities, Queer Histories*. Durham, NC: Duke University Press.

Geissinger, Aisha. 2015. *Negotiating Interpretive Authority in Second/Eighth and Early Third/Ninth Century Exegesis: Shifting Historical Contexts*. Leiden: Brill.

George, Rosemary Marangoly, Indrani Chatterjee, Gayatri Gopinath, C. M. Naim, Geeta Patel, and Ruth Vanita. 2002. "Tracking 'Same-Sex Love' from Antiquity to the Present in South Asia." *Gender and History* 14, no. 1: 7–30.

Ghālib, Lakhnawī. 2011. *Dāstān-i Amīr Hamzah*. Edited by Rifāqat 'Alī Shāhid. Karachi: Oxford University Press.

Gupta, Ankush. 2019. "Trans-Lating Hijra Identity: Performance Culture as Politics." *Theatre Research International* 44, no. 1: 71–75.

Hartman, Saidiya. 2008. "Venus in Two Acts." *Small Axe: A Caribbean Journal of Criticism* 26, no. 3: 1–14.

Hinchy, Jessica. 2019. *Governing Gender and Sexuality in Colonial India: The Hijra, c. 1850–1900*. Cambridge: Cambridge University Press.

'Izzat Allāh Bangālī. 2007. "Gul-i Bakāwalī." In *Gulzār-i Nasīm*, edited by Rashīd Hasan Khān, 603–724. Lahore: Majlis-i Taraqqī-i adab.

Khan, Pasha M. 2019. *The Broken Spell: Indian Storytelling and the Romance Genre in Persian and Urdu*. Detroit, MI: Wayne State University Press.

Kugle, Scott Alan. 2017. *When Sun Meets Moon: Gender, Eros, and Ecstasy in Urdu Poetry*. Chapel Hill: University of North Carolina Press.

Marrewa-Karwoski, Christine. 2018. "Healing Myself: A Woman Recounts Her Struggles after a Court Acquitted the Man She Accused of Rape." Interview by Urvashi Butalia. *Scroll.in*. https://scroll.in/article/876788/healing-myself-a-woman-recounts-her-struggles-after-a-court-acquitted-the-man-she-accused-of-rape.

Merguerian, Gayane Karen, and Afsaneh Najmabadi. 1997. "Zulaykha and Yusuf: Whose 'Best Story'?" *International Journal of Middle East Studies* 29, no. 4: 485–508.

Naim, C. M. 2004a. "Homosexual (Pederastic) Love in Pre-Modern Urdu Poetry." In *Urdu Texts and Contexts*, 19–41. Delhi: Permanent Black.

Naim, C. M. 2004b. "Transvestic Words?: The Rekhti in Urdu." In *Urdu Texts and Contexts*, 42–66. Delhi: Permanent Black.

Najm al-Ghanī Khān Rāmpūrī, Muhammad. 2011. *Bahr al-fasāhat*. Edited by Sayyid Qudrat Naqwī. 5 vols. Lahore: Majlis-i Taraqqī-i adab.

O'Brien, Jodi. 2009. "Berdache (Two-Spirit)." In *Encyclopedia of Gender and Society*, 1:63–65. Thousand Oaks, CA: SAGE Publications.

Petievich, Carla. 2001a. "Rekhti: Impersonating the Feminine in Urdu Poetry." *South Asia: Journal of South Asian Studies* 24, no. 1: 75–90.

Petievich, Carla. 2001b. "Gender Politics and the Urdu Ghazal: Exploratory Observations on Rekhta Versus Rekhti." *Indian Economic and Social History Review* 38, no. 3: 223–48.

Petievich, Carla. 2007. *When Men Speak as Women: Vocal Masquerade in Indo-Muslim Poetry*. New Delhi: Oxford University Press.

Rahman, Tariq. 1988. "Ephebophilia: The Case for the Use of a New Word." *Forum for Modern Language Studies* 24 (April): 126–41.

Rahman, Tariq. 1990. "Boy-Love in the Urdu Ghazal." *Annual of Urdu Studies* 7: 1–20.

El-Rouayheb, Khaled. 2005. *Before Homosexuality in the Arab-Islamic World, 1500–1800*. Chicago: University of Chicago Press.

Şahbā'ī, Imām Bak͟hsh. 2009. *Hadā'iq al-Balāġhat*. Edited by Muzammil Husain. Faisalabad: Miśāl Publishers.

Towle, Evan B., and Lynn Marie Morgan. 2002. "Romancing the Transgender Native: Rethinking the Use of the 'Third Gender' Concept." *GLQ: A Journal of Lesbian and Gay Studies* 8, no. 4: 469–97.

Vanita, Ruth, and Saleem Kidwai. 2000. *Same-Sex Love in India: Readings from Literature and History*. New York: Saint Martin's Press.

Wigh, Sonia. Forthcoming 2024. "From Rahasya to Laẕẕat: Translating Secrets of Sexuality in Early Modern South Asia." Edited by Imre Bangha and Danuta Stasik. *Early Modern Literary Cultures in North India—Current Research*. Oxford: Oxford University Press.

Gwendolyn S. Kirk

# 4

## Spaces of Critique, Spaces of Desire

Gender-Crossing in Pakistani Cinema

In late December 2020, Twitter user @dapakiguy92 posted a fifteen-second clip from the film *Neend* (dir. Hassan Tariq, 1959), which caused a small stir on Pakistani Twitter as it showed doyenne of Pakistani cinema, Melody Queen Noor Jehan, receiving a brief but passionate kiss from another actress (Batool 2020). Some Twitter users applauded or made jokes about the clip, others were dismayed or claimed (falsely) that this was from an Indian movie—hence automatically morally suspect. Despite extensive regimes of censorship, Pakistani cinema has had its share of queer moments; recently, television dramas, such as *Chewing Gum* (dir. Angeline Malik, 2017), web series such as *Churails* (dir. Asim Abbasi, 2020), and a handful of other films and dramas have gained attention for their portrayals of queer relationships and identities (Khan 2020). Yet, as the clip from *Neend* shows, filmmakers in Pakistan have long played blurring lines between homosociality and homosexuality, as well as gender-crossing performances such as drag disguises or representations of characters outside the gender binary such as *khwaja sira*.[1] Kamran Ali, for instance, reads the film *Saheli* (dir. S. M. Yousaf, 1960) not merely as a heterosexual love triangle or the story of a conventional platonic friendship, but as a narrative in which two female protagonists leverage the patriarchal institution of polygamy in order to be together themselves. He writes that attention to cinema "enables me to make visible and audible those instances that may have historically enabled women (and men) in Pakistan to create emotional fields and varied forms of connection to each other" (2020, 119). Although cinema by and large subscribes to heteropatriarchal norms, paying close attention to the ambiguities in gender and sexuality—the spaces of possibility and critique, of "consent and resistance" (Hall 1981, 239)—can attune us to potential alternative readings, an alternative emotional archive available to Pakistani audiences.

This chapter analyzes three Pakistani films that feature gender-crossing and gender-bending performances: *Yakkey Wali* (dir. M. J. Rana, 1957), *Jano Kapatti* (dir. Naseem Hyder Shah, 1976), and *Aurat Raj* (dir. Rangeela, 1979). The former two are in Punjabi, and the latter is mostly in Urdu with some Punjabi scenes, unsurprising as in the Pakistani mediascape Punjabi is a language often associated with comedic and satirical performance. Exploring the contours of these performances helps us to understand the ways in which the breaking down of gendered norms lays them bare, underscores their contingency, and opens them to critique. In particular, the focus in all three films on the struggles of women—even when used as the fodder for comedy—makes a space for a feminist intervention into issues of gender-based violence and patriarchal oppression. The films also chart the resonances between norms of gendered performance and those of class, language, and ethnicity. Finally, following scholars such as Kamran Ali (2020) and Gayatri Gopinath (2000), I read these films not as closed texts, but as sites filled with potential for multiple and contrasting interpretations, productive sites for both queer and heteronormative desire. Although within the narrative of the film the two actresses in *Neend* play the role of sisters, the decontextualization of that clip and its recontextualization on Twitter neatly illustrates the agency that viewers have to interpret cinematic texts through a queer lens. This chapter thus seeks to chart some significant moments of such potentiality, the creation of spaces for questioning norms of gender identities, behavior, and roles, within the Pakistani cinema tradition.

### YAKKEY WALI

*Blurring Gender, Class, and Ethnic Lines*

The film *Yakkey Wali* narrates the story of Lali, a young woman who lives in a rural village and supports her blind uncle and younger brother and sister on the meager income she gets ferrying passengers to and from the railway station in her *yakkā,* a single-axle horse cart. After a series of misfortunes, she leaves her village and travels to Lahore, where she pretends to be a boy in order to continue her profession of driving her *yakkā* while she also seeks for her lost love interest. The film was a financial success and an early hit for new star Musarrat Nazir; however, it was not received entirely positively by the cultural elite. Critic Ahmad Said, writing on the filmmaking history of Lahore in 1962, includes *Yakkey Wali* as one of "those shameful commercial Punjabi films of which their makers themselves appear to be embarrassed" (796).[2] Although Said does not explicitly state what he finds objectionable in this film, the most transgressive content in the film is Lali's blatant violations of gender norms, as she spends about a third of the film in disguise as a man.[3] She is dressed in men's clothing and uses either a hat or a turban to hide her long hair, although she still sports obvious and feminine makeup (lipstick, eyeliner, etc.) and is never without a *sāfa* (a short scarf worn by men and sometimes tied as a turban) that can also be read as a *dupaṭṭa,* a large scarflike piece of cloth commonly worn by women across South Asia, typically covering the chest or head. Although her drag is not much of a disguise to the audience, it is highly successful within the diegesis of the film. Only during a climactic courtroom scene is her ruse detected, when she is ordered to remove her turban, thus revealing her long hair, a powerful symbol of her feminine identity. Here, she frames her choice to live as a man as one of compulsion, asking, "If I hadn't pretended to be a boy, could I have preserved my ʿ*izzat* (honor) here?" Ultimately, she is reunited with her lost love, who saves her from the villains, and in a single brief shot they ride her *yakkā* out of frame and presumably into a conventional, heterosexual marriage—the hero even holds the reins.

Lali is able to pass using her drag, which comprises not just visual transformation via clothes but also linguistic and bodily practices that are gendered male. These include masculine verbs and speech style, as well as bodily practices such as smoking, sitting in a wide-legged stance, and indelicate eating habits (this masculinity is of course also a working-class one). As Butler argues, "In imitating gender, drag implicitly reveals the imitative structure of gender itself—as well as its contingency" (1990, 137–38). Here, the pleasure for the audience lies not in Lali's success at imitation but in their privileged position of seeing through it, being "in" on the joke, and reveling in the bivalency of each action. Nowhere is this more significant than in the moments where the film blurs boundaries between homosexuality, homosociality, and heterosexuality. This play is illustrated in a sequence that illustrates Lali's navigation of these boundaries first in her relationship with Minno, a neighbor girl, and second, in her interaction with a street vendor; both rely heavily on wordplay around the term *dil*, "heart." In the first scene in the sequence, we are introduced to Minno, the daughter of another driver who has struck up a friendship with Lali's sister. Lali arrives home to find that Minno has cooked food for the sister, and asks her why. Minno responds, "*Merā dil kīttā*" (my heart wanted to/I felt like it). Lali again asks why, and the camera cuts from a midshot to a close-up of Minno's bashful face, as she responds, "Ask my heart!" Lali and Minno continue this brief flirtation in a close-up shot-reverse shot sequence that intensifies the intimacy and desire of the moment:

LALI: Your heart even speaks?
MINNO: Your heart never spoke to you?
LALI: It used to, but not now.
MINNO: Even if I say so, it still won't?
LALI: (shrugging) That's up to my heart.
MINNO: If you desire it, it will start speaking.
LALI: (gently places a hand under Minno's chin) My desire is now with your desire.

This light banter is interrupted by Lali's sister, and Lali prepares to leave. As she departs, Minno tells her, "My ears will always be listening for the bell of your *yakkā*," then rushes off, overcome by shyness. Lali raises her eyebrows and whistles in a gesture of surprise. The sequence then cuts to a street scene in which an elderly man at his food stall is calling out to customers to come try his "fresh hearts and livers." The play on the word heart continues here, as Lali orders for a plate of fried lungs. The man replies, "We're out of lungs, but if you say so I'll give you (a) heart." The Punjabi word for heart in this context lacks a plural marking as well as a definite or indefinite article, and this scene leverages this ambiguity for comedy as the phrase could mean, "I'll give you (a plate of) hearts," or "I'll give you my heart." The wordplay on heart continues for the rest of this scene, underscoring a friendly banter that is simultaneously a homosocial performance between two male-presenting characters, but also potentially can be read as a heterosexual flirtation, as the audience knows of Lali's hidden female identity. Chris Straayer offers the term "temporary transvestite film" to describe those films in which characters are compelled by various external forces to disguise themselves as members of the opposite sex within the diegesis of the film. He argues that such films "often support heterosexual desire at the narrative level and challenge it at a more ambiguous visual level where other desires are suggested" (2003, 425). In this scene of *Yakkey Wali*, in addition to visual cues, the ambiguous desire in the scene also uses the multivalency of the word *heart*, both a tasty snack and a symbol of love and desire. Perhaps the danger of this flirtation is somewhat mitigated by the man's age and the fact that we know he does not see through her disguise, but their exchange nonetheless opens simultaneous possibilities for heterosexual and homosexual readings.

Drag enables Lali not just to cross gender boundaries, but also those of ethnicity and class as she negotiates the cosmopolitanism of the city. She is depicted crisscrossing the geography of Lahore, from the walled city to Faletti's hotel, and interacting with speakers of different regional and class identities in its cosmopolitan space. One of the film's most famous songs, the *ṭappa* "*Kallī Sawārī Bhaī, Bhāṭī Lohārī Bhaī*," features shots of Lali driving her *yakkā* and intercut with those of other *yakkā* drivers singing about the different places in the city. Bhati and Lohari are the names of two gates of its walled city, and the song also mentions landmarks such as McLeod Road and the Shahi Mohalla, emphasizing that her male persona has given her free and unaccompanied access to urban spaces. This song also plays with Lali's ambiguity in her new role, both in content (several of the lyrics have double meanings) and also its form. Even though Lali is dressed in male clothing, the *ṭappa* genre itself is often associated with female singers particularly during weddings, or as a sung duel between male and female singers. Moreover, Lali's crossing is not merely one of gender, but she also uses her disguise to transcend boundaries of ethnicity and class. In one particular sequence she is shown as multilingual, speaking Siraiki, Sindhi, and Potohari with her passengers, and also encountering an Urdu-speaking *muhajir* family who are portrayed as highly comical and foreign.[4] The exaggerated ethnic stereotypes portrayed in this sequence center Lali's Punjabi identity as an unmarked one; just as her unmarked male identity gives her complete access to explore the city, she is also able to navigate social difference and transregional encounters with ease.

Perhaps Lali's greatest transformation occurs when she uses her drag to perform both another gender and another class. Dropping a passenger off at Faletti's Hotel, a posh colonial-era landmark dating back to the 1880s, she expresses interest in seeing what goes on in such a fancy place. He responds, "You can't go in there; only people in suits and boots (i.e., European attire) can go. Or people dressed like I am. And you need to know a little 'yes-no' as well." The passenger (clad in a *shērwānī* and pajama, clothing associated with bourgeois city dwellers) alights from the *yakkā* as Lali, in close-up, plays with the two words and a smile crosses her face: "Yes, no. No, yes. Yes, no, no, yes!" The camera then cuts to the interior of Faletti's where Lali, now clad in her own *shērwānī* and *qaraqulī* cap similar to her passenger, strolls into a nightclub, cigarette dangling from her mouth and bumping into things as she looks around in wonder at the place. She engages in a brief conversation with two English-speaking women in dresses, who quickly grow frustrated by her two-word vocabulary, and ends up unknowingly ordering a whiskey and water. Lali's eyes scan the room from her table, and then she sits down dejectedly, saying to herself, "I can't see the one for whom I've come here anywhere." The sequence ends with a song, a jazz band in tuxedos begins to play. Here, the filmmakers play with the generic expectations of film songs at the time—countless South Asian films from this era feature cabaret numbers (early iterations of the "item song"). However, subverting the audience's expectation of a sultry, possibly Anglo-Indian, woman in a Western-style dress, we see Lali's eyes light up as a woman in a silken *shalwār qamīz*, holding a traditional reed fan, twirls out onto the dance floor and begins singing in Punjabi. Lali has come face to face with her previous identity, in a moment of both alienation and recognition. The music shifts from jazz to Punjabi folk, and in several close-up shots we see Lali, head in hand, watching her wistfully as the familiar has now become strange.

JANO KAPATTI

*Transforming the Punjabi Woman*

*Jano Kapatti* featured one of the last performances by comedian Munawar Zareef, who played the title role acting as a woman, Jano. Jano lives in a small village where her fiery personality and propensity for getting into brawls has earned her the nickname *kapattī*—a woman who is sassy, hot tempered, and quick to fight. In many ways this character presents an archetype of classic Punjabi film heroines, who are "bolder, openly flirtatious, and often fight alongside the men rather than stand on the sidelines" (Kirk 2016, 48–49), this in contrast to the often more passive, tragic heroines of Urdu cinema of the period. In portraying Jano Kapatti, Zareef leverages the capacity of drag to distill and amplify key aspects of femininity. He wears heavy makeup and false breasts, sports large jewelry and long hair, speaks using a comic falsetto, and prances and minces in an exaggerated feminine style. Jano's only sister is married to an abusive alcoholic, a relationship that serves as the catalyst for most of the film's plot. His younger brother, Ishaq, is the object of Jano's unrequited affections; he in turn is enamored with her rival Shano. Jano's fierce personality and confident nature cause her some trouble, as she is drawn into conflicts that regularly make her the target of sexual harassment and threats of sexual violence, provoked perhaps by the threat her bold personality poses to the patriarchal order. At one point she is surrounded by four male attackers who shout, "Now tell us if you think a woman can compete with a man!" Through Jano's eyes, the audience sees a remarkably sympathetic portrayal of the daily tribulations that women face, including abusive marriages, sexual harassment, and the challenges of finding a suitable spouse. Another example occurs when, due to a chronic, mysterious pain in her abdomen, Jano regularly gets shots from the free dispensary, run by an Anglo-Indian brother and sister. The brother, enamored of Jano, continually tries to be the one to administer the shot (in her buttock), and we see Jano cleverly negotiate his harassing attentions, ensuring that she only receives her shot from his sister. Later in the film, defending herself from a rape attempt at the hands of her drunken brother-in-law, Jano throws him out of a window and then collapses in pain. She is rushed to a hospital in the city for emergency surgery.

We see Jano's sister begging the doctor to operate, even at the risk of Jano's death; the doctor replies by telling the sister that if the operation is a success, he will be able to give her an amazing piece of good news, of an event that has never happened in Pakistan before.[5] The film may also reference gender-affirmation surgeries (then called sex-reassignment surgeries) happening elsewhere in the world, a practice that had begun to expand greatly in the 1960s and 1970s (Zurada et al. 2018). Jano's sister gives permission for the procedure, although for the viewers the reason for and any detail of the surgery have been obscured. Certainly, any kind of extensive description would have risked opposition from the censor board, and so the brevity of the scene and lack of detail may have been an intentional choice on the part of the filmmakers. There is also a chance this erasure was unintentional, perhaps a result of some small error during digitization. Alternatively, as suggested by the choppiness of the editing in this particular sequence, it reflects censoring the film, either at its time of release by the censor board or perhaps informally over the ensuing decades. What does come though is that Jano's *kapattī*-ness, her defining characteristic, was not a flaw after all. Rather, modern science has instead given her the ability to retrofit this aggression and boldness into a male body where these personality attributes are understood to be positive rather than negative.

Following her surgery, Jano emerges as Jani, a transition that is celebrated by the village (with the exception of the infatuated Anglo-Indian doctor), as her widowed mother now has a son, and her poor sister now has a brother for protection. To my knowledge, this film thus represents the first representation of any kind of gender-confirmation surgery in South Asian cinema.[6] Jani in fact undergoes a double transition. He first transitions not only into a male identity, but (with the help of some girls who frequent a local club for "liberal" women) into an urban, whiskey-drinking playboy.[7] Intrigued by his gender transition, they swarm around him, and in the next few scenes that feature Jani, we see him drinking, dancing, and frolicking in swimming pools with a group of women. One song features a highly seductive dance by his main love interest, filled with shots of the two cuddling and close-ups of her swaying hips mirrored by a swaying camera, emphasizing the intoxication of the two. As the song ends, she lies back on the floor and Jani begins to climb over her prone figure; in a series of rapid cuts we see lights dimming, shoes being kicked off, and a few brief close-ups of the intertwined bodies of the two. It is as explicit a sex scene as one could imagine for a Pakistani film of the 1970s, and potentially even more titillating by dint of the curiosity audiences may have had regarding the details of Jani's surgery. Yet, Jani's identity has not quite reached its final form. After several months of waiting for his return from the village, Jani's mother is ready to give up hope, fearing that she has lost him to a life of sin in the city. She makes one last effort to retrieve him by traveling to the club, whereupon seeing her sorrowful face he immediately repents and leaves for the village, capitulating immediately to the system of patriarchal honor that compels him to return for the sake of his mother and sister.

This is Jani's final transformation, not just into any man, but into an ideal Punjabi man: rural, strong, aggressive, hypermasculine, pious and temperate, and protective of his honor at all costs. As Sevea (2014) writes, in Punjabi films "the ability to protect one's *izzat* (honor), which is vested in the body and chastity of women (who are under the guardianship of men), openly display arms and ammunition, exact revenge, and rise against the state's law and order machinery are heralded as markers of masculinity." Additionally, the rurality of the ideal Punjabi man is consistently emphasized across most Punjabi cinema, and this film is no exception. Back in the village, at last the audience is shown the fully transformed Jani. No longer clad in bell-bottoms and a jacket, but rather in a Punjabi *lāčā-kurtā* (long waistcloth and tunic), rifle in hand, he bursts in on the villains to thwart them single-handedly. His transformation is also a vocal one, as he delivers his dialogues in the classic Punjabi film *baṛhak*, a style of shouted challenges and insults (Kirk 2016, 135–45), making a pointed shift from both his comic falsetto in the first half of the film and the soft drunken slur that characterizes Jani's urban iteration. He single-handedly chases off the entire gang, and grabs his brother-in-law—his erstwhile rapist—by the collar, shouting that he will spare him only for the sake of his sister.

The transformation into a manly man is, however, mitigated in two important ways. First, although he was shown as somewhat sexually assertive before his gender change and was also shown as engaging in sexual activity during his time in the city, ultimately, he remains unpartnered at the end of the film. When his mother suggests he marry Shano, he refuses, telling her as he turns and faces directly into the camera: "I will not marry any girl until my country is self-sufficient in its food supply," thereby epitomizing the masculine virtues of self-control and patriotism. The matter is dropped and Shano is finally engaged to marry Ishaq. Second, during the final act of the film, Jani is surprisingly absent. Although we have seen his fighting ability as confirmation of his masculine prowess, he does not appear in the climactic fight scene of the film until after the villains have been defeated and the conflict resolved. In a sense, although Jano/Jani is the title character, he is erased as the true hero of the film and replaced by cisgender Ishaq, whose masculinity was never in doubt, and who completes the key actions of defeating the villains and restoring the patriarchal order. Jani's transgender identity precludes him from engaging in these heroic acts, and in the final scene he is relegated to comic relief. Arriving at the end of the climax, he stumbles upon the corpse of one of the villains and shouts to the entering policemen: "Don't take this *nilga* away, we're going to share the meat with our neighbors!"[8] He is then misgendered in the final line of the film, delivered by Ishaq, his former love interests. Ishaq teases him using the feminine verb form saying, "What nonsense are you speaking?" Although Ishaq immediately corrects himself to the masculine term, the aspersion on Jani's masculinity has been cast.

Just as in other cinematic traditions, there are myriad examples of men engaging in drag performance for comedic effect within the diegesis of the film. Perhaps no artist was more famous for these performances than Munawar Zareef himself, who used drag as a comedic disguise in perhaps dozens of films, including notably *Rangeela aur Munawar Zareef* (dir. Nazar Shabab, 1973), *Sacha Jhoota* (dir. Zafar Shabab, 1974), and countless others. In a similar vein, he occasionally acted in roles as a *khwaja sira* character, as in *Taj Mahal* (dir. S. T. Zaidi, 1968), making drag performance and gender play a keystone of his career. However, Zareef's performance as Jano stands out because rather than playing a man dressing as a woman for comedy or disguise, Zareef plays a cisgender female character for the first half of the film. Although the campiness of his performance brings it an undeniably comedic element, and of course audiences would have recognized the actor as being the male Zareef, this film is certainly unique in this regard. As noted Pakistani filmmaker and cinephile Omar Ali Khan points out:

> The first half of the movie features Munawar Zareef ripping it up as an actual biological woman rather than a man playing a woman or disguised as a woman. He is actually a woman and recognized and adored by most of the town as such despite his reputation as a "kapatti" or a super freak. Zareef lets fly in his favourite avatar as a speed-talking Punjabi village belle and does the perfect pastiche of the typical Punjabi Lollywood heroine of the era.... His performance is mesmerizing and ridiculously and viciously humorous and beautifully displays an artist at the top of his game performing the skit that he feels absolutely at home with; that of a woman. (2016)

Notably, Khan is also the director of the art horror film *Zibahkhana* (2007), which itself prominently features play with gender-crossing as one of its main antagonists, Baby, is shown to have been born a boy, who at some point transformed into a terrifying figure in a blood-spattered burqa. In *Jano Kapatti*, we also see the first representation of a transgender man in South Asian cinema, with of course an appropriate amount of caution against imposing twenty-first-century identity categories into the context of 1970s Pakistan, and also the caveat that this transman is played by a cis male actor. Momina Masood (2019) has argued for reading *Zibahkhana*'s Baby in fact as a queer, anarchic woman. However, Jani is not allowed the same anarchic agency to dismantle and destroy patriarchal systems. Instead, he becomes a model of heteronormative Punjabi masculinity, even as at the end of the film he is not only rendered somewhat asexual (despite his previous experiences with the "free thinking girls"), but also relegated to the role of comic relief while the real (cisgender) masculine hero saves the day.

AURAT RAJ

*Vocal Drag and Transgressive Power*

The cult classic 1979 film *Aurat Raj* features an unprecedented mixing of gender roles, behavior and sartorial norms, and vocal and linguistic practices. A fantasy film played out largely in an extended dream sequence, the narrative charts abused housewife Sofia's rebellion against her drunken, womanizing husband. The husband decides to follow a classic strategy from the "Muslim Social" film genre by misbehaving in order to force his wife to petition for a divorce, thereby ridding himself of his wife while avoiding having to pay her *haqq mehr*.[9] Fed up with her plight and that of countless other women, Sofia becomes the leader of the "Aurat (Woman) Party," which contests elections against the "Mard (Man) Party" and the Āzād Umīdwār ("independent candidates," i.e., a *khwaja sira* party). Convincing all the men to vote for her through song and dance, she comes to power and becomes the new Pakistani head of state. Immediately she is approached by a group of shady Westerners (in another kind of identity crossing, all played by Pakistani actors speaking in exaggerated Anglo accents), who offer to sell her a powerful bomb with curious effects: this bomb will cover the entire nation with a smoke that turns all women's voices to men's, and all men's voices to women's. Sofia, determined to buy the bomb and have her revenge on men, mortgages the entire country to the Westerners in order to buy it, also subtly implicating the West for disrupting "traditional" gender roles. The bomb is bought and detonated, and for almost the entire remainder of the film the dubbing of the actors' voices is done by performers of the opposite gender. That is, when heroine Rani (or any other female character) opens her mouth, a low-pitched male voice emerges, voicing her character, and when strongman Sultan Rahi speaks, it is in a high-pitched, exaggeratedly feminine female voice, often helpless and breathless. There are clear elements of the carnivalesque in these role reversals, but perhaps most interesting again is that the power to cross inheres in large part not merely in a visual gender transformation, but in voice. After all, President Sofia has not actually called for a gender reversal—men are still men and women are still women—but specifically a vocal reversal, a nationwide performance of vocal drag.

Although this was not an explicitly stated effect of the bomb, to accentuate these vocal changes, men's clothing and bodily movements become feminized; men are portrayed with long hair and wearing makeup, donning brightly colored *shalwar qamīz* and wearing *dupaṭṭas* for modesty over their heads and chests. They use feminized exclamations such as "*hāī Allah!*" (oh my God!) and move their bodies in mincing, feminine ways. Their access to public spaces is also limited, and with the transposition of voice women now fearlessly roam the streets, drive trains, and command armies, while men are suddenly forced to move carefully and protect their honor within a more circumscribed social space. However, they have not become women. They retain their facial hair, and they do not wear padding to suggest or wider hips or breasts (as Jano did); their bodies under their clothing are unchanged. Moreover, although the voices that emerge from their mouths are undoubtedly performed by female dubbing artists, they remain—jarringly—*grammatically* masculine, creating an even more complicated layering of linguistic gender transgression.[10] Similarly, the women in the film have not become men with the effects of the bomb; although they wear pants and shirts and military and jail uniforms their body shapes are not disguised, and they too retain feminine grammatical morphology. President Sofia forces her formerly unfaithful husband to dance for her and her companions' entertainment; she also takes advantage of her position of power to engage in her own infidelity with hypermasculine Punjabi film hero Sultan Rahi. Shehram Mokhtar has read these reappropriations of masculine power as a series of "hackings" through which the women in *Aurat Raj* interrogate and refigure the gender binary (2018).

Of course, comedic disjunctures also lay the ground for critiques of established gender roles and norms. In one particular scene, a reversal of a well-worn filmic trope, a group of giggling, burqa-clad teenagers coming home from school (who are discussing stereotypically feminine topics of jewelry and movies) is stopped and sexually harassed by a gang of pants-clad, cigarette-smoking women on the street. Again, as in the other two films, the film creates a moment that is both highly comedic, but also highlights the issue of harassment and gender violence and the negotiations women must perform in order to preserve their honor. He attempts to shame them by asking, "Don't you have a father or brother at home?" This is of course a reversal of the stock phrase, "Don't you have a mother or sister at home?" deployed by women when harassed, asking their assailants to relent by relating their own plight to those of the women in their harasser's family. However, their pleas are unsuccessful, and one of the youths, Ghumman, is abducted by a woman, Hameeda, the sister of one of Sofia's chief lieutenants. Hameeda and her gang carry Ghumman off by autorickshaw and are about to rape him. The boys implore another woman, cycling by on the street, who saves the abducted youth by shooting Hameeda, pronouncing, "No honorable sister can stand back and watch her brother's honor be stolen!" The shooter's husband laments, "I've become a widow," here combining the explicitly feminine gendered term *bēva*, "widow" (for which there exists no masculine equivalent), with the masculine gendered verb *ho gayā hūñ*, "I've become."

Once again, the unexpected disjuncture of gendered elements provides the impetus for comedy, but also, through satire, the potential for critique in its portrayal of street harassment and gender-based violence. Male audience members may enjoy the spectacle of trouser-clad sexually aggressive women, but also are forced to identify with the victims of these pervasive crimes, routinely depicted as helpless and weak. Meanwhile female audience members may both identify with the victims but also, for once, delight in their gender having the upper hand in such encounters, as women are not only the perpetrators but also the heroes in this scenario. However, women cannot remain in the position of power; the female government is shown to have badly mismanaged the country and a war breaks out. As Sofia is gunned down in the final battle the film fades to her husband shouting, "No!" as he wakes up from his dream. Of course, the entire chain of events has been merely his drunken nightmare of a world in which men are as vulnerable as women, causing him to sympathize with their plight and see the error of his ways. Mokhtar suggests that this reordering involves a recuperation and refiguring of masculinity, as the husband has "reformed" (2018). However, I argue that the ending is somewhat less revolutionary. Sofia actually insists, until almost at the end of the film, that she still wants a divorce, stating that she will not remain married to the husband who has wronged her. In response, her husband chases away their divorce lawyer and offers a single sentence by way of apology: "This cruel man seeks his punishment." Although he is repentant, and she relents and embraces him in a happy ending, ultimately it is still his agency as patriarch that acts to preserve the marriage.

CONCLUSION

These three films explore gender-crossing in markedly different ways. *Yakkey Wali* aligns with the conventions of a temporary transvestite film, while *Jano Kapatti*, in a historic first of South Asian cinema, charts the gender transition of its main character from one side of the binary to the other. Following these, *Aurat Raj* disrupts the conventional binary simultaneously through multiple gendered layers of voice, dress, and embodiment. Additionally, I also want to emphasize that in all three texts, voice and translanguaging play a critical, yet often overlooked, role in the indexicality and citationality of gender. All three films engage in wordplay with masculine versus feminine verbs, and the utility of language in performing not just gender but also class and ethnic drag is clearly illustrated in these films. In *Aurat Raj*, the linguistic choice to feature the urbane, sophisticated Waheed Murad singing a desperate lament in Punjabi, while Punjabi cinema hero Sultan Rahi employing not only a female voice, but also formal Urdu, also heightens the topsy-turvy, carnivalesque aspect of the film. As in the other two films, not only are gender boundaries crossed but also class and ethnolinguistic ones, as well as crossing the urban-rural divide. The films rely on a variety of strategies—dress, voice, language, and representation of space—to achieve this effect. This suggests that the films' gender play intersects with various other identity factors, allowing the audience the pleasure of seeing characters cross through multiple kinds of social roles and spaces.

In all three films, the narrative resolution aligns with heteropatriarchal norms; everyone returns to their normative gender identity. This resonates with Straayer's analysis of the standard plots of "temporary transvestite films" in Hollywood, and is true even of *Jano Kapatti*, where, due to the audience's knowledge that pretransition Jano is played by a cisgender man, her transition into Jani is seen as restoring some kind of "natural" gender order. Yet, as Straayer writes: "The fact that the plot is generic strongly suggests that his process is never finished, and that the generic system fulfills the viewer's desire to return again and again to a less-closed situation" (2003, 413). In the case of an artist like Munawar Zareef, gender-crossing performances were clearly a staple of his repertoire that contributed to his vast success, but such performances can be commonly found across Pakistani film traditions, in Urdu, Punjabi, and also Pashto cinema (Amir 2020, 13). This suggests that the repetition of the trope of gender-crossing performance in Pakistani cinema indicates the instability and contingency of the construction of gender in this society, even as we often associate Pakistan with a context of rigid gender roles and clearly demarcated gender boundaries in almost every sphere of life. For their audiences, such films offer an opportunity for them to delight in the play across gender lines; they open up rare spaces for subversion of gender norms, for crossing the normative limits of desire, and for critique of the heteropatriarchy.

Although the critique is most overt in *Aurat Raj*, all three films make use of the comedic elements of gender role reversal to show the misogynistic violence that would certainly have been a lived reality for the women in the audiences. They play with the trope of the *maẓlūm aurat* (oppressed woman) in ways that allow for explicit critique; for example, Jano's lament of "Oh God! *Why* am I a *girl!?*" in many ways encapsulates the portrayal in all three films of the disadvantages and disempowerment faced by women in realms of property, power, marriage, and sexuality. Additionally, the treatment of sexuality in the films (be it the reclaiming of female sexual agency in *Aurat Raj* or the ambiguity surrounding homosexuality and homosociality in *Yakkey Wali* and *Jano Kapatti*) consistently undermines the heterosexual order, affording queer interpretive possibilities to viewers and, as Ali suggests, offering scholars at least limited traces and glimpses of alternative affective archives (2020, 127). The films are careful to constrain feminist or queer imaginaries within their narratives, but yet they open up spaces of ambiguity and possibility, emphasizing the contingency of the heteropatriarchy and allowing audience members to image their own crossings and plays of language, class, and space along with gender and sexuality.

NOTES

The author would like to thank Nida Kirmani and Abdul Aijaz for extremely helpful conversations around the films under discussion that contributed greatly to the development of this chapter. She would also like to thank Omar Ali Khan for introducing her to *Jano Kapatti,* and also for his innumerable contributions to Pakistani film and film history.

1. A traditional third gender category found in different societies across South Asia; *khwaja sira* is often the preferred term in Pakistan as other variants such as *hijra* can be seen as pejorative by members of this often-marginalized group. It is also important to recognize the porous boundaries of this category; some *khwaja sira* identify as transgender women, some as intersex, and some as third gender, while not all transwomen in Pakistan identify as *khwaja sira.*
2. In fact, Said blames the "current crisis" of the film industry on these "shameful" Punjabi films: "Pičhle tīn čār baras se is sanʿat mēñ jō boḥrān shurūʿ huā is kī sab se baṛī vaja voh sharmnāk sauqiyāna panjābī filmēñ thīñ jin par ab un kē banānē wālē khud bhī nādim naẓar ātē haiñ. Yeh filmēñ '*Māhī Munḍā*' aur '*Yakkē Wālī*' thīñ" (196).

3   Notably, he contrasts *Yakkey Wali* and *Mahi Munda* with a few *sāf suthrī* ("clean") Urdu films, an early example of the hegemonic discourse that dismisses nearly all Punjabi cinema as vulgar and lowbrow.

4   Interestingly, this suggests that the stock identity categories that are commonly seen in Pakistani cinema today—stereotypes of Sindhis, Pashtuns, Punjabis, and Urdu-speaking *muhajirs*—are a more recent innovation, and the ethnic and linguistic categories most relevant to audiences have shifted significantly from this time. *Muhajir* is a term referring to people who migrated from India to Pakistan following the 1947 Partition; although this term can indicate migrants of any ethnic group, it most typically refers to Urdu-speaking people from UP and Bihar.

5   Here lies an ambiguity based on the only available prints of the film; unfortunately (and as is the case with many Pakistani films) *Jano Kapatti* has not been well preserved, and can only be accessed in unofficial, pirated form. This means that the prints available, in addition to being of less than ideal sound and picture quality, are riddled with small cuts and cut-off lines. This has implications for the analysis of a key plot sequence, the surgery scene, which seems to be missing a few key lines of dialogue due to such excisions or interference. There is an abrupt transition from the previous scene, which suggests that at the beginning of this scene the doctor announced the possibility of Jano's gender reassignment, and as a viewer in 2021 we are left with clearly missing details about the surgery and its background, including a potential connection to Jano's mysterious pain.

6   Although there may be a few scattered others, at the time of writing only one other South Asian film, the yet-unreleased *Man to Man* (dir. Abir Sengupta), was found to have portrayed a gender-confirmation surgery.

7   The women are referred to as the *Zindā Dil Club dī āzād khayāl sahēliyāñ*: the free-thinking/liberal girlfriends of the Happy Go Lucky (literally, "living heart") Club.

8   The Punjabi term for a *nilgai*, a large species of antelope (*Boselaphus tragocamelus*).

9   This term refers to money or property granted to the wife in a Muslim marriage contract; it is either payable at the time of marriage or, commonly, only in the event of a divorce initiated by the husband. If a woman initiates the divorce she generally will forfeit her *haqq mehr*, hence the common film trope in which a husband tries to drive his wife to seek divorce in order to avoid having to pay her *haqq mehr*.

10  That is, they use standard Urdu/Punjabi gender agreement in verbal morphology; women still use feminine verb forms to talk about themselves and men still use masculine verb forms to refer to themselves. The somewhat weaker equivalent in English might be to retain the same gender pronouns (Urdu and Punjabi do not have gendered pronouns).

## REFERENCES

Abbasi, Asim, dir. 2020. *Churails*. ZEE5. OTT Series.
Ali, Kamran Asdar. 2020. "On Female Friendships and Anger." In *Love, War, and Other Longings: Essays on Cinema in Pakistan*, edited by Vazira Zamindar and Asad Ali, 114–31. Karachi: Oxford University Press.
Amir, Wajeeha. 2020. "Ajab Khan Afridi in Pashto Cinema: Changing Representations and Shifting Identities." Unpublished manuscript, December 28, 2020.
Arnold (@dapakiguy92). 2020. "Noor Jahan . . . wtf???" Twitter. December 27, 2020. https://twitter.com/dapakiguy92/status/1343126652881145857?s=08.
Batool, Zehra. 2020. "Pakistanis React to Madam Noor Jehan's 'Kiss with Another Woman' in Viral Movie Scene." *Parhlo*. December 28. https://www.parhlo.com/noor-jehans-kiss-with-another-woman-video/.
Butler, Judith. *Gender Trouble: Feminism and the Subversion of Identity*. London: Routledge, 1990.
Gopinath, Gayatri. 2000. "Queering Bollywood: Alternative Sexualities in Popular Indian Cinema." *Journal of Homosexuality* 39, nos. 3–4: 283–97.
Hall, Stuart. 1981. "Notes on Deconstructing 'The Popular.'" In *People's History and Socialist Theory*, edited by R. Samuel, 227–40. London: Routledge.
Khan, Mina. "Screening Lesbian Relationships in Muslim Contexts Across the Global South." Unpublished manuscript, December 28, 2020.
Khan, Omar Ali, dir. 2007. *Zibahkhana*. Film.
Khan, Omar Ali (Swami Ji). 2016. "Jano Kapatti (1976)." *Hot Spot Film Reviews*. November 13. https://www.desimoviesreviews.com/index.php/2016/11/13/jano-kapatti-1976/. Accessed **date**.
Kirk, Gwendolyn S. 2016. "Uncivilized Language and Aesthetic Exclusion: Language, Power and Film Production in Pakistan." PhD diss., University of Texas, Austin.
Masood, Momina. 2019. "Visions of Queer Anarchism: Gender, Desire, and Futurity in Omar Ali Khan's *Zibahkhana*." *BioScope* 10, no. 1: 75–90.
Mokhtar, Shehram. 2018. "*Aurat Raj*: Hacking Masculinity and Reimagining Gender in South Asian Cinema." *Ada: A Journal of Gender, New Media, and Technology* 13: 2018. Accessed January 15, 2021. https://adanewmedia.org/2018/05/issue13-mokhtar/.
Rana M. J., dir. 1957. *Yakkey Wali*. Film.
Rangeela, dir. 1979. *Aurat Raj*. Film.
Razzaq, Adeel, writer. Kitni Girhain Baaki Hain, episode 13, "Chewing Gum." Directed by Angeline Malik. January 29, 2017. https://www.dailymotion.com/video/x59zxs2?playlist=x61en4.
Said, Ahmad. 1962. "Film." *Nuqūsh* 92: 785–97.
Sevea, Iqbal. 2014. "*Kharaak Kita Oi*: Masculinity, Caste, and Gender in Punjabi Films." *BioScope* 5, no. 2: 129–40.
Shah, Nasim H., dir. 1976. *Jano Kapatti*. Film.
Shahab, Nazar, dir. 1973. *Rangeela aur Munawar Zareef*. Film.
Shahab, Zafar, dir. 1974. *Sacha Jhoota*. Film.

Straayer, Chris. 2003. "Redressing the 'Natural': The Temporary Transvestite Film." In *Film Genre Reader III*, edited by Barry Keith Grant, 417–42. Austin: University of Texas Press.
Tariq, Hassan, dir. 1959. *Neend*. Film.
Yousaf, Shaikh M. dir. 1960. *Saheli*. Film.
Zaidi, S. T., dir. 1968. *Taj Mahal*. Film.
Zurada, Anna, Sonja Salandy, Wallisa Roberts, Jerzy Gielecki, Justine Schober, and Marios Loukas. 2018. "The Evolution of Transgender Surgery." *Clinical Anatomy* 31: 878–86.

Syma Tariq  5

# Partitioned Listening

Sonic Exercises Outside of Archival Time

The end of the British Raj and the 1947 Partition of India and Pakistan[1] delivered statehood on the condition of identitarian violence, a moment that punctured centuries of colonial subjugation, classification, and extraction and divided impossible multitudes anew. Embedded in paradox and lasting complexity, Partition—"independence"—never lived up to its promise of fulfilment. Encountering the impossible event of Partition through the oral historical records is messy and conflicting. The very idea of Partition, as literary scholar and queer theorist Madhavi Menon writes, "insists on an opposition between two wholes that are presented as holistic despite having just been butchered in two" (Menon 2015, 118).

Like other territorial partitions in the twentieth century (and this is a less discussed aspect), 1947 also saw the large-scale destruction of historical records. Like Palestine in 1948 and Ireland in 1922, evidence of colonial rule was intentionally burned, bombed, and hidden by India's partitioners, the ashes of empire scattering over new ground zeroes.[2] Much of what remained of this material from across decolonized Asia and Africa is still hidden away from public view under the orders of the UK Foreign and Commonwealth Office. The release of material pertaining to the 1947 Partition via the Mountbatten Papers has been recently vetoed by the Cabinet Office, despite consistent requests for it to be opened.[3]

My series of sound/text works *Partitioned Listening*, produced in the context of my doctoral research, responds to 1947's contemporary memory boom, marked by the widespread collection of tens of thousands of testimonies, in tandem with the genealogies of silence that the new archives contain. As an experimental and subjective historical engagement with Partition's memorial infrastructure, my research aligns with Menon's argument that it is a "condition within which we all labor" (121). While seeking out testimonies about the event, meshed in their narrative contexts and archival regimes, Partition here is proposed as a sonic condition within which there is also a labor of listening. The proliferation of speech—after decades of taboo, erasure, and silence in both the heart of empire as well as its former colonies—is considered here through the lens of historical destruction, speculating on the noise of continued devastation amid the silencing and splitting of epistemic worlds.

This essay departs from the first two works in my audio series *Partitioned Listening* in order to elaborate on their intentions and processual modes of knowledge production. Rather than approach Partition as a finite event relegated to the past, the works attest to the ongoing testimonial politics of the archive that fixes Partition as a singular act involving opposing forces. Menon's "queer theory" of Partition is useful ground for this approach: in her fable on Partition and universalism, kindly read aloud for the first sound work detailed in the next section, she argues for a queer version of universalism that "refuses both norm and antinorm," a universalism that recognizes that partitions do exist no matter how much they are wished away in the false claim of unity. Her brand of universalism "asks us to take even more seriously the idea of partitions that *do not cohere,* and it does so universally" (120, emphasis added).

Crucial to the idea of Partition as a sonic condition is the notion that instead of merely listening to difference—often across borders—we listen with it, because "we already live divided lives" (129). Aided by a practice that interpolates sound and text as a means to question Partition's sonic-archival sense of time and, shakily, space, my research ultimately sounds out one question: How, as partitioned subjects, can and do we listen?

## VOICES IN THE ARCHIVE

To "counter-listen" to testimonies in the archive is an effort in destabilizing what philosopher Nikita Dhawan calls "hegemonic 'norms of recognition,'" which "determine what can be read, heard and understood as intelligible and legible" (Dhawan 2012, 47). *Partitioned Listening: "You Trust Your Memories?"* (henceforth PL001) takes as its starting point the bonfires of imperial paper that coincided with Indian and Pakistani independence. Moving through various "Partition voices," somehow placing myself within the burgeoning culture of collecting tales of loss and trauma, it recognizes that the archival desire to document that which is forgotten, missing, or absent from history has important impulses. Given the scale of Partition's legacies and effects and the aging of witnesses, whose voices in some way replace the void left by missing written documentation of the event, the delay in the projection and production of Partition's public memory must be attended to.

At the same time, historicizing Partition as an event for the archive stages a politics that privileges the experience of violence and trauma (of some people), and frames these experiences as inevitable; this is why the processes of new archives, museums, and broadcasts must also be attended to. The event-ness that Partition inhabits is burdened with inescapability, particularly when we consider the colonialist and postcolonial nationalist narratives around tropes of the violent other, or discourses of "communalism" and the "riot."[4] As certain narratives have colonized Partition's public memory, its ontological nature as an event is carved out—partitioned, even—from the rest of history. Its status as a "uniquely devastating event," as historian Yasmin Khan writes, "works to place it beyond the bounds of comparative accounts and, perhaps, to silence its echoes in contemporary global politics" (Khan 2019, xxii).

The new archival projects that in some way depend on the ordinary voices of Partition vary: some are museal in tone and agenda from the outset, mimicking state archives in their self-assigned neutrality; others are rhizomatic networks, crowdsourcing the voices of "survivors" and witnesses who are mostly kept hidden away until opportune moments for funding or exposure. There is a dynamism involved with the digitization and curation of testimony, their copies "traveling" as part of exhibitions or shared academic initiatives. A memorial or museum or archive dedicated to Partition was deemed impossible for decades, but now they are visibly plentiful. There is now, as Kaur writes, a "disturbing paradox" in Partition's contemporary memorial turn, where "even as the project of maintaining oral history and the memorialization of Partition continue to attract great currency outside of academia and in the public sphere, it remains confined to the narratives of upper-caste survivors" (Kaur 2017).

Pioneering feminist scholarship from the late 1990s onward did much to counter this erasure.[5] With their intersectional Kamla Bhasin, Urvushi Butalia, Veena Das, Ritu Menon, and others have used radical investigatory approaches, prioritizing a politics of care in their research and publishing, particularly when recovering Partition's "recovered women" from nationalist narratives, or centering the stories of communities that were never supposed to be archived. and intersubjective approaches to history and anthropology—and grappling with unfathomable trauma—what binds these thinkers across disciplines is their centering of listening, and the challenges that arise from listening to voices that cannot always fully speak in the face of patriarchy and trauma. Crucially, their own listening is also laid bare over time, which expands the ways in which our pasts can be studied: not just listening to Partition stories told and sealing them in text form, but also sensing them through others' ears, reckoning with the contradictions and complexities over and into the everyday.

Oral history, of the kind that is stripped of this politics of the everyday and relegated to the inevitability of the past and the enclosure of the archive, has been the backbone of the "'memorial industry' that has grown out of the belated realization of Partition as collective trauma" (Kabir 2009, 488). In the end, as the event-memories of hegemonic classes are reproduced as public memory, voices are more likely to become Partition artifacts when the story's good and certain palatable norms are met—and increasingly, when narrators are filmed, named, and signed over with ideally some of their own personal belongings too. The palimpsestic truth values of the archive are made clear through its reconstitution over time—collection and categorization are entangled with institutional survival amid discourses of universalism, nation-building, historical redress, "giving voice to," and performative reparation. Partition's oral archival turn then brings up a question "at once old and new: whose wounds can be preserved, exhibited, and remembered in the public domain?" (Kaur 2017).

## "TIME IS RUNNING OUT"

Historian Ariella Aïsha Azoulay formulates the archive as a regime—one that has taken shape over centuries, well before it existed in physical form. This pins it to the colonial longue durée, as the archive was only thinkable "after millions of people in different places were already forced to embody imperial archival categories, part of a growing and unstoppable ruling operation of classification, tagging, and naming of different groups to form a human index" (Azoulay 2019, 164). The "institutional time lines" of the archive are similarly categoric through its temporal milestones, "in the form of wars, conquests, revolutions, constitutions, laws, establishments, institutions, foundations, and inventions, initiated and imposed by imperial powers. They operate as shutters, slicing the commons into pieces" (167). Azoulay's own encounters with the archive alongside a Palestinian companion—who we can also consider a partitioned subject—entails a rejection "of all the archival designations that since 1948 has made him an 'infiltrator'" (165).

As mentioned, oral history has produced important and relevant knowledges that work against such erasure, historicizing life-worlds the archive never intended to include. Producing oral history for and through the archive, however, means succumbing to the archive's authority, which ensures that "events, objects, and people are in their 'right place'—temporally, spatially, and politically" (168). Artist Shaina Anand makes a strong case for refiguring the archive as a space of alliances, "against dissipation and loss, but also against the enclosure, privatization and thematization" that concerns them globally—even digital archives, she writes, "take fortresses as their model" (Anand 2016, 79–80, 85). This leads to a call for contemporary archival impulses that go against such enclosure, that "challenge us to think through the productive capacities of an archive beyond the blackmail of memory and amnesia" (108).

The progression and linearity of archives—in their exchanges of access and labor as well as processes of ordering and categorization—jar with some of oral history's temporal forms. A largely cited motivation for contemporary Partition projects is at first a coherent one, that the Partition generation's stories are to be lost forever if not recorded, and so we are told: time is running out. This differs from the listening-centered feminist work on Partition mentioned in the previous section, as such work reveals a contrasting temporal position—time does not run out, but goes on and on, implicating the undocumented across history. This resistance against time is foundational in the act of conducting oral history according to the Italian Communist oral historian Alessandro Portelli, for whom telling a story "is to take arms against the threat of time, to resist time, or to harness time. That a tale is a confrontation with time is the attempt to carve out a special time in which to place the tale—a time *outside* time, a time *without* time" (Portelli 1991, 59). Portelli's concern with orality and time also extends to the literal time it takes: the "substantial shifts in the 'velocity' of narration, that is, in the ratio between the duration of the events described and the duration of that narration" (Portelli 2016, 51). In an oral narrative, several years can be covered in a matter of minutes, whereby a moment can be devoted many interviews over several days in its retelling. This contrasts with the given-ness of archival timelines that decide that time can and does run out—and when it does, history is delivered.

Perhaps one way to unfix the rigid dividing lines of Partition, then, is to also refuse its timelines—unlearning the archival regime, to follow Azoulay, but also rejecting outright the master's clock and maps, as the lawyer and theorist Rasheedah Phillips writes. For her, time is the experience of remembering, not "something that defines and predates the memory," too dynamic to be "embodied and frozen in mapped space" (Phillips 2018, 45). Quoting Giordano Nanni, she writes, "the conquest of space and time are intimately connected. European territorial expansion has always been closely linked to, and frequently propelled, by the geographic extension of its clocks and calendars" (45).

Philosopher Achille Mbembe also rejects (colonial) time and the hegemonic nature of its progression, proposing instead a "time of existence and experience of entanglement" (Mbembe 1989, 16). The time of "African existence," he writes, is neither linear nor sequential, where "each moment effaces, annuls, and replaces those that preceded it, to the point where a single age exists within society. This time is not a series but an interlocking of presents, pasts, and futures that retain their depths of other presents, pasts, and futures, each age bearing, altering, and maintaining the previous ones" (16). Like Phillips's ongoing work on black quantum futurism, Mbembe's interlocked and paradoxical experiences of time—which is used as a conceptual frame for the second of my audio works—can be thought together with Portelli's axes of storytelling, Azoulay's refusal of the archive's regime, and Phillips's dismantling of the master's clock. These alternative time-spaces are fitting when considering Partition as a sonic condition: a condition replete with rupture and possibility, *all the time.*

Perhaps working with sonic time-spaces in this way can help us overcome the partitioning of people and places, but also the partitioning of past, present, and future. This "counter-listening" might help supplement the missing historical record, but just as important, goes against the archive in order to "actually use and consume things, to keep them in, or bring them into, circulation, and to literally throw them forth (Latin: *proicere*), into a shared and distributed process that operates based on diffusion, not consolidation, through imagination, not memory, and towards creation, not conservation" (Anand 2016, 81).

## PARTITIONED LISTENING

Following Dhawan, *Partitioned Listening* takes the issue of representation at the heart of the politics of speech and silence—"who speaks for whom alongside what is being said" (Dhawan 2012, 48). The "epistemic violence" of imperialism, exemplified through its archival regime, is not just economic and territorial, but a "subject-constituting project" (50). The liberal democratic idea of speech as always and already politically enabling then needs to be questioned.

Tools and methods from sound studies and sound art can be a way to do that, despite the discipline's lack of attention to voice. As composer and academic Cathy Lane argues, "In sound arts we do so much listening, to the environment, to other species, to objects, to other forms of matter. But so little of that listening is to people" (Lane 2017). According to philosopher Salomé Voegelin, listening allows for "the consideration of reality and meaning from the mired position of living in a world: the reciprocity, complexity, and consequence that brings with it. It is us, the inhabitants of these possible worlds, who as listeners realize their actuality through the invested complexity of our generative reciprocity: being in the world" (Voegelin 2014, 30). Voegelin's theories of listening are placed firmly within the field of sound arts, attuning to a "sonic sensibility" with caveats—listening does not automatically produce a better world or a better philosophy, and it does not necessarily hold a superior ethical position to the visual. Theories of listening that focus on the relationship between self and sound through the medium of sound art can ignore art's institutional regime—keeping listening's political possibility separated from the means of (sonic) production. Listening's power, in the end, lies in "show[ing] us the world in its invisibility: in the unseen movements beneath its visual organization that allow us to see its mechanism, its dynamic and structure, and the investment of its agency" (3).

Engaging with archival sound collections, cultural scientist Anette Hoffmann has documented the impact of close listening to colonial acoustic archives that are understudied outside of the more schematized realms of ethnolinguistics and ethnomusicology. This close listening "makes audible that archived sound files at times speak in ways that are contrapuntal to the object status attributed to them by the recordists and in archival documentation" (Hoffmann 2015, 3). *Partitioned Listening*, though dealing with very different sonic material, makes similar demands on the postcolonized archive and its contra/dictions, particularly if we also take Partition archives as conditioned by colonial knowledge production and destruction—part of the same continuum that enacted nineteenth-century recordings of colonized subjects on wax cylinders. The "disembodied" voices that Hoffman listens to are "much like ethnographic objects in the museum, stored in a way that disconnected them from a body of knowledge, or theorising, or poetry (or all of these)" (7).

PL001 begins and ends with Menon's fable, cut in two. It posits "Partition" and "Universalism" as neighbors ("though never good friends")—Partition trails Universalism, making gains off people's particularities, which Universalism had always "traversed with indifference." PL001 ends with the second half of the fable which—excuse the spoiler—results in Partition overpowering Universalism, both living "unhappily ever after" (Tariq 2020a).

Multiple narratives emerge between Menon's fictive truths, disordering the timelines of Partition's archival regime. One is a partial tale, described and contextualized through my narration and the ominous, textural sound design by Monia Dafa: the deliberate destruction of the colonial record across the fading British Empire, starting with a fire in Delhi in August 1947—the event-time of partition. Partition's (oral) infrastructure of memory therefore occupies the same cognitive space—a space filled with listening—as the (destroyed) colonial (written) record.

My position as a listener, as well as narrator, is made audible through parallel narratives. PL001's title, "You Trust Your Memories?," is a question I ask my maternal great-uncle, *nana abu*, within the piece, as well as of the listener/reader in the universal. This echoes a stance of "critical proximity" adapted and developed by artist filmmaker Onkyeka Igwe in her research on colonial film and bureaucratic archives in Nigeria and in the United Kingdom. Adjoining dance, touch, and sound to recover women's performative anticolonial resistance across time and space, her term "nods to critical distance, the way of knowing championed by Western positivist empiricism. The critical in critical proximity attempts to place historically illegitimatised ways of knowing alongside hegemonic knowledge frameworks in the same value chain" (Igwe 2020, 45). It "allows for the body, with all of its baggage, to function, be recognised and be valued as archive" (52).

In PL001, *nana abu* describes a Partition "riot," which he witnessed as a six-year-old in 1948 in Allahabad, India. The recording was made at his house in Islamabad, Pakistan, in 2019, amid the chaos of a multigenerational family visit just before dinnertime. The sonic disruptions (kids, cousins, and aunts) that soundtrack his story told humorously despite the violence it contains, sound the production of different memories produced together, differing languages, and accents, and noise. Because of this "noise," the interview is unlikely to suit an archive's collection. As part of a "counter-listening" strategy, however, it reveals certain protocols that determine what it is to be heard and how we are supposed to listen. My question to *nana abu*, "Did you see any British at that time? Police, soldiers, people?" at first maybe seems odd for a Partition interview, but this was intentional—Allahabad was historically a chosen city by the British, who declared it as the capital of India for one day, when the Crown took over sovereign rule after the 1857 mutiny, a turning point for ramped-up colonial governance and subjugation in British India. I knew the actors I was asking about probably weren't there, but I wanted some evidence of this sense of abandonment on the recording. I did not make myself invisible, and I did not conduct the interview in the form of the individualist chronology that is favored by established archives: pre-, during, and post-Partition. Rather, I asked about the presence of colonial power. This aligns with historian Ravinder Kaur's critique of contemporary Partition history, in which "the 'human' subject... is often a free-floating agent disconnected from the realm of politics" (Kaur 2017).

The not quite verbatim transcript of what is voiced provides a space of translation, partial explanation, and reference, but also of documentation. The different roles of the transcript—which can also be read like a script—disrupts the stability of the (fictive and nonfictive) truths contained within. Artist researcher Shahana Rajani's recorded tour of the remains of a *gurdwara* (Sikh place of worship) destroyed by a Partition massacre in Karachi, Pakistan, is excerpted in two parts in PL001. Listening to these clips, it is clear that Rajani has given the tour several times before, with scripted notes. Early on, her voice brimming with facts, dates, other people's memories, and her own postmemories of Partition, she is interrupted by the guardian of the building. The conversation that also introduces the three of us attending the tour—which switches to Urdu and is not transcribed—is left in the piece rather than edited out, revealing (to Urdu speakers, but also not) our positionality within this site of history, as re-listeners. This recording—not intended nor suitable for an archive either—carries worlds of temporal violence within it, but also through its intimate forms renders unstable the dialogic categories thrown out in the story we are listening to—the "mob," the "Punjabi Muslims," and the "massacre."

Tropes and stereotypes resonate in sonic artifacts elsewhere in the piece: the steam train rolls into a clip from a BBC documentary on India, its hoots announcing British temporal regularity as a bearer of progress and modernity: the master's clock. In the end, the hoot is turned into a lament, illustrated by the narrator who intones: "It was perhaps ironic that the railways, which had helped to unite British India, now carried its people apart." In the same clip, the thin voice of Lord Mountbatten, the Raj's last viceroy, is described as "charming." The contra/dictions are left to be heard—rather than listening to a supremacist view of the past as legible (especially as the presenter's estimation of the numbers who lost their lives falls factually short), we listen with and through it with imaginative difference. The political possibility of listening, following Voegelin, partly lies in the refusal of cartographical representation and mapping, and so it instead becomes "a practice of walking and listening, doing and redoing. There is no measure, there is no map, just the present materiality unfolding in our ears—hearing our own geography" (Voegelin 2014, 25). As different sonic devices and extra-/archival voices are collaged together in PL001, none sit easily on their own, so their truth value remains insecure, especially to my own sonic memories—the temporal toots of a train, the laughter accompanying an account of violence between communities, the performance of imperial power.

### HUM DEKHENGE

While PL001 renders audible the complexities of "witnessing" Partition through various historical tracks and dialogic exhortations, *Partitioned Listening: "We Shall Witness"* addresses Partition's sonic condition through the trajectories of the (sonic) fragment and the fragment's copy (Tariq 2020b). The piece, hereafter referred to as PL002, does this by sounding out three renditions of Faiz Ahmed Faiz's revolutionary Urdu poem *Hum Dekhenge* (We Shall Witness or We Shall See), and the repetitive refrains of Jana Natya Manch's Hindi protest-performance *Hum Bharat Ke Log* (We the People)—an interactive public performance that asks simple questions of its audience about their national, Indian, identity.

According to Jennifer Dubrow, *Hum Dekhenge*'s sparse textual and performance history (it was even taken out of an edited collection by Faiz himself) meant the poem would ordinarily have been little known (Dubrow 2020). The poem, written in 1979, was also censored in his lifetime—a specific verse was permanently excised from Faiz's complete works, *Nuskha-e-Ha-e-Wafa* (Thomas 2019). This history of *Hum Dekhenge*'s interruptions is not surprising—not only did the poem target the power and corruption of Pakistani dictator Zia ul Haq and his military regime, but Faiz's use of Quranic language and metaphor in the poem deliberately rubbed up against the harsh and conservative Islam that Zia's regime enforced on Pakistani society. In *Hum Dekhenge*, Faiz connects Qayamat, the Islamic day of reckoning, to Communist revolution.

The first time I encountered *Hum Dekhenge* was in London in January 2020. My mother was playing a YouTube video on her phone—in it, protesting women were sitting on the ground at Shaheen Bagh, Delhi, India, loudly singing the lyrics, drumming and clapping. I was already familiar with Faiz and the radical details of his biography—from his agitation and militancy in Pakistan to the Afro-Asian writers' publication, *Lotus*, he edited when in exile in Beirut. His poem on the 1947 Partition, *Subha e Azadi*, encapsulates with brutal subtlety the displacement of one's soul within the movements of history. But I had not heard this before, and with an initial delve into *Hum Dekhenge*'s con/texts, was surprised at the centrality of Islam in what I registered as, at first listening, an Indian feminist protest song. Most notably, as Dubrow writes, is the invocation of the Persian Sufi Mansur Al-Hallaj's famous exclamation, "*An ul-Haq*," translatable as "I am God" but also "I am Truth," which "references the Sufi critique of religious (and other) authority and invokes a fundamentally mystical way of perceiving and understanding God. This was meant as a criticism of Zia ul Haq's government, which imposed Sharia-inspired religious laws (known as Hudood) on the country, but the critique can easily be transposed on to any human or political authority that takes away or threatens humanity's fundamental relationship with God" (Dubrow 2020).

The poem's resurgence in India—and its anthemic status at Shaheen Bagh, the most famous of the many women and queer-led occupation sites in early 2020—occurred in the context of the resistance against the National Register of Citizens (NRC) and the Citizenship Amendment Act (CAA), both Islamophobic laws initiated by the BJP government to tie citizenhood to religion, rather than residence.[4] The identitarian violence enforced in these laws, like many times before, becomes a condition of statehood, and the vanishing of the protest sites because of the onset of COVID has rendered this moment fabulous, almost mythical. As referred to in PL002, students singing lines from *Hum Dekhenge* were reported to the police, as some believed the song not just to be anti-establishment, but anti-Hindu. The recitation of *Hum Dekhenge* in this context holds such power because it interrupts narrative hegemony as it has been ordained over time, a symbolic act of complexity that reveals the fragility of historical dichotomies—Communist/Muslim, faithful/faithless, Urdu-speaking/Hindi-speaking. Though not explicitly referring to 1947, here the relationship between silence and speakability is again forced up against the workings of public memory across partitioned terrain. Against the order of the present and the inevitability of the past, *Hum Dekhenge*'s artifactualization, like Menon's queer universalism, coheres around incoherence.

The first rendition heard in PL002 is performed by singer Iqbal Bano at the Al-Hamra Cultural Center in Lahore, Pakistan, in 1986—two years after Faiz had died, two years prior to Zia's death, and thirty-four years before the institution of the NRC and CAA in India. The performance, widely accepted as legendary, took place at the Faiz Mela, a regular celebratory event run by the foundation set up by the poet's surviving relatives. These events were open to the public, "attended by workers, peasants, trade union activists, students, teachers, men, women, children and everyone in between" (Hashmi 2019). The recording we hear of Bano is actually the *second* time she performs *Hum Dekhenge* in Al-Hamra, because of the overwhelming response of the audience to the first rendition and their demands for an encore. As Faiz's grandson remembers that raucous night when Pakistani authorities raided the homes of organizers and participants afterward looking for any recordings to obliterate: "Many copies were confiscated and destroyed but my uncle Shoaib Hashmi had managed to get a hold of one copy and anticipating the crackdown handed it over to some friends who promptly smuggled it out to Dubai where it was copied and widely distributed" (Hashmi 2019). Some of these copies made it into India.

At pains to interrupt Bano and her band, as well as the audience's fiery response to its anti-establishment verses, my vocal annotations are brief during the instrumental breaks—setting the scene, journalistically, but also asking broad questions of the status that events hold in our memory, questions implicated in the sonic and political situation of this performance:

> *What makes an event, an event?*
> *Does an event exist if it doesn't end?*
> *Does an event exist if there are no witnesses?*
> *Does an event exist if it is not archived*? (Tariq 2020b)

When we listen to the Delhi protest clip extracted from YouTube, the second rendition of *Hum Dekhenge* heard right after the fiddles of Bano's band fade out, our listening is transformed. This version, with its drumbeats and ringtones and background hum of agitation, captured on a smartphone mic that was likely thought of as secondary to the recording of visual footage, might be spatially and temporally displaced from the "original" context, but aligns with it politically. *Hum Dekhenge*'s cry against tyranny—already embedded with its projected imagination into the future ("we *shall* witness")—is circulated and brought forth out of time. Against collection and enclosure, listening with *Hum Dekhenge* and its fragments provokes our understanding of this time—as Mbembe writes and lawyer Bernard Keenan reads aloud here—as "made up of disturbances, of a bundle of unforeseen events, of more or less regular fluctuations and oscillations" (Mbembe 1989, 16).

The third and final rendition of *Hum Dekhenge* in PL002 is in the form of a slowed-down performance by artist Fazal Rizvi, produced for the piece and performed outdoors, his voice and harmonium addressing the sky and what sounds like a single crow. We have heard the harmonium already before we were led to this point. We have also heard crows, signifying mass death, in the BBC report of PL001. We have heard the words already and we have heard the political power of their utterance too. In this final act of repetition and return, Rizvi sings *Hum Dekhenge* with a carefully altered pitch and decreasing tempo—the poem's "sonic possible world" (Voegelin 2014) laid bare through its subjective and temporal fluctuations. This rendition evokes the future more tentatively, perhaps, because of its fragility as a solo performance and not-always-fully controlled slowing pace. This is particularly evocative when considering the second direct translation in the transcript of "*hum dekhenge*" is written as "we shall see," rather than "we shall witness," which somehow in English loses its urgency and becomes more tentative in terms of its future-facing political imaginary. With this final version, our own listening is contrapuntal, interfering with the decades that have been chronologized and the twenty-five minutes of the audio essay's length. Partition as a sonic condition becomes, to adapt Phillips's conception of time, "the subjective duration of 'now' interacting with other nows" (Phillips 2018, 45).

Returning to Nikita Dhawan's politics of speech and silence, "partitioned listening" is a hopeful exercise to subvert listening and render it a disruptive tool for testimonial histories and archives that hold their own genealogies of silence. In PL003, titled "I Hear (Colonial) Voices" and published in the journal *World Records*, the voices of "colonial servants" who witnessed Partition and the documents and photographs belonging to others who were there at the "time" are correspondingly silenced and sounded out. What remains are the voices of the oral historians who ask (from the listener's perspective) unanswered questions, my selective fragments from the archive's catalogue index and physical collection material, and the deteriorations and (manufactured) repetitions of the digitized oral history tapes. The absence of colonial voices in the work, voices not heard in part for reasons of self-censorship to protect their living descendants and reputation according to the archive's protocols, are positioned alongside annotations of my own encounters with the "safer" written and visual evidence. As well as listen, here I look, sifting through materials that exist from this about-to-be partitioned landscape.

Dhawan argues that silence is not "necessarily a passive act of submission or repression. It can be a challenge to the monologue of dominant discourses that ruptures the power play between speakers and listeners, and creates conducive conditions for the 'invisible,' the 'unsaid' to emerge" (Dhawan 2012, 59). If the power of listening can show us the world in its invisibility, this subversion of traditional "logocentric strategies of resistance" means giving oneself over to silence in discourses, the silences that have ordered our time and history. In yielding to silence, absence, and erasure emerge practices and conventions of historical research that hold a much-needed consideration of our auditory sensibilities and sonic agency. Considering Partition as a sonic condition—one within which we all labor—then gives us the possibility to push beyond the parameters of colonized public memory-making practices and reencounter for ourselves impossible multitudes.

NOTES

1. The research presented in this essay is grounded in the UK and Pakistan and, from a distance, contemporary Indian history as well. This is out of an interest in my own origins, politics, language, and familial affinities as well as a sonic/archival interest in Partition and colonialism. This focus therefore excludes connected partitions and multiple and specific conditions of violence against Indigenous, displaced, low-income, and lower-caste minorities. I acknowledge that many places across the partitioned subcontinent—particularly Kashmir, Assam, Chittagong Hill Tracts, Baluchistan, and North West Frontier Provinces—and the countless violated, missing, displaced, and dead within and beyond partitioned borders are erased from the mainstream conversation in the United Kingdom, India, and Pakistan. See *A Thousand Channels*, Episode One (www.colomboscope.lk/a-thousand-channels), for examples of collaborative audio art that listens to linguistic enclaves, seditious poetry, imperial history, and stories of statelessness via East Bengal/East Pakistan/Bangladesh and the Indian Ocean.
2. This consideration of the destruction of colonial evidence relies on Ian Cobain's *The History Thieves*, which outlines episodes of British state secrecy, drawing on declassified documents and court proceedings, including the notable case of the missing evidence of the Mau Mau insurgency and massacres in Kenya. It offers a stark insight: even if Operation Legacy—the secret operation to destroy and hide colonial documentation—officially ended in the 1970s, the British state continues to conceal colonial crimes, from Northern Ireland to Indonesia.
3. As an example of this active and ongoing concealment, the unredacted Mountbatten Papers are at the time of this writing still being blocked for release by the United Kingdom Cabinet Office at great expense. These papers are believed to shed light on how the then-viceroy of India dealt with Partition, and it is doubtful whether they will see the light of day. See for context Jon Ungoed-Thomas, "Anger Over 'Grotesque Abuse' of £600,000 Case to Keep Mountbatten Papers Secret"; and Haroon Siddique, "Cabinet Office Blocks Publication of Lord Mountbatten's Diaries."
4. See Ganendra Pandey's *The Construction of Communalism in Colonial North India*.
5. For more context see Jhalak M. Kakkar, "India's New Citizenship Law and Its Anti-Secular Implications."

## REFERENCES

*A Thousand Channels*, Episode One. Colomboscope and FOLD Media, 2021. https://www.colomboscope.lk/athousandchannels-episode-one.

Anand, Shaina. 2016. "10 Theses on the Archive." In *Autonomous Archiving*, edited by the Artikisler Collective, 78–94. Barcelona: DPR.

Azoulay, Ariella A. 2019. *Potential History: Unlearning Imperialism*. London: Verso.

Butalia, Urvushi. 1998. *The Other Side of Silence: Voices of Partition*. New Delhi: Penguin.

Cobain, Ian. 2016. *The History Thieves*. London: Portobello Books.

Das, Veena. 2007. *Life and Words: Violence and the Descent into the Ordinary*. Oakland: University of California Press.

Dhawan, Nikita. 2012. "Hegemonic Listening and Subversive Silences: Ethical-Political Imperatives." In *Destruction in the Performative*, edited by Alice Lagaay and Michael Lorber, 47–60. Amsterdam: Rodopi.

Dubrow, Jennifer. 2020. "Faiz, India and Protest." *Dawn*. July 5. https://www.dawn.com/news/1566933.

Faiz, Faiz A. 2013. *Faiz: Fifty Poems*. Selected and translated by Mahmood Jamal. Karachi: Oxford University Press.

Hashmi, Ali M. 2019. "When Iqbal Bano Defied Zia's Dictatorship to Sing 'Hum Dekheinge' at Alhamra." *Medium*. September 4, 2019. https://medium.com/@nayadaurpk/when-iqbal-bano-defied-zias-dictatorship-to-sing-hum-dekheinge-at-alhamra-81f971eebe3d.

Hoffmann, A. 2015. "Introduction: Listening to Sound Archives." *Social Dynamics: A Journal of African Studies* 41, no. 1: 1–14.

Igwe, Onyeka. 2020. "Being Close To, With or Amongst." *Feminist Review* 125: 44–53.

Kabir, Ananya J. 2009. "Hieroglyphs and Broken Links: Remediated Script and Partition Effects in Pakistan." *Cultural and Social History* 6 no. 4: 485–506.

Kakkar, Jhalak M. 2020. "India's New Citizenship Law and Its Anti-Secular Implications." *Lawfare*. January 16. https://www.lawfareblog.com/indias-new-citizenship-law-and-its-anti-secular-implications.

Kaur, Ravinder. 2017. "Curating the Wound: The Public Memory of Partition Remains Woefully Caste-Blind." *Caravan*. August 7. https://caravanmagazine.in/vantage/public-memory-partition-remains-caste-blind.

Khan, Yasmin. 2019. *The Great Partition: The Making of India and Pakistan*. New Haven, CT: Yale University Press.

Lane, Cathy. 2017. "Listening and Not Listening to Voices: Interrogating the Prejudicial Foundation of the Arts Canon." *Seismograf Special Issue: Sound Art Matters*. November 15. http://seismograf.org/en/fokus/sound-art-matters/listening-and-not-listening-to-voices-interrogating-the-prejudicial-foundations-of-the-sound-arts.

Mbembe, Achille. 1989. *On the Postcolony*. Berkeley: University of California Press.

Menon, Madhavi. 2015. "Universalism and Partition: A Queer Theory." *differences: A Journal of Feminist Cultural Studies* 26, no. 1: 117–40.

Menon, Ritu, and Kamla Bhasin. 1998. *Borders and Boundaries: Women in India's Partition.* New Delhi: Kali for Women.
Pandey, Ganendra. 2012. *The Construction of Communalism in Colonial North India.* Delhi: Oxford University Press.
Phillips, Rasheedah. 2018. "Mapping Time Mapping Space: Dismantling the Master's Clock." *Funambulist* 18, July–August: 20–25.
Portelli, Alessandro. 1991. *The Death of Luigi Trastulli and Other Stories: Form and Meaning in Oral History.* Albany: State University of New York Press.
Portelli, Alessandro. 2016. "What Makes Oral History Different." In *The Oral History Reader*, edited by Robert Perks and Peter Thomson, 48–58. Oxon: Routledge.
Siddique, Haroon. 2021. "Cabinet Office Blocks Publication of Lord Mountbatten's Diaries." *The Guardian.* May. https://www.theguardian.com/uk-news/2021/may/15/cabinet-office-blocks-publication-of-lord-mountbattens-diaries.
Tariq, Syma. 2020a. "Partitioned Listening: 'You Trust Your Memories?'" *The Contemporary Journal* 3. December 5. https://thecontemporaryjournal.org/issues/sonic-continuum/partitioned-listening-001-you-trust-your-memories.
Tariq, Syma. 2020b. "Partitioned Listening: 'We Shall Witness.'" *The Contemporary Journal* 3. July 7. https://thecontemporaryjournal.org/issues/sonic-continuum/partitioned-listening-002-we-shall-witness.
Tariq, Syma. 2022. "Partitioned Listening: I Hear (Colonial) Voices." *World Records* 7. December. https://worldrecordsjournal.org/partitioned-listening/.
Thomas, Kavya. 2019. "Singing 'Hum Dekhenge' in Hard Times: Why a Pakistani Poem Echoes India's Pains 40 Years Later." *The New Leam.* December 28. https://www.thenewleam.com/2019/12/singing-hum-dekhenge-in-hard-times-why-a-pakistani-poem-echoes-indias-pains-40-years-later/.
Ungoed-Thomas, Jon. 2021. "Anger Over 'Grotesque Abuse' of £600,000 Case to Keep Mountbatten Papers Secret." *The Guardian,* November 7. https://www.theguardian.com/uk-news/2021/nov/07/anger-over-grotesque-abuse-of-600000-case-to-keep-mountbatten-papers-secret.
Voegelin, Salomé. 2014. *Sonic Possible Worlds: Hearing the Continuum of Sound.* London: Bloomsbury.

Geeta Patel

# 6

## Miraji's Poetics for Queering History

Wandering from town to house, a wayfarer misplaces
the road that gathers him home. That which was once mine
and your belongings, both foresworn
from memory. Mine and yours no longer known.
*Nagarī nagarī phirā musāfir ghar kā rāstā bhūl gayā, kyā hai merā, kyā hai terā,
apnā parāyā bhūl gayā.*
As I turn to look at everyone passing by, I find—
they all nurse one simple reproach: Why,
when I can recall everything so fully—
Has my time forgotten me?
*Jisko dekho us ke dil meN, shikvā hai to itnā hai. HameN to sab kuch yād rahā par
humko zamānā bhūl gayā.*
—Miraji

### HAS MY TIME FORGOTTEN ME, MINE AND YOURS NO LONGER KNOWN

*Translation Theory from the Global South*

Born in Lahore, Pakistan, the Urdu modernist poet Miraji (1912–1949) commenced his forays into translation and lyric as a wayfarer, wandering from town to house, as it were, by rummaging in Lahore libraries in the 1930s for literary guidelines, lodestones, and compasses garnered from volumes that had been ferried across oceans. Among the plethora of writers and poets that Miraji salvaged in his searches was Sappho (c. 630–570 BCE). Renowned as a lyricist from the Greek island of Lesbos, the scraps left behind of Sappho's verse sing of her heartbreak and desire for women and men, giving us some traces of her own peripatetic life (Alvi, Chaudhry, Khan, Kolb, Patel, and Shahbaz 2020). In the essay Miraji composed on Sappho's life and for which he translated her lyric, published in his collection *Mashriq o Maghrib ke Naghmen* (Songs from the East and the West), he introduces her through an epigram, an oft-rehearsed depiction of Sappho ascribed to the Athenian philosopher Plato: "The Seventh Muse."

How can bringing Miraji and Sappho together into a montage as wanderers speak to queer histories that settle in colonial Lahore?[1] How does that same montage unsettle what a Lahore already unsettled by Partition might mean by allowing Miraji's epigram of "the seventh muse" to jostle, rub up against, walk alongside, lean on, and perhaps overlay the epigram-cum-"translation" that opens this chapter? (Can one even call it translating?) Miraji's epigram invokes a goddess who presides over learning, a spell of contemplation, a pondering. The epigram I have selected highlights *bhūl gayā*, the phrase (*radīf*) that repeats at the end of each couplet in a series of rhyming verses (*ghazal*), with which poets play as they sculpt meaning. I chose to translate *bhūl gayā* in a way that ferries its multiple resonances from Urdu into English, including mislay, forget, misplace, absentmindedness, mistake, lapse. Implicit in this pairing is a novel approach to Miraji and his work that highlights his contributions as a theorist of queered histories, in addition to but also through the poetics and translations for which he is best known.

As Miraji contemplates Sappho's life and lyric, he pursues history keyed *through* translation, and traverses history *as* translation, finding his way not by returning home in any simple way to a place like Lahore, but by transiting through myriad genres of *bhūl gayā* in the course of mislaying, misplacing, forgetting, and lapsing. I will return to this movement by and by. In the meantime, the first sections of this essay open a byway through which I can turn to Miraji not merely as a translator of Sappho, but as a queer Hindustani lyricist born in Lahore who died in Bombay, longing for Pakistan, someone who tells stories through translation and in so doing lays down a concourse for theorizing queered histories, archives, and translation.

Queer histories, queered as narratives that root around in pasts to reconstitute what has been forgotten, *bhūl gayā*, forage in archives for queer characters and off-kilter genres of living. Certainly in South Asia, if those archives are rendered eventually in English, scholars and activists often lean on translations from local languages to make possible what they feel they must enable. Underwriting the viability of these translations that reach into the historical as a process of *remembering* rather than forgetting, however much that process has been undercut, subject to critique, caviled against, commissioned through an askance, is a thin skein of longing for veracity, which constitutes what those histories carry with them out of the archives as a believable object or analytic. Without some small vestige of accuracy and reliability, it is as though the very project of queer history in translation is predestined for a cul-de-sac or scripted through an impossible impasse. *Bhūl gayā* in this reading stays where it appears to belong, as foreplay to finding en route to remembering.

But *bhūl gayā*, as my epigram suggests, was also Miraji's *maqsad*, his intent, his alignment, the necessary condition that brokered something else through mislaying as forgetting. This something else, as we shall see, emerged in his essay on Sappho as a capacious grammar of surmise—uncertainty, hesitations, coincidence, possibility—made possible through bringing translation to history (aka queering history). In order to show what led Miraji here, to these particular theoretical invocations in the gestures of surmise, I first need to detour through the Lahore of the 1870s, where *bhūl gayā* assumed the form of a colonial enterprise.

## A WAYFARER MISPLACES—THE ROAD THAT GATHERS HIM HOME

A whole slew of projects underwritten by translation from English into local languages, with Urdu merely one of many sites, were orchestrated in the mid-nineteenth century following the 1857 War of Independence when so many were killed. Some of these colonial projects, many of them housed in Lahore (now in Pakistan), funded the composition of refurbished lyrical forms with the enticement of prize money awarded for literally descriptive, thematically based poetry. British colonial administrators such as Colonel Holroyd, responsible for education policy in Punjab, organized poetry symposia in Lahore in the 1870s, abetted by the endorsement of Muhammad Hussain Azad and the Anjuman-e Punjāb (Assembly of Punjab).[2]

Altaf Husain Hali (1837–1914), who had witnessed some of the extraordinary virulence of 1857, was one of the purveyors of this new poetry as both a poet and a critic. Hali earned his living correcting translations from English into Urdu in the nineteenth century at the crowded Punjab Book Depot in Lahore. One can easily envision him, pen in hand, scribbling away, surrounded by stacks of teetering files. As a lyricist, translator, and theorist of literary matters, it was as though his meticulous labor filtered into both his verse, which was written in this new key, as well as his monumental though brief critical monograph, *Muqaddmah e She'r o Sha'irī* (Prolegomena of Lyric and Poetics), which extolled these new genres of versification. Hali maintained that his feeling for English literature was inculcated as he cleaned up translations.[3] The intent, *maqsad*, of these ventures was oriented toward transmuting the conditions of the composition of lyric, how verse was written and what was written, turning the pleasures coded into the euphoric, anguished, teasing multivocal chanciness of metaphor to drier verse, flattened into literalism while bursting with detail, which tuned into ekphrasis for its semiotic registers. Hali, who was also a philosophical historian of the intellectual lineages encoded into Islam (*madd o jazr e Islam*, ebb and flow of Islam), named this new genre of verse "*necaral shairī*," or natural verse.

Hali composed in this paradox by tuning in to Islamic lineages outside South Asia, notably al-Andalus, to find value for Muslim learning in the subcontinent, even as he siphoned away a bit of the value he accorded local lineages of lyric that included those of his teachers and forebears. Along the way, something of the tongue of lyric was forgone, mislaid, left aside. Out of this detritus, Urdu writers such as Miraji were trying to forage something viable to enable them to continue on.

Projects of translation from South Asian languages into English participated in a long history of shipping traffic that brought translated texts to Britain and Europe as mercantilist artifacts with profound political, philosophical, and literary ramifications, as Manan Ahmed has recently illustrated. Translation as a practice through which governmentality in South Asia was finessed also had a rather protracted legacy, and a large cohort of this legacy from the eighteenth century onward was bent toward translating religicolegal texts from South Asian languages into English. Many scholars have spoken of these interventions, through which deliberately culled, translated works became the authoritative primers to adjudicate legal regimes and produce a novel lineage of legal being as they subverted the clout of South Asian translators in courts and mutated what was customary practice into a more carefully patrolled, text-based regulatory apparatus. The independence mobilizations of 1857 brought something else to the colonial table. Colonial administrators in places like Lahore understood even more explicitly than they had until then that forms of governmentality had to be devised to temper anticolonial resistance that sporadically broke out into full-fledged violence.

One way the colonial government endeavored to ward off the rekindling of violence was through the adoption of universal pensions in the 1860s following the War of Independence. Paradoxically, as the notes administrators appended to pension documents revealed, they did not believe that modulation could solely be achieved through sovereignty established via force majeure conceived of as compulsion to obey inscribed through law and legal mandates. Rather, as was the case with pensions, which tied everyone who received a pension into a kind of faith in those who were responsible for giving it, they judged that they had to come up with more subtle, covert strategies to bind colonized denizens to the state.

Another possible route was through persuasions of the heart (collateralized by capital), which were so deeply felt that they could not be released, something more akin to Antonio Gramsci's invocation of hegemony, control through ideology folded into everyday commonsense or inculcated habit and ordinary desire or dislike. The law enabled and enforced through a facticity of sovereign authority couldn't achieve the same ends. In the ideological lay the grounds of what Ludwig Wittgenstein speaks of in *On Certainty* as belief that was a bit more than commonsense: what was to be valued, how one valorized one's moral worth or culpability. All these came together at this cusp where governance and the aesthetic met. Translation could be said to be the carrier.

Colonized subjects in Lahore such as Altaf Husain Hali translated from English in response to and perhaps to rescript stereotypical caricatures of morally retrograde colonial subjects—those who had been widely circulated by pamphleteers such as Charles Grant in the late eighteenth century. The translator and theorist Wail S. Hassan speaks of translation as an "extension of military, political and economic power," but in some ways these colonial ventures were more than a mere extension and perhaps this is how Hassan intended his elaboration—that force was not sufficient if colonizers wished to burrow so deeply into the habits of those whom they had colonized that little was left untouched (though that neglected smidgen could still flourish explosively, or unexpectedly).

I want to turn to something besides the effects of education in English, through the translation of South Asian materials into English. I want to turn instead to tutelage through English transported into South Asian languages. I want to fathom something about queering history and the questions that have become both quotidian and sacrosanct in these ventures. Projects of translation like the ones undertaken by Hali are the heart blood—or more aptly for Urdu, the *khūn-i jigar*, the liver juice that kept lyric and lovers thrumming and dying oh-so-slowly—of governmentality in the colonies that managed to finesse what queer historians return to over and over. A fantasy of loss of a past, of self, of being, as Anjali Arondekar has so pointedly shown, underwrites, as animus and animating, historical accountings of queer considerations, of Atlantic slavery, of communities who inveigle their pasts through the stories of archives gone missing. So many projects where the variegated patinas of loss send them to archival scrounging to salvage possible pasts or memories seem to sift almost inadvertently, even as they might do otherwise, through some notion of veracity and fidelity, as I pointed out in my opening paragraphs. Translation conjures other transactional economies—those that can fold into colonial management and an insistence on fidelity, but also flourish into what Indrani Chatterjee and, in her *silsilah* (genealogy), I call counterteleologies, where, at the very least, truth is composited through, with a rigorous attentiveness to truth value.

To see how one can theorize translation to account for what Hali, and Miraji after him, were grappling with, I ferry in the word *tarjumah* from Urdu via Arabic (and via pre-Semitic languages) and fold it into the Sanskrit root *tr—taratī*, transport, transmute, swim over, from which the word *avatār* is born. As Wail S. Hassan emphasizes when he translates Abdelfattah Kilito's magisterial readings of passages that Arabic texts wend through time in *Thou shalt not speak my language*, *tarjumah* brings biography/life, explanation, and interpretation together.[4] *Tarjumah*'s possible line of descent through the Arabic root *rajama* also conveys damned, reviled, soothsaying, uncertain, unreliable speech.[5]

And the effect of translation, *tarjumah, taratī*, understood in this way, was not just to make Anglicized ideas amenable to a larger Urdu-speaking audience, but to make one's tongue over. It made Urdu so utterly something else that the words one used changed, and rather than what one was *compelled* to write, how and what one *wished* to write henceforth was amended. Language itself changed. Urdu was expected to assume another life, another unreliable avatar, a vernacular, become amenable through translation. That all languages mutate, absorb, collude, hybridize is a truism; in how they do it lie the politics that underscore what is at stake. For Altaf Hussain Hali, fleeing the desecration in Delhi to find more hospitable possibilities in Lahore meant turning away from his own teachers and literary forebears, edging away from Farsi (the language of Mughal governance, finance, jurisprudence) toward English, not as his tongue, but as one necessary ancestor. Hali's anguish at this loss was profound. The excitement of new possibilities that *tarjumah* might open for Hali moderated, assuaged by their unreliability. As Homi Bhabha suggested a while ago in his discussion of colonial makeovers, mimesis, in imitating a colonizer, is also an incompleteness carried in by Hali's grief, or perhaps his ongoing melancholia.

When scholars speak of target languages, they, unlike Hassan, rarely bring to the surface this failure, the politics that transmute the language into which translation takes place as one rendered friable, fraying, in the crucible of colonial governance. Perhaps this is what Gayatri Spivak ought to have intended, though she did not articulate it quite in the way I mean it here, when she says in her essay "The Politics of Translation" that "the writer is written by her language, of course. But the writing of the writer scripts 'agency' and [whatever falls under its name in a way that might be different].... 'Safety' is the appropriate term here, because we are talking of risks, of violence to the translating medium" (Spivak 2021, 320–21). Translating is dangerous business, *tarjumah, tr* turns one's language into the vernacular of the damned.

## WANDERING FROM TOWN TO HOUSE, A WAYFARER MISPLACES THE ROAD THAT GATHERS HIM HOME

Miraji (*Sana Ullah Daar*) was arguably one of the most inventive, theoretically nuanced prose masters and lyricists in colonial South Asia. Literature, in all its shapes and guises, provided the venue through which Miraji became a wayfarer, a traveler. He began culling, picking, and choosing what he went on to translate from the books piled in public libraries in Lahore, as he sat ensconced behind the massive neoclassical Georgian façade of the Qaid-e āzam Library or hunched over a desk under the soaring vaulted ceilings of the glorious neo-Islamic Government—Punjab Public

Library. Translation gave Miraji his "archives of belonging," to misquote Susan Sontag. On the streets of Lahore and in homes, South Asian poets met and formed conclaves such as the *Halqa e arbāb e zauq*—the circle of the men of taste—to ponder and exchange prose and lyric. Journals such as *Adab-i latīf* were circulating the writing of the day. Miraji's 1930s Lahore, then, was a city that brimmed with literary and political possibilities that emerged from the jostling of different communities. And in the excitement that was so much a part of its traffic, it resembled the city that Hali lived in. At the same time, because its literary life did not orient itself toward British initiatives, this later Lahore was profoundly different from Hali's.

Miraji himself is often given life through accounts of him settled into and as though growing out of the cities in which he lived. Cities, as Neloufer de Mel has shown us in her research on Jaffna and Colombo, people their architecture through juxtapositions of map to description with somewhat unexpected ramifications (de Mel 2020). Anīs Nāgī, who writes a biographical essay on Miraji, draws him out in the context of the family home in Lahore, where Miraji had turned one tiny room into a *sahar khānā*, a poet's magical garret. The house was tucked into the winding lanes of MuzaNg, its façade tightly closed. But Nāgī renders that description through details (ekphrasis) that could easily have been excavated from maps delineated in the *Imperial Gazatteer*'s architecture of governmentality or via E. M. Forster's Chandrapore in his opening paragraphs from his novel *A Passage to India*, emphasizing as Nāgī does "the narrow and torturous lanes, [the] mean and gloomy appearance" of the area. Colonial cartographies calibrate morality, and the translation of those older streets into a refurbished colonial lexicon of decrepitude carries over into Nāgī's portrayal of Miraji as lacking in moral fortitude, what we might see from our vantage point now as a portrait of a somewhat Dionysian madman.

But perhaps this is unwittingly apt in its way. For in the translations to which Miraji turned his hand extensively in Lahore, he searched assiduously for those lyricists who refused or were refused propriety. It was as though Lahore itself, having been the space where translation foreclosed its own opening gestures, now threw up the possibilities for kinship that translation might have wrought, whether they were tucked into verses by geishas, or French symbolists, or Sappho. In both Hali's and Miraji's case translations were the places through which literary family trees were refashioned, but oriented very differently. Both were genres of "disruptive kinship," François Noudelmann's "elective as opposed to genetically ordained affinities"—families without parents (Apter 2013, 14). But Miraji's (un)*translatables* stood outside language families, finding their path through "broken ties, soul mates, monsters," while Hali's kept on reaching for hope of a family.

## MIRAJI'S UNTRANSLATABLES

### A Kinship of Broken Ties

Miraji made an art of reading closely. However, he was an unfailingly unreliable translator—and this is where he ventured his theoretical and philosophical insights on translation and what translation could promise or forestall as it produced queered histories. In her monograph on world literature Emily Apter suggests in *Against World Literature* (20) that *only* if we *don't* make a virtue of poising what is amenable to being translated *against* what is untranslatable, demanding that they oppose each other in a Manichean fashion, can we see something of import emerge. Hassan massaged this opposition slightly differently, allowing sacrilege into the very conditions of language itself and refusing the tensions that often surface when eros (desire) pulls against thanatos (death), and translation was settled at the boundary between life and love and death or decimation. For Hassan, the afterlife that translation (and through it the archive) promised happened not when eros and thanatos were set apart from each other as though they were contrary and at war, but when they were juxtaposed, bounced around, and played with productively in concert.

Miraji would appear to concur with Apter in some ways, and he would quite assuredly have acceded to Hassan's account in the translations and in the deftly drawn essays Miraji composed on the poets he translated. Miraji translated widely, choosing poets from a rogue's gallery of writers, towed from different times and parts of the world, who would never have featured in the earlier translations of someone like Hali. They offered him a conclave from which he could extract an alterior archival kinship—*bānke, teDe*—of broken ties.

When Miraji found his way to Sappho, he intimated that she had found her voice over time through translation: that she herself had been brought to life so many times as herself, in translation, and every translation replenished Sappho as archive. But as a queered figuration she also faced imaginative resistance, in the ways in which Neloufer de Mel proposes, from translators who excised her from their annals. In his essay on Sappho, Miraji speaks of the ebb and flow of translation as tolling the tales of her demise (thanatos) and rebirth from the crypt of forgetting through love (eros) each time a translator found her again. Sappho died in the hands of her interlocutors, the quarry, Miraji explains, of Christian pogroms against immorality. As a woman lyricist who sang the delight and torment of love for other women, she violated the religious sentiments of those who envisioned themselves as holding a higher moral and religious ground. Miraji chronicled Sappho's life by charting her loves, how she had died a little death each time she lost one, found her being again as she hitched her feelings onto another. She became a poet whose biography, as narrated by Miraji, began in exile, and ended with a chase, away from her own land, her *vatan*, to pursue a boatman she loved, which led to her spectacularized suicide. Sappho's own life required her to find her place over and over every time she lost it. So being lost was nothing special: death and rebirth, eros from thanatos were quotidian, even as they might have choreographed the flow of disappeared and resalvaged forms that are often called into presence when archives are redeemed for value.

By figuring Sappho as a queer songster who could incite imaginative resistance, Miraji called upon his readers, as translators, to face their own imaginative resistance to what they read, to tussle with their refusals to accept what they encountered, so that they could eventually release that resistance and fall into the text, become intimate with it, in a process that Miraji called *hamdardī*—sharing pain. In so doing they would breach what had once seemed untranslatable to them because it felt morally suspect. *Hamdardī* cannot be resolved into fidelity or veracity.

By the time Miraji had begun his own sojourn as a doyen of Urdu modernism, Hali's ekphrasis had become the method of the day. Ekphrasis in the guise of literary realism, *haqīqat parastī, ai'nā dārī* (infatuation with truth, mirroring), was political aesthetic. Ekphrasis, art mirroring life through its welter of detail, was deemed the most salvific and viable route to a robust indictment of the violence that permeated everyday life in colonial settings. Only if one could describe fully, could one respond appositely. Miraji took this on theoretically through his translations. One could align his process somewhat with the tripartite one given us by Spivak in "The Politics of Translation": logic and rhetoric working in silences in and around words (326).

Though Miraji himself wrote enigmatic (*mubham*), philosophically playful, obscure verse as a riposte to his contemporaries' devotion/ *parastī* to realism, he did not entirely shun detail. His essay on Sappho is chockablock with historical material on Greek lyric of the time. It has minutely, tenderly crafted depictions of Sappho's lifeways, her desires, her exiles, her political engagements. But Miraji turned ekphrasis on its head. He understood that details that record and authenticate make us imagine that we hold previously forgotten historical facts in our hands with ease, allow us to succumb to what Alisa Lebow terms *epistephilia*—an excessive, overweening preoccupation with knowing that haunts the practice of documentary realism and dogs value invested in an archive (Lebow 2006, 227).

In his essay on Sappho, Miraji resorts to several strategies to undercut epistephilia. To get to *tarjumah* you have to marshal interdisciplinary resources and registers—the political, the historical, the scientific, the economic, the aesthetic. Translation is interdisciplinary and so also are the routes to arrive at it and to garner its import. Everything Miraji describes lovingly is laid out through the conditions of its production, the putative authors he draws on and their failings accounted for multifariously and mindfully. And all the details are spoken in the grammar of surmise, fleshed out as merely a possible past, what may have been but equally could not have been. Miraji theorizes the archive for us in one of his essays on poetics—for him, its art (as all literature is liable to be) is as a translation of, a transit through, life—*adab zindagī kā tarjumah hai*. And translations are options we settle upon but could just as easily release. An exhortation and challenge to naturalism, mirroring life or nature, documentary realism and epistephilia.

As with all the essays that Miraji composed on poets whose lyric he translated, this essay too enunciates a politics of language and gives us an entrée into a philosophy of translation as history birthed under colonial constraints. He writes about his cohorts having lost their way after 1857, their tongues adrift, their path to a future murky. When filiations are sundered Miraji suggests that poets rattle around with no place to go. But poets can rattle around productively: they can scrounge lineages from scraps and bits left behind—as we have to with Sappho, who, as archive, shows up in fragments. The issue is not *that* you do it but *how* you do it, and where it leads you. The method, the "how" in the "what you do," is the other lesson that Sappho allows him to pursue.

In this way, Miraji's essay on Sappho forges responses that speak to the narrowest fissures through which violence comes to reside in the ordinary. This is an essay that brings theory to life not by addressing loss directly, head-on. Rather, it achieves its effects by taking on ideologies, such as mimesis and epistephelia, that planted their tentacles deep into the political grammar, desires, and words crafted by Miraji's compatriots. The essay's plotting and queered grammar of the evocations of desire, love, anguish, joy, gender, history, and governmentality incite *indirect* commentaries. What happened to Urdu instantiates a paradox of lyrical archives that are *bhūl gaya,* forsaken but not entirely gone, and here is where Miraji establishes the worth of translation, and thus also the archive, as indirection.

Since Miraji's aim, or *maqsad,* was nothing less than the unraveling of hegemonies in their minutest capillary flows, Miraji's rhetoric steered toward the most potent and virulent of their effects. This was the incubation of realism (the anti-love-lyric lyric), the literary form that was believed by fellow writers to be the most efficacious political aesthetic for a compelling critique of colonialism: *haqīqat parastī,* the twentieth-century rendition of Hali's naturalism (*necaral*) or mimesis—much of it magnetizing around the place of and the status of women. To target the literalism of mimesis, Miraji had to evade, or slide past the crudely literal, veering instead to an arsenal of rhetorical gestures of indirection and possibility, from allegory to metaphorics, slyly insinuating through them other venues for gazing, for intellectual labor, for fancy—*takhayyul,* a word that fused thinking with dreaming, both of which were terms essential to Miraji's repertoire.

Miraji brings Sappho to readers in the opening of the essay via the annals of classical authors, such as Plato and Plotinus, and with them something askance is birthed. Classical enchantment loses its gloss somewhat, first because Sappho appears to be the very embodiment of depravity. Then, though Miraji launches his essay by giving both Greece and Rome their due, he quickly undercuts that stance with a searing exposé of the dire state of gendered subjects in Greece, an indictment of a Greek democracy that failed some of its most vulnerable denizens, and an implicit condemnation of the late eighteenth- and early nineteenth-century British use of classical archives by Blackstone and others to bolster their colonial legal and policy initiatives. One way to view passages like these is as a kind of exploratory archival historiography that doubles as colonial critique.

Much of the rest of his essay reiterates the vocabulary associated with surmise: *andāzah* (estimation), *ho saktā hai* (it might have been), *mumkin hai* (it's possible), *hu'ā hogā* (it might have happened), *lāzmī* (what must be). In closing this chapter, I will offer possibly the most salient features of what Miraji might have hoped to achieve with "Saffo." One is tucked into the word "*shāyad*" perhaps, conjecture, surmise.

"Perhaps" is the signature of prophecy. In this sense, Miraji's essay on Sappho is a recital, an inventory of the syntax of surmise, of what might be in the guise of what might have been or must have been. History is conjectural, but not merely so. The possibilities history brings to bear, Miraji seems to say, bear the heft of futures that are thrown from it. The past, then, is as prophetic as the future, the present lying in their wake (suspended between *abad* and *azal*, between eternity and time without an ending). Is this Walter Benjamin's angel of history, facing the past? Almost everything that has the texture of historical truth about Sappho, translated with meticulous tender care so that it comes across as a vivacious present—beginning with Sappho's mother's rush across the sharply scented pine forests of Lesbos to Mythilene with her young children following upon her father's death, her library of contemporary resources, her staunch political stances against authoritarians and dictators, the spirited conclaves poets who composed in concert—is hedged in by surmise, perhaps this was so. All these are prophetic futures by which Sappho's voice would live in the time given by Miraji to fellow sojourners (Miraji 1958, 324–28). And because we are speaking of Greece, the heartland of what Europeans deemed the classical, whose registers grounded colonial claims for themselves and the prophetic future they proposed for those they had colonized, the grammar of surmise gently deflected the censuring surety of their pens. Even as Sappho's past unraveled the labyrinth in which Urdu found itself and unobtrusively smoothed away its lost past in surmise and what is possible.

The lexicography of surmise, lodged in the poetry Miraji translated in his own inimitable style, expands the sparseness of the Sappho's fragments into lyrical, dreaming history. Fidelity is not Miraji's stance, recomposition is. In tuning Sappho's voice to Miraji's own lyrical one, he resurrects her for Urdu and calls Sappho back in translation where the translations improvise, dance, and flow far beyond the phrases left behind, even as they stay true to something in the fragments. In this rebirth, Sappho marries and loves both men and women. And love after all is all about surmise. Who hasn't turned to guesswork when they hurtle into love: from potential to possible? Is it true, can it be true, how certain am I, does she or doesn't she, am I imagining it? All such familiar phrases when love hails us, overtakes our senses, turns us into bumbling, bubbling fools.

The deepest rapport that Miraji as a poet and translator developed with Sappho, the one where he began to fold into her, involved her love for another woman, Atthis. Here Miraji hails readers, asking them to feel for her—as *hamdard*—in a kind of acutely shared listening through which a reader comes to experience Sappho's joy and love and suffer her grief. It's as though Miraji's voice emanates from Sappho's, flowing easily into confluence with the verse. Miraji is found as Sappho sings in Urdu, whether in ecstasy or deep mourning, jealousy, or joy. In love's fervor, loss loosens its tenacious grip. And here is where Miraji asks readers and the poets who belong to *jadīdiyāt*, those who are modernist, for *hamdardī*, to share feeling or belong to the same pain. To bring *takhayyul* to *takhlīq* in *ikhlāq* as *tarīkh*—to bring imagination to creatively birth composition in morality as history.

It's as though Sappho's love releases Miraji from any leftover assumptions that queer history need be parsimonious, that it stick assiduously to the realist mimetic proprieties *(ai'nādārī)* archival investigations often bring with them. Miraji then commences a conversation with/ as Sappho—a *guftagū*—and this is where *takhayyul* can be fostered. He does this through a dramatic flourish: taking the Greek form of the symposium and translating it into a loosely filled *mushairā* (a *mehfil*, a gathering of poets). Miraji stages this *mushairā*/symposium/*mehfil* toward the end of the essay, creating a venue for possibility where Sappho trades love lyric, overflowing, bustling with metaphoric nuance and specificity, with three poets who share her lyrical sensibilities. One is an Urdu poet from Miraji's own time, Akhtar Shīrānī, who has a fluid facility with ardor. The second is Mīrābai, the medieval mistress of mystical love, whose Braj verses, through the centuries, have been recomposed over and over under her name. The third, farther back in history, is Bhatṛhārī, a fifth-century BCE grammarian, philosopher, and adept at Sanskrit lyric brimming with feeling, whom Miraji also translated. To abet this lyrical tête-à-tête, Miraji translates Mīrābai and Bhatṛhārī into Urdu. And through them, Sappho is drawn into Miraji's Urdu, a tongue loosened through metaphor, and it is an Urdu that flits between Arabic, Farsi, Braj, Hindustani, with a dash of Sanskrit. The target language, Urdu, lives as something else in translation, in *tarjumah*, in *taratī*. It sidles away from the lyrical lexical rhythms that Altaf Husain Hali's translations from English once had it bear. But even as I translate Miraji's Urdu back into English, the source language that gifted Miraji his queer/ed archives, it is clear to me that English, too, does not remain itself. Miraji's verses barely match up to any English versions that one could hold onto as their precursors, and mine slide away even further. What is the target language and what is an origin are inescapably sullied. Both are in peril, and neither can quite find its way home. A lesson to which Walter Benjamin, writing about ten years before Miraji wended his way toward translation, was well attuned (Benjamin 2021).

But the converse between poets is neither absentminded nor haphazard. Poets are pulled toward one another through metaphor. It's as though metaphors were alive, vibrant, thrumming, voluptuous, prickly, gutting. They throw out resonances, create moods, speak to one another. The bulbul calls out to the nightingale, the flushed earth summons earth garlanded in color, and willy-nilly drags Mirabai toward Sappho. Metaphors have claims on people and people have claims on metaphor—the result is an ambience in which both partake. Metaphors do, and in their doing fidelity and veracity fall away in each translation that Miraji expands vertiginously to make the historical archive capaciously queer enough to embrace the task of releasing what was wrought for Urdu in his time from loss.

We often dream ourselves through archives. Surmise how we would cleave to possible pasts through guidelines or crumb trails laid along our particular found and foundational archival nuggets. Queer archives will lead us to queer presents, donate queer epistemes—so the story goes. It has an insidious attraction, however much we hold it abeyance. But how might we queer the desires we invest in queer archives? I stalk doubled archives: the archival paths Miraji traced folded into the archives that leave bits of him behind for us. To notice that Miraji laid out a route for us through Sappho, found in a library in Lahore: archives are translations, wonky, friable, tentatively playful, and their work may possibly lie elsewhere than where it appears to belong.[6] Who's to say that the impossible possibility of the symposium in Miraji's essay on Sappho that brought together poets across languages and centuries did not take place in colonial Lahore? A Lahore that Miraji continued to reach for, long after he had left it behind. The Lahore, in Pakistan, he longed to return to just before he died.

*Tarjumah zindagī kā adab hai, tārīkh sirf mumkin.* (In translation lies life's literariness, its art, history is the merely possible.)

> Wandering from town to house, a wayfarer misplaces
> the road that gathers him home. That which was once mine
> and your belongings, both foresworn
> from memory. Mine and yours no longer known.

*Nagarī nagarī phirā musāfir ghar kā rāstā bhūl gayā, kyā hai merā, kyā hai terā, apnā parāyā bhūl gayā.*

My Urdu melding with Miraji's melding with Sappho's in a Lahore to which I have never been, except through Miraji's queer histories and my family's memories. Broken ties of filiation.

NOTES

Several readers, to whom I am deeply indebted, showed me how to think through what I had mislaid, *bhūl gayā*, and helped me find possible pathways: Anjali Arondekar, Indrani Chatterjee, Anannya Dasgupta, Neloufer de Mel, Evelynn Hammonds, Richard Handler, Nizar Hermes, Deborah Johnson, Omar Kasmani, Amina Yaqin. Devi was with me, and my wife Kath Weston's tender rigor runs through every phrase; without her this chapter would never have been. This is written for Shamsur Rahman Faruqi, who is entirely responsible for my work on Miraji, and for my mother, whose memories animated my own writing. My mother, entirely insouciant about Miraji's queerness, ferreted tidbits about Miraji's life for my research—my writing returned her to the pleasures of her own childhood.

1   My own relationship to Pakistan and Lahore is complex, and torqued through Bombay, where I was born. I began my archival work on Miraji in Urdu bookstores on Mohammed Ali Road in Bombay with my mother's assistance, even as my own sense of Lahore is based both on archival work and on memories nursed by my mother's family, most of whom came from Lahore. I could not have written on Miraji, who was shunted aside in India but remembered in Pakistan, without materials carried by hand to me from Pakistan, sent by my students, bookshop owners, Miraji afficionados, poets, and critics such as Jamil Jalibi (who compiled the largest volume of materials by Miraji). Ironically enough, given Pakistan's own fraught engagements with queerness to which this volume speaks, my first popular pieces on *queer* Miraji were published by *Dawn* in Karachi.

2   See Laurel Steele, Frances Pritchett, and Shamsur Rahman Faruqi's disquisitions on this period and these events.

3   *Islah*, or correction, which was a technical term in "classical" poetics, is picked up by Hali (and Azad) to mean progress as well as correction (or progress through correction). *Iṣlāḥ* taken this way becomes a cornerstone of Hali's aesthetic philosophy (Patel 2002; Pritchett 1994). Hali serves my purposes as an effective exemplar who brings a range of theoretical invocations to the fore; the "history" of this time is of course much more complex.

4   I am indebted to Mohammed Sawaie and in particular Nizar Hermes for helping me with *tarjumah*. Nizar sent me to Hassan—which helped me rewrite my section.

5   Lineages of translation that don't rely on biblical exegesis and transmission and are therefore less beholden to literalism and a transparent translator are explored in the collection by Tariq Khan. The discussion of Telugu in this collection turns to "rupantar" (changing form) and anuvād, speaking after, as two possibilities from Sanskrit that don't following the moral and religious failures that unfaithful renderings bring with them, which hamper theories that assume, however inadvertently, biblical translations as their forebearer; see also Chatterjee.

6   Archives are so frequently coopted as well, as Joanne Barker points out in her introduction to *Critically Sovereign* (2017, 15).

REFERENCES

Apter, Emily. 2013. *Against World Literature: On the Politics of Untranslatability*. London: Verso.

Arondekar, Anjali. 2020. "The History of Sex: Object Matters." *History Workshop Journal* 89: 207–13.

Barker, Joanne, ed. 2017. *Critically Sovereign: Indigenous Gender, Sexuality and Feminist Studies*. Durham: Duke University Press.

Benjamin, Walter. 2021. "The Translator's Task." Translated by Steven Rendall. In *The Translation Studies Reader*. Edited by Laurence Venuti, 89–97. New York: Routledge.

Chatterjee, Indrani. 2019. "Response to Panel: The History of Sex: Object Matters." Annual Conference of South Asia Studies. Madison, WI, October 2019.

de Mel, Neloufer. 2020. "Literary Lineages: Cambridge South Asia Online." Centre of South Asian Studies, Cambridge University, UK, December 2, 2020.

Faruqi, Shamsur Rahman. 1992. "A Survey of Urdu Literature, 1850–1975." In *Modern Indian Literature*, vol. 1, edited by K. M. George, 420–42. New Delhi: Sahitya Akademi.

Hassan, Wail S., trans. 2008. *Thou Shalt Not Speak My Language*. Syracuse, NY: Syracuse University Press.

Khan, Tariq. 2017. *History of Translation in India*. Mysuru: Central Institute of Indian Languages.

Lebow, Alisa. 2006. "Faking What: Making a Mockery of Documentary." In *F Is for Phony: Fake Documentary and Truth's Undoing*. Edited by Alexandra Juhasz and Jesse Lerner, 223–37. Minneapolis: University of Minnesota Press.

Miraji. 1958 (repub.). *Mashriq o Maghrib ke Nagmen* (Songs from the East and the West). Lahore: Punjab Academy.

Nāgī, Anīs. 1991. *Mīrājī ek bhaTkā hu'ā shāir* (Miraji: A Poet Amiss). Lahore: Pakistan Books and Lahiri Sounds.

Noudelmann, Francois. 2012. Les Airs de famille. Une philosophie des affinités. Paris: Gallimard.

Patel, Geeta. 2002. *Lyrical Movements, Historical Hauntings: On Gender, Colonialism and Desire in Miraji's Urdu Poetry*. Stanford, CA: Stanford University Press.

Patel, Geeta. 2014a. "The Queer Subject of Urdu Modernism: Miraji and Gender Part 1." *Dawn*. April 13. https://www.dawn.com/news/1099395.

Patel, Geeta. 2014b. "The Queer Subject of Urdu Modernism: Miraji and Gender Part 2." *Dawn*. May 11. https://www.dawn.com/news/1105439.

Patel, Geeta. 2020. "Sappho's Ephemera." In *Against the Canon: Urdu Feminist Writing*. Edited by Haider Shahbaz. *Words without Borders*. March 3, 2020. https://www.wordswithoutborders.org/article/march-2020-urdu-feminist-writing-sapphos-ephemera-miraji-geeta-patel.

Patel, Geeta, Asad Alvi, Amna Chaudhry, Mehak Faisal Khan, Anjuli Fatima Raza Kolb, and Haider Shahbaz. 2020. "Urdu Feminist Writing: New Approaches." In *Against the Canon: Urdu Feminist Writing*, edited by Haider Shahbaz. *Words without Borders.* March 3, 2020. https://www.wordswithoutborders.org/article/march-2020-feminist-urdu-writing-new-approaches.

Pritchett, Frances. 1994. *Nets of Awareness*. Berkeley: University of California Press.

Spivak, Gayatri. 2021. "The Politics of Translation." In *The Translation Studies Reader*. Edited by Laurence Venuti, 320–38. New York: Routledge.

Steele, Laurel. 1981. "Hali and His Muqaddamah: The Creation of a Literary Attitude." *Annual Review of Urdu Studies* 1: 1–45.

Nael Quraishi 7

## This Is Home after All

Home is: a place, a person, a thought, a sound, a memory, an abstraction, fluid.

I often find myself looking out my living room window observing the surroundings. All my senses fixated by the slight glimpses into the lives of the neighboring families. The somehow comforting sounds of the afternoon chaos from the streets behind. The breeze perfumed with the savory scent of onions, garlic, and ginger frying in oil. The dominant sounds of men in the distance. The caws of a crow perched by my window paired with the buzzing of generator units interrupted by the distant thuds of a tram on its tracks.

Through these acts of observation and looking through window frames, while physically staying put in one place, my mind is offered moments for contemplation as it flirts with other memories of homelike places. Triggered by the slightest relatable element, it searches for a similar vignette of a memory from a place that in the past also felt like home, reaching out onto another reality. In an instant, everything beyond my living room window is transformed. A fluid combination of reality and fact that exist in the past, present, and future. A constant collision of geographies dotted with the daily mundaneness of life exploring the ideas that the mind re-creates. It reveals perhaps the most realistic version of what one's personal home looks like.

FIG. 7.1. Wesselstraat.

FIG. 7.2. Den Hertigstraat 1.

FIG. 7.3. Den Hertigstraat 2.

FIG. 7.4. Rimpa.

Asad Alvi

## After Heather Love, and Others

سوزِ غم دے کے مجھے اس نے یہ ارشاد کیا
*those* were the words I heard, in a state of half-sleep
جا تجھے کشمکشِ دہر سے آزاد کیا *words*, lodged in some unconscious tissue
risen to the surface, unexpectedly     the m/other tongue
"handing me the *soz,* the heat, of sorrow, he said, go, I release you, from time"
whose words were they now     I asked dreamily
*Josh,* I murmured, smiling     then
I remembered Ghalib نغمہ ہائے غم کو بھی اے دل غنیمت جانیے
بے صدا ہو جائے گا یہ سازِ ہستی ایک دن "even the song of sorrow, O heart
is a blessing... voiceless one day will be the lute of life"
why did I remember him     as if the two, removed in time
but bound by the thread     of the same word
words, committed to the *hafiza,* to memory
in childhood, resurface in this way     and I
feel backwards with them
exposing my wounds
in another language

MEHFIL

Vanja Hamzić

# 8

## Temporal Nonconformity

### Being There Together as *Khwajasara* in a Time of One's Own

"Here in Pakistan, we say *khwajasara*," Kajol, an office clerk, told me, sitting upright in the relative comfort and safety of the quarters of a nongovernmental organization she worked for, walled off and tucked away in a sleepy middle-class neighborhood of Lahore. "We become *khwajasara* when a spirit, called *murid,* enters us," she continued, placing her hand gently on her chest. "Once *murid* is within oneself, one feels very special about oneself and then one can consider oneself *khwajasara*" (Hamzić 2016, 156; Hamzić 2019, 49).[1] We become, when, once, then... These markers of an identitary process, of being "initiated into a temporal life of language" (Butler 1997, 2), and community, meant then, for Kajol—as they mean still and as they had meant before for members of her gender-nonconforming collective—a dis/orienting experience transgressing the sedimented notions of linearity and progress in time. Christian but partaking in *khwajasara* cosmology (which was, in turn, firmly located within the larger, popular Punjabi, Indic, and Muslim hieropraxis), born into a "low caste," yet resituated within *khwajasara*'s own kinship system and a whirlwind of recent legal and civil society developments, Kajol was living her life within and between different temporalities. Having a spirit within herself, a community—often described as "traditional" in contradistinction with the emergent trans and queer senses of the self in Pakistan—and a "respectable" job, she embodied an increasingly complex web of temporal directions, which characterize contemporary *khwajasara* lifeworlds, but are also, as we shall see, seemingly inextricable from *khwajasara* selfhood across time.

While this communal designation, also transliterated as *khwaja sira* or *khawaja sira*, of a feminine-presenting, gender-binary-defying South Asian subjectivity—more widely known as *hijra* (pl. *hijre*)—is nowadays peculiar to Pakistan, it conjures up and re/memorializes a much longer and wider Muslim and subcontinental past. *Khwajasara* of today claim an etiological link with *khwājasarā'* or *khwājasarā'ī* of yore, who were often designated male at birth but then castrated in their youth before being sold into Muslim imperial or other elite service.[2] As their Persian title suggests, *khwājasarā'* ordinarily, though not exclusively, served as guardians of the secluded women's quarters (*zanāna*) at the Mughal and other South Asian courts. Twenty-first-century Pakistani *khwajasara* see this as their own past. As Bindiya Rana, a Karachi-based *khwajasara* leader, once told me, "We even have certain documents of our *khwajasara* ancestors, when they received some tip or a reward from the Mughal emperor" (Hamzić 2016, 162). However, such claims have been largely dismissed as tenuous, not least because of the coexistence of elite—if oft troubled and derided for their "lack of manliness"—*khwājasarā'* and the supposedly "less dignified" *hijṛā* subjectivity throughout much of the eighteenth and nineteenth centuries, the latter ostensibly more resembling the contemporary *hijre*, including Pakistani *khwajasara* (Hinchy 2013, 8; Hinchy 2014, 277; Hinchy 2019, 23, 28, 148, 260).

In a similar manner, *khwajasara*'s pursuits of their own presents and futures are increasingly threatened by the enterprising gaze of neoliberal futurism (Pamment 2019b, 141–51; Mokhtar 2020) as well as neoconservative "rescue" operations, seeking to extirpate *khwajasara* from their larger networks of solidarity and sociality, labeled by such operations as "lesbian, gay, and bisexual persons whose claim of rights has deeply divided societies" (Farhat et al. 2020, 31). Each relying on a crude, universalizing use of transgender, albeit for different purposes, these disciplining attempts espouse what Elizabeth Freeman (2010, xxii, 3) has referred to as "chrononormativity," or the hegemonic use of time to organize individual and collective human bodies toward certain elite goals, be it late capitalist "maximum productivity" or a forcibly homogenous time of the nation-state. The result is a *stretch* in *khwajasara*'s own temporal and communal practices, a disorienting demand in language, social and political life to conform to either the insipid nationalized notions of respectability (*sharafat*) or to what Aniruddha Dutta and Raina Roy (2014) described as "the expanding category of transgender" in South Asia (320), in need of decolonization and dissent (Dutta 2019, 2).[3]

Such a stretch can cause damage—it can *distemporalize*. In a different context, Safet Hadžimuhamedović and I (Hadžimuhamedović and Hamzić 2019) have described distemporalization as a project of denial of time—a denial of historicity, futurity, or change, which is a significant element of various constructions of "otherness." We have also taken distemporality to signify a refusal of, and intervention into, qualitatively specific temporal lifeworlds, such as that of *khwajasara*. And, as with the conscription into a politics of *sharafat* or a commodified, docile, "recolonizing" notion of transgender, such projects usually include a demand for a retemporalization into another "world," be it of globalized gender regimes or an illusory "respectable" Pakistan.[4]

This chapter engages the temporality of *khwajasara* communal experience by examining not only the processes of distemporalization but also a variety of ways in which this Pakistani gender-nonconforming subjectivity has shared in the larger South Asian and Muslim memories and performance of gender and sexuality, while forging alongside a space and a time of their own. I have sought elsewhere (Hamzić 2019) to account for the specifically spatial aspects of *khwajasara* political, social, familial, and spiritual lives, focusing on *thereness*—a property of dwelling with kindred souls—such lives would entail. But, as I now argue, being there together for *khwajasara* has also meant a great deal of idiosyncratic, multidirectional time-making—oriented toward the pasts, the presents, the futures, and sometimes altogether different temporalities—often at odds with the time-making in their wider sociopolitical environments. This chapter revisits several tell tale instances of such temporal diversity and nonconformity, asking how those relate to *khwajasara* knowledge-production about the self and the world in thereness and, also, in what ways they could contribute to the growing concern with temporality in critical subjectivity studies.

First, I turn to *khwājasarā'* and *hijrā* historical subjectivities to account for the distemporalizing effects as well as some potentially productive tensions between present-day *khwajasara* and *hijra* views of the(ir) past and those of the(ir) historians. One needs to question whom such temporal interventions are *for* and how they travel, in meaning and intent, in a historical "postness" (Freeman 2010, xiv) of empire, colonial modernity, and Orientalism, or when rendered into a history of the present—a critical endeavor that recognizes as futile any (empiricist) struggle to hold the meaning of gender and sexuality in place (Scott 2011, 1–22). Second, I briefly examine a site of *khwajasara*'s present/future-making. At this site, *khwajasara* are literally made part of another, virtual world, but find ways to disrupt or "rewire" such transformation. There, as Omar Kasmani (2021) avers, an "ongoing futuring" (99) takes place, in which "not only locally specific meanings around gender variability are being pushed out and projected anew" (98) but "a register of new world making" (107) emerges, "making temporality a key character in this process" (106).[5] Third, based on divergent *khwajasara* experiences of temporality and distemporalization as well as a range of decolonial queer, Black, and trans/feminist *timely* studies, I ask how time matters differently in the postcolony.[6] Or, more concretely, how do the selfhoods and bodies that matter and churn Pakistan's desires travel through multiple communal, national, and colonially induced formations of time? And what does such interruptive time traveling *do* to their senses of being present as they are?

## PRESENTING THE PAST: ON BEING "BACK IN THE DAY"

So many *khwajasara* stories of the(ir) past begin with an indeterminate time that is applied as a medicament to heal history's wounds (Freeman 2010, 7), inflicted through generations on their body and soul. "Back in the day, only *khwajasara* knew what it meant to have good manners," Saima told me, sitting among her *khwajasara* disciples (*chele*) in their lower-class household (*dera*) in Lahore. She recounted such time as a proof of respect (*izzat*) that *khwajasara* had enjoyed and as a didactic device, which was supposed to teach her young *chele* the value of good manners. "In Mughal times," she continued, "*khwajasara* used to serve at the imperial courts, to educate people, to give them good manners, to teach them how to be well-behaved." But, Saima sighed, turning to her *chele*: "Unfortunately, nowadays, *khwajasara* are ill mannered. They can barely help themselves, let alone teach the others" (Hamzić 2016, 280; Hamzić 2019, 36). Recalling these Mughal times (*Mughalan da wela*) was not so much about locating societal *izzat* into the precise era of the Mughal Empire (1526–1540, 1555–1857) as it was about recounting a Muslim and Indic spacetime *before* colonialism and the violent dispossession of the historical subject positions (*khwājasarā', hijṛā*) to which Saima and the other *khwajasara* and *hijre* trace their communal histories. Or, as Bindiya Rana explained to me, "Once the white men came to India," its previous rulers were "forced to take customs of the white men, and to receive all sorts of orders from them." While previously "considered to be closer to God because they were a mixture of both genders," in the colonial period "*khwajasara* were less and less sought after and they eventually had to [abandon Muslim elite service and] go and live among themselves" (Hamzić 2016, 159).

Rather than romanticizing or fixating on an imperial Muslim polity, Saima's and Bindiya Rana's stories were specifically told against the tides of the "official" histories that had relegated *khwajasara* and other gender-nonconforming subjectivities into a liminal, transhistorical space. Before the recent spike in *khwājasarāʾ* and *hijṛā* historiographies, which this chapter briefly considers, academic literature on *khwajasara* and *hijre* had variously described them as "hermaphrodite prostitutes," "sex-perverted," "sexo-aesthetic inverts coupled with homosexual habits," or even "abominable aberrations."[7] These studies carried on the same scorn for sexual and gender nonconformity that European writers since the eighteenth century accorded to South Asian *hijṛā* and (at first to a lesser extent) to *khwājasarāʾ* subject positions. And, to be sure, they mirrored the abuse and ridicule that so many *khwajasara* and *hijre* continued to experience in their immediate surroundings. To summon a different communal past meant to preserve a sense of self-dignity and *izzat*, which did not simply conform to the external expectations of *sharafat*. After all, quite a few of Saima's *chele* engaged, among other professions, in sex work as well as kindergarten education (both within the confines of their *dera*), a practice that hardly squared with more mainstream, middle-class notions of respectability. Rather, for Saima and Bindiya Rana, "back in the day" was a time of their own, out of sync (Rao 2020, 27) with (post)colonial time, presenting and futuring an idiosyncratic decolonial register of *izzat* suffused with regenerative and didactic properties.

Besides, as much as their dwelling together—as kinfolk, as coworkers, and as a spiritual community—equipped *khwajasara* with exploratory senses of the subject (Hamzić 2019), it also provided for a plural understanding of the(ir) past. It included, for example, a sense of a *prenatal* temporality. Thus, Kajol told me, "If certain matters in the mother's womb are mixed in a particular way, there comes a girl; with some other mixtures, a boy comes out. And with another special mixture, in which a spirit (*murid*) is involved, *khwajasara* emerges." A *murid*'s intercession may have also made possible what Bindiya Rana explained as the link between a *khwajasara*'s communal seniority—as a *bare* or *bare-bare guru* to other *khwajasara*—and her longevity. Some of the highly ranked *khwajasara*, she said to me, were "between 105 and 120 years of age" (Hamzić 2016, 281).

An *originatory* temporality was also often invoked, which among Pakistani *khwajasara* was linked to the ancient Indian princess of an uncertain period, called Mainandi. As Kajol recalled:

> It all started in India. It started with Mainandi. Mainandi was born *khwajasara*. A man came up to her and said, "Mainandi, you are so graceful. Can I be like you?" She said, "No! Please ask forgiveness from God! You cannot be *khwajasara*. You are *zenana*." But he went to the field of sugarcanes and he sliced off one sugarcane. He sharpened it and, with it, he emasculated himself. Then he went back to Mainandi and said, "Look, I'm like you now! Am I not *khwajasara?*" But Mainandi was so depressed that she asked God for forgiveness and to open the earth beneath her. So, a crack appeared beneath her feet and swallowed her. (160)[8]

This temporality comes forth not only as a link with an Indic past, but also as a longtime marker of difference in *khwajasara* cosmology and communities between those who are said to be born intersex, those who are not but undergo ritual emasculation (*nirban*), and those who "imitate *khwajasara*" (*zenana*), even though such subdivisions are sometimes porous and overlapping (Pamment 2019a, 299). And it serves to remind *khwajasara* of the beauty of *nirban*, an initiation into the *khwajasara* lineage and a bodily, spiritual, and temporal re/turn. As Neeli Rana, a Lahore-based *khwajasara* leader, told me, "When a *khwajasara* becomes *nirban*, she sometimes takes Mainandi's name. Because, once you become *nirban*, you also become very beautiful" (Hamzić 2016, 160). The special charisma (*baraka*) that *khwajasara* were widely seen to possess, endowing them with the powers to bless and curse, could also be linked to this originatory event and Mainandi's intercession.

Finally, some Muslim *khwajasara* who had made pilgrimage to Mecca and Medina fondly recalled meeting *aghāwāt* there, whose Arabo-Turkic honorific suggests that they were—just like the historical *khwājasarā'*—designated male at birth but then castrated in their youth, and who, because of their unique *baraka*, served as the guardians of the tomb of Prophet Muḥammad in Medina as well as at the Great Mosque of Mecca, since about the mid-twelfth century (Marmon 1995, 31–112). While such meetings indeed could have taken place in or around these sanctuaries, of even greater importance is that *khwajasara* pilgrims thought *aghāwāt* "to be just like themselves" and having a common gender and spiritual destiny, thereby completing "a trans-historical cycle of gender-variant thereness, across [the] spaces and times" (Hamzić 2019, 51) of Islamicate societies.[9] And it is precisely within those societies that *aghāwāt* of yore—some, tellingly, of known South Asian origin (Lal 2018, 98)—built their senses of communal belonging and temporality.

Histories of Islamicate societies account for a complex web of genders and sexualities, or rather bodily characteristics, acts, and proclivities that are diversely read—and misread—as identitary patterns, communal practices, and distinct ways of being-in-the-world. *Aghāwāt* and *khwājasarā'* are but two out of myriad terms of art used in Muslim historical sources to record the affairs of castrated individuals—clumsily lumped together and described as "eunuchs" in most European accounts and translations—whose rise to prominence was often linked to a form of elite servitude. The popular euphemisms included a reference to bodily difference (such as *khiṣyān*, "the castrated ones"), types of military or domestic service (*khuddām*, *ṭawāshiyya*), and most commonly, honorifics (*aghāwāt*, "sirs, lords") (Hamzić 2019, 36–7). In the Delhi Sultanate (1206–1526), terms such as *majbūb* were used both "technically," to connote "total" as opposed to "partial" penectomy, and as an insult (Jackson 1999, 73). In the Mughal Empire, particular professions, such as *nāẓir* ("superintendent") or, indeed, *khwājasarā'* ("master of the palace," or more precisely, of the secluded *zanāna*), came to be equivalent with the subjectivity of castrated individuals, who often hailed from as far away as Abyssinia (Hamzić 2019, 36, 38; Bano 2009, 418).

Despite their high office, distinct *baraka*, and awe (*hayba*) they reportedly commanded, these castrated individuals formed their own societies and networks of kinship and patronage—partly, no doubt, in search of a repose from outward hostilities, which often stemmed from their perceived bodily and behavioral difference. Examples of such hostilities abound, including distinct gender and sexual connotations. Thus, the terse Żiya' al-Din Barani, in his *Tārīkh-i Fīrūzshāhī* (1860–1862 [1357]), regaled in calling his nemesis Kafur all sorts of names, from "mutilated" (*nāqṣī*) to "penetrated" (*mābūnī*), referring to Kafur's alleged sexual relationship with the Delhi Sultanate ruler, 'Ala' al-Din Khalji, as "severed at the front, torn at the back" (*pīsh barīde, pas darīde*) (369, 391; Sarkar 2013, 50). In a similar manner, the *Mir'āt-i-Sikandarī* (Sikandar b. Muḥammad 1889 [c. 1611]), recounted the abuse the independent sultan of Gujarat hurled at Ḥujjat-ul-Mulk, his castrated ennobled subject: "O fool, what shall I say to you? If you were a man, I would have reviled you by calling you a coward; if you were a woman, I would have called you unchaste. You are neither man nor woman, but the bad qualities of both are present in you" (126). A few years earlier, envious of the Mughal *khwājasarā* Iʿtimad Khan's many successes, ʿAbd al-Qadir Badaʾuni (1986 [1595]) resorted to a less direct form of critique, quoting in his *Muntakhab al-tawārīkh* an alleged *ḥadīth* against the counsel of women, the rule of boys, and the management of *khwājasarā* (2: 63–64). Badaʾuni's gender bias is evident throughout his writings; for instance, in the *Najāt al-rashīd* (1972 [1581]), he warned "that men should refrain from dressing up like women and vice versa" (Majid 2010–11, 250).

Castrated ennobled imperial servants were often—though not always—accused of "effeminacy," which made them more recluse and possibly closer to other gender-nonconforming palace dwellers, such as "sober and active women"—as they are referred to in the *Āʾīn-i Akbarī* (Abuʾl Fażl 1873 [c. 1592–1602], 1: 46–47)—who succeeded *khwājasarā* as inner guardians of the Mughal *zanāna*. They were, like them, often of foreign origin and seen as "manly" because of their refusal to veil and for being "highly skilled in the management of the bow and other arms" (Manucci 1907 [c. 1708], 2: 332). The term Muslim historical sources often used was "the effeminate" (Arabic: *mukhannath*, Persian: *mukhannaṣ*), which has a long and complex social and theological history and the same Arabic trilateral root *kh-n-th* found in the legal term *khunthā*, denoting an intersex person.[10] For example, in the Delhi Sultanate, Minhaj al-Siraj Juzjani (1963–64 [c. 1259–60]) identified the *mukhannaṣān* in his *Tabaqāt-i Nāṣirī* as one of social ills causing the sultan to become "entirely enslaved by dissipation and debauchery" (1: 457). The term evidently did not apply solely to castrated individuals, but it *was* used against them, indicating that the boundaries between the "severed" (*khāṣī*) and "born that way" *aghāwāt, khwājasarā*, and other gender-nonconforming subjectivities were not always so clear-cut. Indeed, in 1621, Emperor Jahangir (1980 [1627]) recorded in his *Tūzuk-i Jahāngīrī* the arrival of castrated individuals who were gifted to him, noting that "one of these was a *khunṣa*, having both the male organ and the private parts of a woman" (373).[11]

It is, of course, not possible to fully ascertain the effects of the manifold forms of institutionalized violence and sexual and gender bias on *khwājasarā* subjectivity formation. The available accounts of *khwājasarā* were chiefly penned by elite men, who were sometimes their enemies or who envied their beauty, education, wealth, or other perceived privileges. One exception is Bakhtawar Khan, a prominent *khwājasarā'* and historian at Emperor Aurangzeb's court, who penned such works as *Ā'īna-ye bakht, Bayāż, Rīāż al-awlīā'*, and—most famously—the *Mir'āt al-'ālam*, completed in 1667–68. The *Mir'āt*'s preface recounts how fond the author was of historical studies, always wanting to write one, while the conclusion relates to various poets, including the author. But one cannot assume a deeper sense of the self from this or the other, largely impersonal, Bakhtawar Khan works (1979 [1667–68]; Elliott 1877, 7: 145–65). It is, however, possible, that *some khwājasarā'* responded to the demands of an elite sense of propriety by assuming less ambiguous masculine positionalities. Thus, Jessica Hinchy (2018), who studied *khwājasarā'* in eighteenth- and nineteenth-century Awadh, argues that "*khwāja-sarā'ī* in Awadh displayed aspects of dominant forms of elite masculinity in order to secure the loyalty of followers, suggesting that androgyny was not the only interpretation" (151) of their gender identity, at least as far as Awadh is concerned.

As an elite subjectivity, *khwājasarā'* still left a much more indelible mark in Muslim historical sources than the *hijṛā* subject position, which chiefly appeared elsewhere and more recently, that is, in the accounts of late eighteenth-century European travelers, the East India Company's officials, and, later, colonial administrators, medical doctors, and ethnologists (Hinchy 2019, 28–30). My purpose here is not to rehearse such encounters, or the language used to describe people who, at first, appeared to the European observer as "human beings called hermaphrodites," wearing "the habit of a female and the turban of a man." The same observer, then, in a manner typical of such accounts, was compelled "to examine some of these people: my visit was short, and the objects disgusting" (Forbes 1834, 1: 359). Suffice it to say that such early colonial "knowledge" of the lower-class *hijṛā* subject position gradually became the basis for similarly worded local accounts. Thus, a typical description in English, penned by Khan Bahadur Fazalullah Lutfullah Faridi (1899), alleged that *hijṛā* communities "feign themselves women and some of them devote their lives to the practice of sodomy and gain their living by it" (21). This was in sharp contrast with the few remaining earlier non-European sources, such as the eighteenth-century legal documents, issued on behalf of Śahu I, the ruler of the Maratha Empire, which referred respectfully to its *hijṛā* (Marathi: *hijḍā*) community and bestowed on it specific revenues and rights (Preston 1987).

Instead of returning, as it is repeatedly done, to the sites of colonial knowledge-production, I find it potentially more productive to engage with the recent surge in historical *hijṛā* and *khwājasarā'* studies, which, in a nutshell, challenge present-day *khwajasara* claims of a common ancestry with the historical *khwājasarā'*. The argument goes that because the historical *khwājasarā'* "presented themselves as masculine, . . . in contrast to femininely dressed" historical *hijṛā* communities (Hinchy 2019, 23), the two "categories should not be conflated" (Hinchy 2013, 8). They performed "distinct social roles in the eighteenth and nineteenth centuries" (Hinchy 2014, 278), and, while the *hijṛā* subject position continued its existence—though not without major legal and economic challenges—into the twentieth and twenty-first centuries, *khwājasarā'* "did not survive the historical transformations of colonial modernity in South Asia" (Hinchy 2018, 166).

Here, the challenge is to resist the seductive unidirectional meaning-making in the colonial archive and to question *how*—as Anjali Arondekar (2009) states—it "has emerged as *the* register of epistemic arrangements" (2), with a modest hope to propose, instead, "a different kind of archival romance" (1)—one that is cognizant of *any* archive's "fiction effects (the archive as a system of representation) alongside its truth effects (the archive as material with 'real' consequences)" (4). I respond to this challenge by offering but a single insurrectionary vignette that *might* disrupt the logics of the (colonial/archival) extinction of *khwājasarā'*.

If, as it is often claimed, the gradual but certain decline in elite patronage forced *khwājasarā'* to disappear "into narrow alleys and streets of Delhi" (Lal 1988, 198) and other urban centers, where did they end up? What were their new sources of subsistence? Whom did they befriend and work with? One possible clue lies in Dargah Quli Khan's *Muraqqaʿ-i Dihlī*, a riveting diary of his stay in Delhi from June 1738 to July 1741. Although in noble service, he quickly became an enthusiastic and enterprising chronicler of the city's life, across classes and professions, including its many entertainers. And it is there—among vivid descriptions of sex workers, dancers, mimics, and musicians—that the reader finds Taqi, a castrated individual, who is "a personal favorite of the Padishah and has access to His Majesty's private chambers," but who keeps a "gardenlike home" in the city in which, "like flowers of many colors, young men are always present." Most tellingly, "wherever there is a boy who is unhappy with the male apparel, Taqi's searching eyes spot him," and "wherever Taqi sees a soft and tender boy, the gardens envy such a discovery." Taqi, Dargah Quli Khan concludes, "is the master and patron of all sorts of catamites because they know that Taqi has carried this art to new heights"; and Taqi is also "the leader of all the castrated ones, who feel proud to be Taqi's disciples" (Dargah Quli Khan 1993 [1738–41], 97–98; Dargah Quli Khan 1989 [1738–41], 155).

Could this be a rare account of a *khwājasarā'* settling in a *hijṛā* environment, transgressing the former boundaries of class and profession? Could it signal the way at least some *khwājasarā'* gradually merged with the *hijṛā* and other sexually and gender-nonconforming lifeworlds, rather than disappearing into oblivion? Taqi's life story, traversing the spaces and subjectivities of an embattled and impoverished ruling class and those of a buzzing metropole, resonates with Bindiya Rana's claim that, due to the major "social changes, *khwajasara* were less and less sought after and they eventually had to go and live among themselves. Before they used to live in the palaces; now, they were living in their own dwellings" (Hamzić 2016, 159). Such communal re/memorializations, after and in spite of systemic distemporalization, call for what Lisa Lowe (2015) has termed "history hesitant." In historical research, she writes, "hesitation may provide a space, a different temporality, so that we may ... reckon with the connections that could have been but were lost and are thus not yet" (98). Or, sometimes, such connections persist and they *are*, albeit within communal spaces and time-keeping practices that quietly resist hegemonic temporalities and their academic agents.

TRANS ON THE MOVE AND *KHWAJASARA*'S
WORLDING OF TIME

Having briefly come to Lahore for a range of activist meetings, Bindiya Rana was finishing up her lunch. "You know," she told me between bites, "the governments in Pakistan change constantly—today it's one person, tomorrow it's someone else—and we wouldn't want to be part of that environment more than we have to, really" (Hamzić 2016, 167). *Khwajasara*, of course, contested elections, successfully engaged the state legal system, and organized protests and even the first Trans Pride March on December 29, 2018 (Hamzić 2019, 47–48), proving extraordinarily savvy in navigating the country's political, social, legal, and religious landscapes. But this sense of an abject, volatile temporality of everyday politics seems to have guarded them from becoming too involved, resorting, instead, to what Faris Khan has described as "a form of translucent citizenship—a mode of belonging which involves not only demands for equal rights from the state but also the right to remain hazy to broader publics" (1–2). The temporal aspect of such "haziness" is important, too. In keeping workable distance from an unhomely time, *khwajasara* continue to *world* (habituate, structure, materialize) a time of their own, a distinct set of timely orientations in politics, social work, and selfhood that, for a moment, might seem to chime well with some other, more hegemonic, systems of time-reckoning, only to quickly retreat to its separate domain.

I focus on a well-known example, "recent" inasmuch as it is proximate to the temporal locus from which the present text is wrought and from which its futural sensing takes place, which might offer a glimpse into *khwajasara* present/future-making. This glimpse is really just that—fleeting, speculative, momentary—pointing to the way a *khwajasara* political activist and *guru*, Neeli Rana, dealt with an external chrononormative demand on her time. It relates to the 2017–18 #ChangeTheClap campaign, launched by the Pakistani office of a large international advertising agency, BBDO Worldwide, on behalf of the Asia Pacific Transgender Network, a transnational nongovernmental organization. The key element of this social media campaign was a ninety-second video ("We Are APTN" 2021a), produced by Rocketman Films, in which *khwajasara* are urged to change *tali*, their idiosyncratic hollow clap, into the more "respectable," conventional clapping of applause. Other videos were also produced featuring trans and *khwajasara* activists and a trans model—all widely lauded online and endorsed by a range of Pakistani celebrities ("We Are APTN" 2021b; We Are APTN" 2021c; We Are APTN" 2021d; Saad 2021). The campaign's final element was a Meta Messenger application, named Meeno Ji: the World's First Transgender Bot, a virtual "transgender woman and a teacher by profession," who was happy, as far as her coding allowed, to answer "any question you may have about transgender people" (@TheMeenoJi 2021; Pamment 2019b, 141–51; Mokhtar 2020).

It was, of course, only a matter of time before the neoliberal politics of transnational donorship, middle-class national "respectability," and advertising and entertainment industries combined to propose—or rather launch—a remodeled and retemporalized "ideal version" of *khwajasara* subjectivity, subsumed under the larger, hegemonically deployed notion of transgender. In her incisive analysis of the campaign, Claire Pamment (2019b) describes *tali* as a combative, differential performative, "its effects dependent on the spaces and temporalities upon which it is unleashed"

(142), a quintessential *khwajasara* tool of self-signification, contact, and resistance that may disrupt, rather than conform to, quotidian forms of social hostility and cisheteropatriarchal violence. The campaign robs the clap of its multiple performative possibilities, turning it instead into an implicitly stigmatizing gesture. Indeed, in the main video, "street" *khwajasara* protest and curse the (staged) violence that is inflicted on them; they are pushed around, called names, sneered at, and ejected from a "respectable" (*sharif*) neighborhood, but they are not allowed to speak. Instead, Kami Sid, described as "transwoman model," wows her upper-middle-class audience on a catwalk and turns directly to the camera to ask, "Never thought people like us could get that far, right?" The idea is that changing the clap and changing (cis) people's mindset, as Kami Sid explicitly suggests, are somehow inextricably connected. Other "respectable" figures—a "transwoman engineering student," a "transman activist," and a "transwoman social worker"—briefly make appearances but do not speak. This social worker is none other than Neeli Rana, made up and dressed to impress, which clearly works because a man in the video gives up his seat on public transport for her ("We Are APTN" 2021a). As Pamment (2019b) suggests, the video explicitly confers approval on "these 'deserving' transgender subjects" at the cost of "street" *khwajasara* "who don't conform to these images of class respectability or have access to formal education or jobs in the NGO sector or fashion industry" (146).

Meeno Ji, the Facebook Messenger bot, goes one step further in distemporalizing *khwajasara* and, for that matter, the larger formations of trans in Pakistan too. The same "respectable" figures from the main video make their appearance once again, introduced as Meeno Ji's friends, but not only can they not speak in their own voices; they are literally turned into cartoonish, vectorized images. What speaks, instead, when prompted, is a series of coded scripts, constructed out of the information available on various trans websites in the United States, which is largely useless to Pakistani trans or nontrans users of any class. Words such as "khwajasara," "tali," "the clap," or "hijra" are not part of its repertoire (@TheMeenoJi 2021; Pamment 2019b, 147–48). Neeli Rana's avatar is given a dignified, kind but serious, look, her black hair flowing down one side of her face, a golden earring shining on the other side.

For a while now, trans—as an identitary orientational aid, as a register of both difference and commonality with the re/claimed *khwajasara* or the formations of queer—is on the move in Pakistan. It has been enshrined in law in a wide sense, "as per self-perceived gender identity."[12] It intersects a variety of activist and communal political explorations and self-designations and it has reached deep into Pakistan's social strata, where its variant transgender is sometimes (mis)used neoconservatively, to divest it from the larger queer Pakistani connotations (Farhat et al. 2020, 31). As Omar Kasmani (2021) has proposed, in an attempt to outline its futural shapes, trans in Pakistan "kicks off a capacious contact zone, triggers encounters, and generates momentum with implications, which impact but also exceed local conditions" (107). The issue, however, is that some of these discursive and material moves can have serious distemporalizing, depoliticizing, and silencing effects on Pakistani *khwajasara*—and trans, nonbinary, and other gender-nonconforming—communities. In the extreme cases of neoliberal futurism, as with Meeno Ji and her friends, such moves can even *entirely displace* trans and *khwajasara* subjectivities with an Americanized bot, where all that is left is an avatar of the former self.

How then, do prominent *khwajasara* activists, such as Neeli Rana, negotiate those demands on their time and subjectivity? Her appearances in the #ChangeTheClap campaign were not only in the main video, where she gracefully takes her seat on public transport, or as a virtual friend of the Meeno Ji bot, the latter commodification being, in fact, done without her prior knowledge or participation (Pamment 2019b, 148). She also speaks in a short black-and-white video, stylized as a personal testimony of "Neeli Rana, transwoman social activist" ("We Are APTON" 2021d). And it is in this video—despite its heavy editing and English subtitles, which often take away from the complexities she tries to convey—that her voice and a distinct *khwajasara* temporality break out of the campaign's neoliberal frame.

"*As-salamu alaikum*," she says, introducing herself as a social activist for "transgender community." But later in the video, she clarifies that she works for a "platform she co-founded," called Khawaja Sira (which she pronounces: *khwajasara*) Society. "It is Pakistan's first organization where each staff member is from the *community*," she says. The English subtitle translates this as "from transgender community." But the use of this English word in *khwajasara*, trans, and queer Pakistani contexts has been deliberately more ambiguous.[13] She speaks of violence that she experienced at a wedding party. The context suggests that she was there with other *khwajasara* to perform *badhai*, their traditional rituals of blessing. But fighting erupted, leading to severe violence against *khwajasara*.

"They beat us all night, some were *raped*. I faced so much *violence* that I can never forget that night," Neeli Rana continues, her voice firm but heavy. "When we went to the *police station* in the morning, they started blaming us for it. They said that we encourage people to have *sex* with us with all the *makeup* that we put on and the way we dress. That is when I thought that I will fight for myself. If I fight for myself, then I'm fighting for my *gender*. I'm fighting for my *community*." The words in italics are all spoken in English. Neeli Rana's re/memorialization and redress of a harrowing experience invoke the body's own microtemporality, the act of speaking out that both comes deep from a *khwajasara* lifeworld and recenters it, and the language of an activist, imbricating, as it often does, multiple temporalities and senses of the self.

"People really need to change their attitude," she says. "Clapping (*tali*) to mock or hurt someone is not acceptable. Even in Islam, our religion, it is not permitted to hurt someone like that." But the people whom Neeli Rana invites to reconsider their behavior are *not khwajasara*. It is *those*, like children and men in the main video, who misappropriate *tali* to abuse *khwajasara*. There is no mention that *khwajasara* should change their clap, attire, makeup, or behavior. But she does finish assuming a communal "we," ambiguous though as it may be, to provide her own reading of the context in which the campaign takes place and issue a call for more cross-sector and, seemingly, cross-class understanding and collaboration. "If we start working with other people, then this *stigma* will be gone," she says hopefully. "Whatever the profession. Whether it is drama, fashion or working in a factory or a company, if the *community* steps in, this *phobia*, this *transphobia* will start to dissipate and will eventually disappear." This interpretation disorients completely the message of the main video. No longer are *khwajasara* silent victims nor is their *tali*, when used *by* themselves, an "invitation to violence." Quite the opposite: it is protesting and redressing the systemic violence of cisheteropatriarchal men and the police that animate Neeli Rana's activist life. But there is a stretch, and it is temporal. It comes with a chrononormative demand on her time to produce a "legible," widely "usable" account. What she has not said is implied in editing; what she has said is shortened, interrupted, and temporally rearranged to produce a desired outcome. That Neeli Rana still manages to channel a time and complex positionality of her own is a testament to her activist skills and ability to straddle sometimes starkly incongruent worldings of time.

## SHAPESHIFTING TIMES AND POSTCOLONIAL DISTEMPORALIZATION

In his meditation on time and Blackness, Achille Mbembe (2017 [2013]) has argued for an attention to the temporal effects of being and becoming, with time itself described as "that which one inevitably encounters on the path to subjectivity" (120), along with multiple and intersecting forms of domination, which—to endure—inscribe themselves on both the bodies of their subjects and on the spaces those subjects come to inhabit, "as indelible traces on the imaginary" (127). Thus, to experience time in the postcolony "is in part to know no longer where one stands in relation to oneself" (121). Such radical uncertainty is a fundamental effect of colonial and postcolonial distemporalization, dispossession, and erasure of certain formations of insurrectionary subjectivity, but it has also been turned, in the African novel and other decolonial temporal devices, into powerful communal dis/re/orientation aids. Or, as Kara Keeling (2019) has asked, "If we were never meant to survive *as such*, what do we do with 'the time that remains'"? (i). These are invitations not only to *spend time* differently, in a decolonial otherwise, but to account for the ways of both losing and gaining a time of one's own.

At the same time, queer and trans each have been hailed as proleptic devices, with queerness understood as a "mode of desiring that allows us to see beyond the quagmire" of the postcolonial present (Muñoz 2009, 1), while "the transgender body has emerged as futurity itself, a kind of heroic fulfillment of postmodern promises of gender flexibility" (Halberstam 2005, 18). Against such all too prescriptive or hopeful ways of presenting and futuring subjectivity, critical scholarship has called for a renewed attention to the ways sexually and gender-nonconforming subjects inhabit categories of their own making, which are not inherently unidirectional ("progressive") and can have both decolonizing and recolonizing effects (Halberstam 2005, 30; Rao 2020, 15). Such unruly inhabitations, in turn, point to a shapeshifting quality of both queer and trans, which get intersected and coconstituted by a whole host not only of other categories (race, class, caste, religion, language, nation, postcolony...) (Rao 12), but also of the contingency of such terms-of-art as "queer time" or "trans time." If there are no such overarching one-times, if one can only speak of queer- and transforming temporalities (Cadwallader 2014), it becomes clearer that one's focus should also shift to the multidirectional ways sexually and gender-nonconforming people habituate their own temporal diversity. In postcolonial contexts, such diversity is often materially and discursively positioned against not one, but multiple, formations of chrononormativity, from the demands of late capitalist "productive subjectivity" to those of a cisheteronormalizing nation-state. And so, the strategies of embracing and preserving temporal nonconformity differ too, resulting in profoundly idiosyncratic worldings of time.

Thus, we have seen how *khwajasara*'s thereness affords a series of time-making practices and orientations: from an indeterminate, "back in the day" past, where they encounter the(ir) *khwājasarā'* and *hijṛā* histories; through originatory and devotional temporalities, which connect this gender-nonconforming community with the long arc of Indic and Islamicate subjectivity making; to the spacetimes of "today's Pakistan," where an "ongoing futuring" of *khwajasara* and trans subject positions is performed, exemplified in the ways Neeli Rana moves subversively through diverse—increasingly dispossessive and distemporalizing—demands on her subjectivity and time. I have argued that present-day *khwajasara*'s re/memorialization of the historical *khwājasarā'* subject position should be taken seriously, not only as a form of resistance to systemic colonial and postcolonial distemporalization, but also as an act of hesitance, a critical distance, which in historical research can open up to a different temporality from which to think such distemporalization. As for *khwajasara*'s dealings with the demands of both neoconservative and neoliberal futurisms in an era when trans is on the move in Pakistan, I have called for more nuanced understandings of the individual and collective *khwajasara* agency and the art of being present as they are. Those futural dealings may be specific to Pakistan and its political moment in time, but they also reverberate across the subcontinent and beyond, bringing about novel configurations of social life.

NOTES

1    This chapter derives from my long-term fieldwork in Lahore, Punjab, Pakistan, in the eventful 2010s, interruptive and multitemporal as they were, which made each visit unique and bristling with its own senses of communal directions, whether within *kwajasara*'s own networks or the larger sexually diverse and gender-nonconforming social and political formations. I am deeply grateful to each of my many interlocutors over/in time, whose names here either correspond to those they went by (always or in certain contexts) or are changed, if I was so requested. Many thanks to our editor Omar Kasmani too, for an entirely joyful and rewarding prepublication process.

2   For the transliteration of classical Arabic and Persian sources and their historical derivatives in this chapter, I used the IJMES (*International Journal of Middle East Studies*) system, but I omitted the usual diacritics in personal names. Diacritics were not used for the transliteration from present-day South Asian languages. For the sake of clarity, I distinguished throughout between the historical *khwājasarā'* and *hijṛā* subject positions and the contemporary *khwajasara* and *hijra* communities.

3   There is a growing literature on the making of "respectable" *khwajasara* as a national trope, which is related to but should not be confused with *khwajasara*'s own demand for respect (*izzat*). See, for example, Pamment 2019b, 144; Mokhtar 2020, 5; Khan 2019, 10; Hussain 2019, 335.

4   To use the term M. Jacqui Alexander has theorized in her critical writings about Caribbean state nationalism; see, for example, Alexander 1997. Moreover, for the avoidance of doubt, it should be clear that I do not consider every discursive deployment of "transgender," in Pakistan or elsewhere in South Asia, to be hegemonic or temporally and politically damaging.

5   Kasmani focuses on futuring a capacious, asterisked, more-than-identitary trans* in Pakistan; my focus is on futuring *khwajasara*, that is, on specific communal futurities that may or may not travel as far afield as the wider designation of trans or trans* in Pakistan.

6   For a recent study on a variation of this exact question, probing the timeliness of the *queer* postcolony while seeking to provincialize the time of Western modernity, see Rao 2020, 1–32.

7   For a brief survey of the 1950s to 1990s subcontinental literature where these labels come from, see Hamzić 2016, 158, 278, and Hall 1997.

8   For a similar recollection of this originatory narrative, see Abbas and Pir 2016, 163.

9   Marmon (1995) quotes a 1990 interview in the Saudi magazine *al-Yamāma* as, to her knowledge, the latest evidence of the existence of *aghāwāt*. In this piece, an official in charge of the "affairs of *aghāwāt*" reported that fourteen *aghāwāt* "still served at the sanctuary of Mecca and seventeen at the sanctuary in Madina" (111).

10  Or rather a person of an ambiguous or intractable sex, translated as "hermaphrodite" in most European sources. For a discussion on the long history of *mukhannath*, see Hamzić 2016, 94, 97, 278–79.

11  Sarkar (2013, 45) notes that the latter part of the quoted text, in which Jahangir explains how he knows that "one of these was a *khunṣa*," was omitted from a popular English translation of the *Jahāngīrnāma: Tūzuk-i-Jahāngīrī*.

12  §3(2), Transgender Persons (Protection of Rights) Act, 2018. This right to self-identify, removing the need for an earlier proposed gender recognition committee, was, of course, hard-won through the concerted efforts of a group of *khwajasara* and trans activists and their feminist allies, which involved, inter alia, an interaction with the Council of Islamic Ideology (Pamment 2019b, 149).

13  I am grateful to Naseeba Umar, a fellow researcher in the field, for a recent discussion on this topic.

## REFERENCES

Abbas, Qaisar, and Ghiasuddin Pir. 2016. "History of the Invisible: A People's History of the Transgendered Community of Lahore." THAAP *Journal* 6: 162–75.

Abu'l Fażl. 1873 [c. 1592–1602]. *Āʾīn-i Akbarī*. Translated by Heinrich Blochmann, vol. I. Calcutta: Asiatic Society of Bengal.

Alexander, M. Jacqui. 1997. "Erotic Autonomy as Politics of Decolonization: An Anatomy of the Feminist and State Practice in the Bahamas Tourist Economy." In *Feminist Genealogies, Colonial Legacies, Democratic Futures*, edited by M. Jacqui Alexander and Chandra Talpade Mohanty, 63–100. New York: Routledge.

Arondekar, Anjali. 2009. *For the Record: On Sexuality and the Colonial Archive in India*. Durham, NC: Duke University Press.

Badaʾuni, ʿAbd al-Qadir. 1972 [1581]. *Najāt al-rashīd*. Edited by Sayyid Muʿin al-Ḥaqq. Lahore: Idārah-yi Taḥqīqāt-i Pākistān, Dānishgāh-i Panjāb.

Badaʾuni, ʿAbd al-Qadir. 1986 [1595]. *Muntakhab al-tawārīkh*. Translated by George S. A. Ranking, W. H. Lowe, and Wolseley Haig, vol. 2. Delhi: Renaissance Publishing House.

Bakhtawar Khan. 1979 [1667–68]. *Mirʾāt al-ʿālam: History of Emperor Awrangzeb ʿĀlamgīr*, edited by S. S. Alvi, vols. 1–2. Lahore.

Bano, Shadab. 2009. "Eunuchs in Mughal Household and Court." *Proceedings of the Indian Congress* 70: 417–27.

Barani, Żiyaʾ al-Din. 1860–62 [1357]. *Tārīkh-i Fīrūzshāhī*. Edited by Syed Ahmed Khan. Calcutta: Aligarh.

Butler, Judith. 1997. *Excitable Speech: A Politics of the Performative*. New York: Routledge.

Cadwallader, Jessica Robyn. 2014. "Trans Forming Time." *Social Text Online*. July 10, 2014. https://socialtextjournal.org/periscope_article/trans-forming-time/.

Dargah Quli Khan. 1989 [1738–41]). *Muraqqaʿ-i Dihlī*. Translated by Chander Shekhar and Shama Mitra Chenoy. Delhi: Deputy Publications.

Dargah Quli Khan. 1993 [1738–41]. *Muraqqaʿ-i Dihlī*. Edited by Khaliq Anjum. New Delhi: Anjuman Taraqqi Urdu (Hind).

Dutta, Aniruddha. 2019. "Dissenting Differently: Solidarities and Tensions between Student Organizing and Trans-*Kothi-Hijra* Activism in Eastern India." *South Asia Multidisciplinary Academic Journal* 20: 1–20.

Dutta, Aniruddha, and Raina Roy. 2014. "Decolonizing Transgender in India: Some Reflections." *Transgender Studies Quarterly* 1: 320–37.

Elliott, Henry Miers. 1877. *The History of India as Told by Its Own Historians*, vol. 7. London: Trübner.

Farhat, Syed Nadeem, Muhammad Daniyal Abdullah, Shafei Moiz Hali, and Hamza Iftikhar. 2020. "Transgender Law in Pakistan: Some Key Issues." *Policy Perspectives* 17: 7–33.

Faridi, Khan Bahadur Fazalullah Lutfullah. 1899. "Híjdás." In *Gazetteer of the Bombay Presidency: Gujarát Population: Musalmáns and Pársis*, 21–22. Bombay: Government Central Press.

Forbes, James. 1834. *Oriental Memoirs: A Narrative of Seventeen Years Residence in India*, vol. 1. London: Richard Bentley.

Freeman, Elizabeth. 2010. *Time Binds: Queer Temporalities, Queer Histories*. Durham, NC: Duke University Press.

HadžiMuhamedović, Safet, and Vanja Hamzić. 2019. "Distemporalities: Collisions, Insurrections, and Reorientations in the Worlding of Time." Panel organized for the biennial conference of the Finnish Anthropological Society, Helsinki, Finland, August 29–30, 2019.

Halberstam, Jack. 2005. *In a Queer Time and Place: Transgender Bodies, Subcultural Lives*. New York: NYU Press.

Hall, Kira. 1997. "'Go Suck Your Husband's Sugarcane!': Hijras and the Use of Sexual Insult." In *Queerly Phrased: Language, Gender, and Sexuality*, edited by Anna Livia and Kira Hall, 430–60. New York: Oxford University Press.

Hamzić, Vanja. 2016. *Sexual and Gender Diversity in the Muslim World: History, Law and Vernacular Knowledge*. London: I. B. Tauris.

Hamzić, Vanja. 2019. "The *Dera* Paradigm: Homecoming of the Gendered Other." *Ethnoscripts* 21: 34–57.

Hinchy, Jessica. 2013. "Power, Perversion and Panic: Eunuchs, Colonialism, and Modernity in North India." PhD diss., Australian National University.

Hinchy, Jessica. 2014. "Obscenity, Moral Contagion, and Masculinity: *Hijras* in Public Space in Colonial North India." *Asian Studies Review* 38: 274–94.

Hinchy, Jessica. 2018. "Eunuchs and the East India Company in North India." In *Celibate and Childless Men in Power: Ruling Eunuchs and Bishops in the Pre-Modern* World, edited by Almut Höfert, Matthew M. Mesley, and Serena Tolino, 149–74. London: Routledge.

Hinchy, Jessica. 2019. *Governing Gender and Sexuality in Colonial India: The* Hijra*, c. 1850–1900*. Cambridge: Cambridge University Press.

Hussain, Salman. 2019. "State, Gender, and the Life of Colonial Laws: The *Hijras/Khwajasaras'* History of Dispossession and Their Demand for Dignity and *Izzat* in Pakistan." *Postcolonial Studies* 22: 325–44.

Jackson, Peter. 1999. *The Delhi Sultanate: A Political and Military History*. Cambridge: Cambridge University Press.

Jahangir. 1980 [1627]. *Jahāngīrnāma: Tūzuk-i- Jahāngīrī*. Edited by Muḥammad Hashim. Tehran: Intishārāt-i Bunyād-i Farhang-i Irān.

Juzjani, Minhaj al-Siraj. 1963–64 [c. 1259–60]. *Tabaḳāt-i Nāṣirī*. Edited by ʿAbd al-Ḥayy Ḥabibi, vol. 1. Tehran: Intishārāt-i Asāṭīr.

Kasmani, Omar. 2021. "Futuring Trans* in Pakistan: Timely Reflections." *Transgender Studies Quarterly* 8: 96–112.

Keeling, Kara. 2019. *Queer Times, Black Futures*. New York: NYU Press.

Khan, Faris A. 2019. "Translucent Citizenship: *Khwaja Sira* Activism and Alternatives to Dissent in Pakistan." *South Asia Multidisciplinary Academic Journal* 20: 1–22.

Lal, Kishori Saran. 1988. *The Mughal Harem*. New Delhi: Aditya Prakashan.

Lal, Ruby. 2018. "Harem and Eunuchs: Liminality and Networks of Mughal Authority." In *Celibate and Childless Men in Power: Ruling Eunuchs and Bishops in the*

Pre-Modern World, edited by Almut Höfert, Matthew M. Mesley, and Serena Tolino, 92–108. London: Routledge.
Lowe, Lisa. 2015. "History Hesitant." *Social Text* 33: 85–107.
Majid, Afshan. 2010–2011. "Women and a Theologian: The Ideas and Narratives of Abdul Qadir Badauni." *Proceedings of the Indian Congress* 71: 248–55.
Manucci, Nicolao. 1907 [c. 1708]. *Storia do Mogor or Mogul India, 1653–1708*. Translated by William Irvine, vol. 2. London: John Murray.
Marmon, Shaun. 1995. *Eunuchs and Sacred Boundaries in Islamic Society*. New York: Oxford University Press.
Mbembe, Achille. 2017 [2013]. *Critique of Black Reason*. Translated by Laurent Dubois. Durham, NC: Duke University Press.
Mokhtar, Shehram. 2020. "Mediating Hijra In/Visibility: The Affective Economy of Value-Coding Marginality in South Asia." *Feminist Media Studies* 20: 1–14.
Muñoz, José Esteban. 2009. *Cruising Utopia: The Then and There of Queer Futurity*. New York: NYU Press.
Pamment, Claire. 2019a. "Performing Piety in Pakistan's Transgender Rights Movement." *Transgender Studies Quarterly* 6: 297–314.
Pamment, Claire. 2019b. "The *Hijra* Clap in Neoliberal Hands: Performing Trans Rights in Pakistan." *Drama Review* 63: 141–51.
Preston, Laurence W. 1987. "A Right to Exist: Eunuchs and the State in Nineteenth-Century India." *Modern Asian Studies* 21: 371–87.
Rao, Rahul. 2020. *Out of Time: The Queer Politics of Postcoloniality*. Oxford: Oxford University Press.
Saad, Raja. 2021. "Pakistani Celebrities Showing Their Support for Transgenders #changetheclap." YouTube. Accessed May 18, 2021. https://www.youtube.com/watch?v=XM3DBZM7o2I.
Sarkar, Nilanjan. 2013. "Forbidden Privileges and History-Writing in Medieval India." *Medieval History Journal* 16: 21–62.
Scott, Joan Wallach. 2011. *The Fantasy of Feminist History*. Durham, NC: Duke University Press.
Sikandar b. Muḥammad. 1889 [c. 1611]. *Mir'āt-i-Sikandarī*. Translated by Fazlullah Lutfullah Faridi. Dharampur: Education Society Press.
@TheMeenoJi. 2021. "Meeno Ji: The World's First Transgender Bot." Facebook and Facebook Messenger. Accessed May 18, 2021. https://www.facebook.com/TheMeenoJi/.
Transgender Persons (Protection of Rights) Act, 2018 (Pakistan).
"We Are APTN." 2021a. "#ChangeTheClap." YouTube. Accessed May 18, 2021. https://www.youtube.com/watch?v=vGsNPHj_ZdA.
"We Are APTN." 2021b. "Kami Sid #ChangeTheClap." YouTube. Accessed May 18, 2021. https://www.youtube.com/watch?v=M5pGawnwd-k.
"We Are APTN." 2021c. "Mani | #ChangeTheClap." YouTube. Accessed May 18, 2021. https://www.youtube.com/watch?v=bIdmnlN3XI0.
"We Are APTN." 2021d. "Neeli Rana | #ChangeTheClap." YouTube. Accessed May 18, 2021. https://www.youtube.com/watch?v=GyA0M0gsmZM.

Claire Pamment 9

## On the Other Side of the Rainbow?

*Khwaja Sira* Pieties, Politics, Performances, and the Tablighi Jamaʿat

*Khwaja sira* (*khwaja sara*)-trans engagement with the transnational Islamic missionary Tablighi Jamaʿat has risen in visibility alongside Pakistan's transgender rights movements of the last decade (2009–).[1] Social media and television interviews have featured spectacular displays of glitter, color, makeup, and flowing long hair of dancing *khwaja sira* bodies being switched out by white kaftans, beards, and turbans of *khwaja sira* preachers. The dominant narrative perpetuated by Tablighi Jamaʿat leaders and media often emphasize *khwaja sira* people offering *tauba*, or repentance, of their femininity and dance practices, as the vehicle to their "new" religious inclusion. A proliferation of such reformist images occurred around the time that the Transgender Persons (Protection of Rights) Bill was being debated in the Pakistani Senate (2017–18), where *khwaja sira*, feminist, and trans activists advocated for the right to gender self-identification for a spectrum of persons, against practices of regulatory gatekeeping.[2] Amid these legal developments, activists in an LGBTI social media group expressed concern over the *tablighi khwaja sira* images as detransition, working to turn transwomen into men, what some called "desi conversion therapy," apparently anathema to the rights movement. Conversely, as trans activist Mehlab Jameel noted in the group's discussion, this growing religious reformism is a "product of the last two decades of sociopolitical developments regarding trans lives in Pakistan" (Jameel

2017). I follow Jameel's prompt to illustrate the entangled relationships between the Tablighi Jamaʻat and the rights movement, particularly as they coalesce around anxieties about the *khwaja sira* dancer and kinship structures of *guru-chela* (teacher-disciple) lineages.[3] I seek to move beyond essentializing readings of religious repression/detransition by foregrounding a spectrum of *tablighi khwaja sira* embodied navigations through the shifting scripts of liberal-secular rights and religious reform. Performances of repentance on the NGO-madrassa circuit, through to couplings of dance and preaching, index that *khwaja sira* people are finding a multiplicity of pious, political, and/or aesthetic possibilities through their *tablighi* affiliations. As such, while *khwaja sira* engagements with the Tablighi Jamaʻat may in their surface representations be seen to sit at the Other side of the rainbow of queer possibility, in the spirit of this volume, I suggest that closer analysis of *khwaja sira* agencies in, through, and against secular-religious normativities might take us to "unlikely places to think queer" (Kasmani, see introduction, this volume).

My introduction to *khwaja sira* engagements with the Tablighi Jamaʻat came through Almas Bobby, a senior *khwaja sira guru*, dancer, actress, and media celebrity, whom I have known since 2008, prior to their 2009 protests that spurred initial Supreme Court hearings around *khwaja sira* rights (Pamment 2010, 2019a, 2019b). In spring 2019, Bobby appeared in a social media video with the bearded *khwaja sira* Amir Khusro, who is active in the Tablighi Jamaʻat. Wearing simple white clothes and a cap, Bobby announced repentance of their jewelry, long hair, and feminine dress, in preparation for the Muslim pilgrimage of Hajj, and requested to be addressed with the male prefix of Shah ji.[4] Bobby has been a pioneering but controversial figure in the battle for trans-*khwaja sira* rights, who in recent years has propagated narrow demarcations of *khwaja sira* authenticity accusing other *khwaja sira*-trans people of being "fake" ("men" or "gay men") that are taking opportunities away from "real *khwaja siras*" (Pamment 2022). As a critical voice of the Transgender Persons (Protection of Rights) Act, Bobby's new pious masculine comportment seemed to push back against the recently introduced legislation—raising alarm in activist conversations about dangerous role modeling, and "who would be next?" Those within *khwaja sira* lineages—particularly those engaged in *badhai*—were less surprised. As Bobby stressed in media interviews, this preparation for Hajj is neither new nor radical in *guru-chela* lineages, where some senior *guru*s, often in old age, give up feminine adornments, permanently or temporarily, as part of their cultivation of piety for the pilgrimage, and sometimes upon return (CCTV 2019; Shakeel 2019; Reddy 2005, 105; Jagiella 2021, 192). Some explain this removal of feminine signifiers as eliminating the need for being accompanied by a male relative, easing transit through Saudi Arabia, and for many it relays beliefs around death and the Hereafter. As Bobby puts it: "We are not women. We will go to death as men. He who gave us breath, will take us as we came" (in Shakeel 2019).[5] This complicated relationship between gender and religion, the mixing of male and female orthopraxies, the bodily "here" and the "after," alongside some *khwaja sira* people's overlaps with social maleness (Dutta 2013; Nisar 2018) urges us to think beyond any unilinear translation of "transgender woman" into these cultures. Bobby complicates the secular narrative of rights, and also the *tablighi* narrative of religious absence within *khwaja sira* cultures.

Bobby invited me to a religious gathering at her house in Rawalpindi before embarking on Hajj (August 2019). The event was attended by a large crowd: some twenty *tablighi khwaja sira* adherents dressed in white, other *khwaja sira* people of varying sartorial gender presentations, *maulvis,* neighborhood acquaintances, and a few media outlets (see fig. 9.1). Amir Khusro framed Bobby's transformation as a path for others, while promoting their own religious/technical school (Knowledge City Technical College): "If he [Bobby] can change, so our friends can also change. Allah always rewards our struggles. When our friends come to us they don't have any source of income, for that we have made two branches in Rawalpindi. Those who want to do *tauba* and leave song and dance they are welcome—for them there is board and lodging, everything is free, for them we have provided computers and other small skills so they can earn their money." The underscoring of *tauba* or repentance of performance (and of the *guru-chela* kinship structures that support these practices) converges with backlash against these elements in the liberal-secular project of rights. Bobby intercepted this narrative of reform to address other *khwaja sira* people, including her own *chelas*, in the gathering: "Whatever you are doing, do it. We don't have resources and neither is the government helping ... so they can continue doing what they are doing, but also remember to pray. ... So many people are coming towards us. You will not get peace anywhere in the world, except in remembering Allah. No one can be perfect but we should keep trying." Bobby suggests that other *khwaja sira* people should pray but not give up the *guru-chela* system, dance, or other labor they are engaged in. Rather, the urge to "keep trying" or good intention, known as *niyat*, offers leverage for *khwaja sira* people who cannot, or choose not to, give up their femininity, art, labor,

FIG. 9.1. At a religious gathering in Almas Bobby's home in Rawalpindi (August 2019). Almas Bobby (left of center) after handing the microphone to a *khwaja sira* singer (far left) who presents a devotional item cultivated in *guru-chela lineages*. *Khwaja sira tablighis* on the right, including Amir Khusro (far right).

community, and/or expressions of piety. Bobby's gathering offers an orientation to the spectrum through which *tablighi khwaja sira* persons are negotiating piety, from *tauba* to *niyat*, and in collusions and collisions with the project of liberal rights.

## THE TABLIGHI JAMAʿAT

The transnational movement of Tablighi Jamaʿat, which emerged out of the Sunni Deobandi school in India in the 1920s, is underpinned by a missionary commitment to faith revival and renewal, cultivating within members and others core *Shariat*-based individual practices (Masud 2000; Metcalf 2002). The movement's teachings, outlined in the *Tablighi Nisaab*, entail six fundamental qualities: certainty of belief in the *Kalima* (the Muslim profession of faith), *salaat* (prayer), a basic knowledge of the obligations of Islam combined with *zikr* (the remembrance of God), service to other Muslims, *niyat* (the purification of intention), and *dawat* (preaching, often to fellow Muslims) (Ilaahi). For the Tablighi Jamaʿat, preaching is an act of piety, incumbent on all Muslims, and not just the scholarly elite. As such, this voluntarist movement, where individuals contribute their own time and resources, brings together heterogeneous identities, albeit men dominate its public face. Modeling a strictly gender-segregated culture of piety, early writings in the movement describe women as a form of *fitna*, or potential disorder, "always on the verge of moving out of control, of displaying excess, of spilling over," of dangerous sexuality, and a distraction to pious activity (Metcalf 1990, 14). Some scholars have critiqued the Tablighi Jama'at for reinforcing women's subordination at the hands of the patriarchy (Sikand 2002). By contrast Darakhshan Khan and Metcalf locate *tablighi* women's pious agency, drawing from Saba Mahmood's critique of the secular-liberal limits of resistance and her ethnographic research around women's piety in Egypt's *da'wa* movement (Khan 2020a, 2020b; Metcalf 1995, 1998; Mahmood 2012). They illustrate that while it is men who invariably offer the public face of the proselytizing movement, taking part in the annual preaching tours and going door to door, women also participate in practicing individual piety and occasionally going out to preach, provided that they do not mix with unrelated men (Khan 2020a, 2020b; Metcalf 1998).[6] *Khwaja sira* engagement with the masculine public contours of the movement arguably further complicate its gender scripts.

Media have often foregrounded *khwaja sira tauba* or repentance of femininity and dance practices, as the vehicle to their "new" religious inclusion, a narrative propagated by Maulana Tariq Jameel, an influential Pakistani television/social media *tablighi* and recent recipient of the Pakistani Government's Pride of Performance Award. Described by several of my *khwaja sira* interlocutors as a great impetus for their religious reform, one tells that the Maulana "is the tree and we are his branches." In a 2017 sermon, the Maulana invites *khwaja sira* people (Punjabi, *khusra*) into the Tablighi Jama'at:[7]

> Khusras are also the creation of Allah and should also be given dawat [invitation] to Islam.
>
> In a village, near my home town, a preaching group came with old singers and dancers and a song-dance master [to a *khwaja sira* household].... The guru agreed to go with them to the mosque. I asked him, have you ever prayed? He said no, never in my life. He said, people hate us so we never came to the mosque. I presented him food and gave him a lot of respect. I invited him to join the Tablighi Jama'at, he agreed.
>
> Basically, they are men, who turn into khusras.
>
> ...After 3 days [the guru] came back. He did tauba to dance. He began regular prayer, he grew a beard, he got married, Allah gave him kids.

Now you have to look after me, he said. I know no other work except dancing, so you bear my expenses. So I said, okay.

Then he brought more than 10 dancers, they cut their hair, and put turbans on.... (Marhaba Official 2017)

In Maulana's account, *khwaja sira* people are positioned as men with reproductive responsibilities of the patriarchy. Like the *khwaja sira* followers before and after this *guru*, *tauba* is central to their piety, through repentance of dance, feminine adornments, and kinship structures—each cast as a sinful obstacle in the path to Allah. These penitent practices share similarities with what Karin van Nieuwkerk (2013) describes of Egyptian actresses who create an Islamic public sphere through discourses of *tauba*, as "repentant artists." This *tablighi tauba* discourse in scripting a Deobandi-infused exemplary model of *khwaja sira* piety strips *khwaja sira* people of femininity, performance, nonreproductive sexuality, and also pieties cultivated in community kinship structures and genres of performance.

Perhaps the closest scholarship has got to trans-ing gender of the Tablighi Jama'at is Darakhshan Khan's insightful reading of the eighth-century female Sufi mystic Rabea Basri, and her interpolation into the Maulana's sermons (2020a). Rabea serves as an interesting example in considering *khwaja sira* pieties: one Lahori *hijra-khwaja sira* dancer of my earliest interviews in 2008 described Rabea as a *hijra* herself, because of her celibacy and ascetic Sufi ways (Pamment 2010, 33). *Khwaja sira* people have often drawn creatively from across religious orientations (Hossain, Pamment, and Roy 2023), particularly Sufi, Shi'a pieties in public performances in shrines; *badhai* performances of blessings, songs, dances, and comic repartee at births, weddings, and other celebratory occasions; through to political activism (Pamment 2019a; Jaffer 2017; Hamzić 2016; Kasmani 2012; Jagiella 2021). Although some scholarship has tried to draw correlation between Sufi and *tablighi* practices, as Muhammad Khalid Masud argues, the Tablighi Jama'at share more with the reformist activities of the *ulema* in stressing the supremacy of *Shariat* (divine law), whereas Sufis stress *Shariat's* inner meanings (Anwarul Haq 1972, in Masud 2000, xi). The Tablighi Jama'at's treatment of Rabea Basri evidences some of these differences. Known to have defied "abject poverty, slavery and her gender to become Allah's beloved," the thirteenth-century Attar in his *Tazkirat-ul Auliya* includes Rabea Basri as the only woman among the otherwise exclusively male compilation of saintly hagiographies (Attar 1997, 41; Khan

2020a, 185). He explains his rationale: "If anyone says, 'Why have you included Rabea in the rank of men?' my answer is, that the Prophet himself said, 'God does not regard your outward forms.' The root of the matter is not form. But intention.... When a woman becomes a 'man' in the path of God, she is man and one cannot any more call her woman" (in Khan 2020a, 187). By contrast, this gender-defying woman appears married, tamed, and domesticated in Maulana's preaching. Khan summarizes: "The feisty Rabea, who expounded on the annihilation of the self and divine love, the one who wanted to set the heaven on fire and douse the flames of hell with a pail of water, is missing from Maulana Jameel's version. She is replaced by a woman anxious about the *nama-e-amal* [the Heareafter]" (Khan 2020a, 189). Similar to Maulana's narrative of *khwaja sira* religious reform, Rabea is wedded into cisheteronormative limits, with a straightened path to the Hereafter. Khan, however, illustrates malleability in the Tablighi Jamaʿat's high ideals upon women, who, out of social, familial, and material restraints, may not be able to reach an elevated station like Rabea so to be "counted among men." Instead, they engage in a "balancing act between the ideal and the contingent," reminding themselves that Allah looks at intent or *niyat* (Khan 2020a, 184, 194). *Niyat*, as such, offers spaces for pious agents to negotiate rigid religious prescriptions.

I proceed by exploring *khwaja siras'* cultivations of piety in *tablighi* networks through embodied negotiations of liberal-secular orientations *and* dominant religious prescriptions. The first part features Amir Khusro, Umer Farooq, and Abu Huraira, who preach on the NGO-madrassa circuit, foregrounding repentance, or *tauba*, of dance and *guru-chela* affiliations. The second turns to Mehak Malik, who combines preaching with dancing, finding alternative registers to highlight her pious intentionality, or *niyat*.

TAUBA: THE NGO-MADRASSA NETWORK

In December 2017, a few months after Maulana Jameel's *khwaja sira* sermon, a poster circulated on social media platforms promoting a *khwaja sira* training scheme that entailed four months of *tablighi* courses, accompanied by classes in sewing, salon work, and/or catering.[8] Underneath was the caption "before change," spotlighting a hyperbolic image of *khwaja sira* femininity, an individual in make up, jewelry, and a red dress, apparently poised to dance. Opposite was "after change," featuring the same *khwaja sira* person, now with a small beard, cap, and white kaftan, an image of masculine piety cast in the model endorsed by Maulana Tariq Jameel. Headlining the text is the aforementioned Amir Khusro, heavily bearded, pointing their finger upward, as though directing the path to the Hereafter (Wasif 2017).

This poster was distributed not by a religious seminary but instead by the nongovernment organization (NGO) Saffar in Islamabad that purports to work for *khwaja sira* and transgender rights. Since the beginning of rights movements in 2009, respectability, morality, and normative citizenship have strengthened the backlash against *khwaja sira* dance and the *guru-chela* kinship on which these practices rest (Pamment 2019a, 2019b, 2022). Saffar's coupling of religious instruction *and* vocational training marks convergences between religious and secular agendas in urging *khwaja sira*s away from dance, which accompany the rising visibility of Tablighi Jamaʿat *khwaja sira*s in this period of rights. Arguably the austere masculine imaging of the religiously reformed *khwaja sira* meets its match in the puritanical call to apparently feminine domestic labor through "sewing, salon work, and/or catering"—one of countless similar training schemes that have emerged through the rights period from both government and NGO-backed "social rehabilitation" programs. Secular and religious reform collude against the dancer, with promises of social upward mobility and spiritual uplift in the passage to the Hereafter. This is further amplified in Saffar's release of a video sermon by the white-clad and bearded *khwaja sira* Umar Farooq, directing the reform of other *khwaja sira* people:

> Dear brothers . . . only when we walk in the path of Allah will we find our respect. . . . There is the world and the Hereafter—the last day will be decided through our actions in this life. . . . We cannot live according to our desires. We have to know the difference between what is lawful and what is forbidden. . . . We are born into Muslim families but we have now forgotten our identity. I request you to become part of our organization. There is peace in religion. I will also send message to the parents of khwaja siras. Parents who have a child that is fond of singing and dancing should send them instead to us.[9]

Through Saffar's overall campaign, the rhetorical devices of "before" and "after," the world to religion, the forbidden to Islamic sanction, femininity to apparent masculinity, closely align with Maulana Jameel's sermon. Respect, the Hereafter, and peace are presented as the boons of repenting desires, song, dance, feminine comportment, and *guru-chela* kinship.

While Saffar harnessed dominant discourse against the dancer, its deployment of *tablighi* discourse also arguably propelled its own particular organizational agendas, and perhaps also those of its donor agencies. Well connected to media outlets, a year before this campaign, Saffar made newspaper headlines: "Pakistan transgender leader calls for end to culture of 'gurus,'" while announcing a new transgender mosque project (Boone 2016). Although the mosque never met completion, similar to Saffar's madrassa-like training program, it was positioned as a replacement to the *guru-chela* home, the *dera*. Saffar has also been instrumental in voicing opposition to the clauses of gender self-determination and the spectrum of gender variance of the Transgender Persons Act (2018), in support of a petition in the Shariat Court, which alleges the act to be un-Islamic (Pamment 2020). The apparently shifting and divisive nature of Saffar's politics are cause for concern and alert us to how *tablighi* authorities and *gurus* may be orchestrated to advance narrow exclusivist criteria of *khwaja sira*-transgender legitimacy, possibly in a bid for media space and competitive donor funds. However, that the *tablighi* figures have been propped up as just *one* element in Saffar's operations and are not a permanent part of its organizational structures points to other *khwaja sira tablighi* piety, within, on the edges, and beyond NGO and madrassa networks.

Abu Huraira is a *khwaja sira* preacher who runs a madrassa in Lahore, which in autumn 2019 had a membership of forty *khwaja sira* adherents, largely cultivated through active preaching in *deras* and NGOs, but also through the assigned annual tours of the Tablighi Jama'at. During our meeting in their madrassa, I was introduced to several students: one transfeminine person who lives with her biological family in Abbottabad and had come to the madrassa for several days, finding in it community and spiritual fulfilment; a more permanent resident who had left her *dera*; and another who made daily trips to the madrassa and was still part of *guru-chela* kinship, working in alms collection and occasional dance performances. As Abu Huraira describes, many *khwaja sira* people who come to the madrassa dress in simple clothes for prayer and religious instruction, and then return to their feminine dress as they return to work and life beyond the madrassa. Abu Huraira was introduced to the Tablighi Jama'at through the cismale actor Jawad Waseem, a well-known member of the Tablighi Jama'at who himself continues to work in the theater. Likewise, Abu Huraira does not mandate that others should undertake *tauba*, even though that has been their own path. They joined the Tablighi Jama'at eight years previously, after dancing in the Punjabi theater by night, and working as an office typist by day. Amid increased social and religious stigma against *khwaja sira* dance, Abu Huraira described their decision to renounce performance: "I stopped feeling good about it. Islam doesn't allow it. You look like a joker to normal people; they don't give you respect. That is why I left everything." With beard, white kaftan, and turban, they tell of new family acceptance and social respect, and like other repentant artists, an incredible sense of calmness and peace (van Nieuwkerk 2013, 50). While on the surface this speaks to *khwaja sira*-transphobic sociality or the return to masculinity that Maulana Jameel propagates, Abu Huraira describes their return to a "pure" *khwaja sira*-ness, cultivated by pious practices, and in alignment with the guardians (*Aghas*) of Prophet Muhammad's grave in Medina (Marmon 1995):

> I asked Allah for my beard. "Your Prophets have a beard, so please give me one as well." Khwaja siras used to have beards because they were close to Allah. . . . I got rid of feminine dress myself. I started wearing a white dress. I feel good wearing white—the khwaja sira dress used to be naturally white during the Mughal era when we were kept in good will. . . . Old transgenders used to recite the Quran, and people would ask for their prayers, just like we are doing today. . . . The khwaja siras at the grave of Prophet Muhammad, they don't talk to anyone, but are clean and pious. Women's dress was important for dance and singing purposes, but we ruined our bodies. . . . Everyone knows I am a khwaja sira–we don't need to tell who we are. (2019)

Abu Huraira articulates their *khwaja sira* identity beyond the male designator that Maulana Jameel assigns, while interloping "pure" and idealized Muslim "origins." These puritanical strains may work to cast judgment on those who "ruin" their bodies, yet here in this particular iteration Abu Huraira was possibly extending care to my *khwaja sira* friend who had accompanied me to the meeting. Just moments earlier, we had been chatting about how she was still recovering from medical complications caused by the rupturing of her expensive silicone breast implants.

Abu Huraira moves fluidly from madrassa, preaching tours, *deras,* and into NGOs and *khwaja sira*-transgender community-based organization spaces—where they have even offered congregational Quranic recitations on Transgender Remembrance Day. Their madrassa suggests porous structures that enable an "out" for some *khwaja sira* people of various backgrounds and struggles—a refuge however temporary. While Saffar also entails these elements, in its alliances with liberal reform efforts steeped against the dancer and *guru-chela* kinship, and its direct politicking in the Shariat Court against the spectrum of identities of the Transgender Act, it makes abject Others. By contrast, in resisting becoming a poster image of reform and evasive to the narrow legibilities of the media's gaze, Abu Huraira tells that they do not push their own path onto others but instead stress Islam's openness and flexibility.

### *NIYAT*: PREACHING ON THE DANCE FLOOR

Mehak Malik is a dancer, Punjabi theater performer, and social media star, ranked as one of Pakistan's top-ten most popular TikTokers (Taj 2020), with more than 6.3 million followers and 141.1 million likes (as of December 2020). In contrast to other *khwaja sira tablighis* who have renounced their femininity and/or dance, Mehak boldly brings both together. While performing at a 2017 wedding function, adorned in the shimmer and tassels of a belly dancing costume, she pauses her dance, places a *dupatta* on her head, takes the mic and addresses her all-male audience, who are gathered in the hundreds:

> I wasn't sure it was appropriate in my get up, but my heart told me I should speak. I have many fans, well maybe just a few ... however many there are ... I hope this will reach you. ... Whatever my profession, I pray 5 times a day ... and so should you ... Allah says you bow in front of me and I will make the world bow in front of you. (Zafar Production 2017)

Mehak carefully joins profession and ritual obligation (e.g., praying five times a day)—to underscore her *niyat*—so strong that her heart compels her to preach at the dance function. The crowd murmurs, clearly agitated by the interruption of her dance, but Mehak persuasively persists. She proceeds to deliver an Islamic narrative, featuring Hazrat Aisha (the Prophet's youngest wife), who asks the Prophet to tell one thing revealed on the night of Ascent. Mehak delivers the conclusion to her sermon, "Allah said, any person who heals a broken heart will be let in to heaven without question. ... One should not break anybody's heart." The crowd affirms her compassionate telling of Allah's mercy in declarations of "praise to Allah," followed by a roaring round of applause. In the context of strengthened socioreligious stigma against *khwaja sira* dancers, where incidents of extreme violence only seem to be on the rise within these typically male-only gatherings, Mehak's performances of piety masterfully cultivate moral-ethical dispositions in her audiences.[10] Rather than casting dance as sinful or forbidden, she instead takes to task her audience, calling *them* to piety.

In a recorded video fragment of her meeting with Maulana Tariq Jameel, when asked if bodyguards accompany her to dance functions, she responds, "No. Allah is there for me," which prompts even this anti-performance religious authority to affirm, "Wah, you are Allah's saint" (Shutter super star 2019). Maulana's endorsement has apparently facilitated Mehak's participation in Tablighi Jamaʿat tours for short periods, preaching in mosques, between her busy schedule of dance bookings. In these tightly gender-segregated congregations, full of bearded men, Mehak is introduced with male pronouns, but like other *khwaja sira tablighis* she does not conform to dominant forms of masculinity with her androgynous-fitting kaftan, feminine *dupatta,* and vocal registers. Neither is her dancing personae erased in her moments of preaching inside the mosque, but rather explicitly referenced to amplify her *niyat.* As one introduction inside the mosque went: "He [Mehak] gave up two days of performing in plays . . . 10 lakh rupees and royalties. . . . He said, I am giving two days to Allah!" (Some Fun 2018). The sacrifice of giving up dance and its material rewards, if only for two days, underscores Mehak's *niyat*, undoing rigid distinctions between the world and religion, and legitimizing her presence in the otherwise male pious gathering.

The free flow between the world and religion, the wedding function and the mosque, and masculine and feminine gender presentation is nowhere more fluid than in her social media videos, entailing a multiplicity of genre-bending acts. In her popular TikTok channel (@mehakmalikofficial578) and YouTube videos, Mehak skillfully lip-synchs to the Punjabi hero Maula Jatt, as she does to heroines in serials and films and also devotional religious songs by male vocalists (fig. 9.2). In one compilation of TikToks, she lip-synchs to a male voice reciting a Quranic verse in Arabic, while embodying an archetypal image of feminine piety, wearing a *dupatta*, with eyes lifted to the heavens, tears streaming down her cheeks (Mehak Malik 2020). She also offers religious sermons/narratives that have included religiously imbued takedowns of politicians (Shaheen Studio 2018). Sometimes she offers prayers, responding to fans' complaints of illness or hardship (@mehakmalikofficial578 2020)—in what might be described as a digital-age *badhai* presentation. Like her live performances,

FIG. 9.2. Screen grabs of Mehak Malik's Tik Tok videos.

whether in the dance hall or in the mosque, in these TikTok videos, divine love and a purity of *niyat* generate multiple expressions of piety, innovating an expansive body of aesthetic registers.

Amid the anti-performance imperatives that have been foundational to the entrance of *khwaja sira* people into the Tablighi Jamaʻat, it is not surprising that Mehak has opponents. After a siege of hateful social media comments, accusing Mehak Malik of indulging in sinful activity for continuing to assert her femininity and dance, she offered a firm reprimand against those who wage judgments against not just herself, but the wider *khwaja sira* community:

> Whatever I do, is between me and my Allah.
> Before you point fingers, look to yourself! . . .
> We are on the path of Allah with this kind of face, hair and attire (*she gestures to herself*). And you who have beards, you people of the world, why don't you go for tabligh? . . . (*She steps back to put her body profile into the camera's frame.*) I haven't left this, this is my need. It is our duty to spread Islam. Whatever our situation, we will keep on doing it. (Mehak Malik 2018)

158  CLAIRE PAMMENT

Bringing her femme performing body into the camera's frame, she asserts it as a vehicle of her preaching, a matter between herself and her Allah.

CONCLUSION

Mehak's call against judgment is pertinent across the religious-secular spectrum, from her "religious" opponents that claim her Other, to some of the more secular members of the LGBTI group who imply *khwaja sira tablighi* piety to be on the Other side of the rainbow of queer possibility. Saba Mahmood, in her important work on the politics of piety, also cautions against "delivering judgments on what counts as a feminist versus an antifeminist practice, to distinguish a subversive act from a nonsubversive one. While acts of resistance to relations of dominance constitute one modality of action, they certainly do not exhaust the field of human action" (2012, x). The *khwaja sira* pieties I have introduced here prompt us to read beyond a binary of liberal-secular versus religious projects, which often collude against *guru-chela* kinship and dance. While *khwaja sira* engagement with the Tablighi Jamaʿat has offered refuge for some against hegemonies they find in *guru-chela* kinship, dance or elsewhere, so too it has offered for Mehak a powerful defense of the dancing *khwaja sira* body. Over the border in India, the figure of Laxmi Narayan Tripathi as the recent leader of the Kinnar Akhada has been critiqued for bowing down to majoritarian Hindutva ideology (TNM 2018; Stryker 2019; Upadhyay 2020; Bhattacharya 2019). This might be seen, in chorus with the rising numbers of Tablighi *khwaja sira*s, to signal worrying religious orthodoxy among *hijras-khwaja sira* people concurrent with transgender rights projects. Yet, the diverse range of religious expressions through the Tablighi Jamaʿat—not to mention the many other religious spaces that continue to offer *khwaja sira* people world-making possibilities— challenge unilinear futures of religious orthodoxy. Against the grain of "queer secularity," which assumes the "secular self is the only possible way to be successfully *liberal* and *liberated*" (Khan 2020, 136; Puar 2007), *khwaja sira* pious agency across a spectrum of possibilities, desires, and doings signals "elsewheres" to thinking religion "beside" queer (Kasmani 2022; Kasmani et al. 2020). As Kasmani argues, queer like religion offer methodologies for a "dismantling of boundaries that divide what is from what might be" (2022, 157; viz. Nikki Young 2017), disrupting notions of foreclosing relationships between Islam and queerness.

NOTES

1   *Khwaja sara* is a Persian designation, literally "lord of the palace," and such people sometimes held considerable influence at court (Abbott 2020). In the term's revival over the period of *hijra-khwaja sira*-trans rights in Pakistan (Faris Khan 2019; Shahnaz Khan 2016), the vernacular "khwaja sira" is deployed by *khwaja sira*-led organizations and in the Transgender Persons (Protection of Rights) Act (2018), while both "khwaja sira" and "khwaja sara" hold currency in scholarship, media, and spoken language. In alignment with activist organizing, I use "khwaja sira" in this essay. The presence of *khwaja sira* people in the Tablighi Jamaʻat, while noted in earlier periods (Faris Khan 2014, 107; Baloch 2015, 303–6), has arguably risen in visibility since 2017.

2   The Transgender Persons (Protection of Rights) Act gave transgender people (whether "intersex or *khunsa*," "eunuch," "transgender man, transgender woman or *khwaja sira* or any person whose gender identity and/or gender expression differs from the social norms and cultural expectations based on the sex they were assigned at the time of their birth") the right to self-identification (National Assembly of Pakistan 2018). The "capaciousness" of these recognitions (Redding 2019) evokes what Faris Khan (2019), Kasmani (2021), and Shroff (2021) celebrate as open-ended futures. Yet, as Kasmani and others warn, such "progress" also gestures to other structural inequities that may come to be sedimented, including the privileging of some ways of gender nonconforming over others (2021, 108). Even the legal act itself entails a provision against begging (National Assembly of Pakistan 2018; Redding 2019), and in implementation may carry over the Supreme Court's concern with delineating "real" from "fake" transgender people (Redding 2019; Pamment 2022), and potentially criminalize forms of *khwaja sira* occupation and kinship.

3   The *guru-chela* system of chosen families is organized into houses, or *deras*, that offer for many a refuge from unhomely natal families and a new home beyond the systemic violence of heteronormative society. Careful not to romanticize the *dera*, which for some entails its own violence and hierarchies, Hamzić describes its liminal qualities as an "anchor [of] . . . spatial and identitary journeying towards collective thereness" (2019, 36). In early legislative discussions in the Supreme Court of 2009, *gurus* were named as "violat[ing]" "rights of respect," "forc[ing]" dance and "begging," and "enslave[ment]" (Pamment 2022). Despite the more inclusive gender spectrum of the Transgender Persons Act (2018), its anti-begging clause raises concerns about the potential criminaliza-

tion of occupation; a similar critique has been expressed about legal recognition of *hijras* as transgender in India (Saria 2019, 6–10).

4   This video is no longer online; for a comparable one see Pak Tea House 2019.

5   Another guru explicates these beliefs: "Allah has sent us as a man. You will go back the same way you are sent. You cannot go back as a girl. This is a reality" (anonymous, personal interview 2019).

6   Scholarship has increasingly complicated understandings of the Tablighi Jamaʻat's gender arrangements, but presents a limited heteronormative lens for understanding *khwaja sira* engagement. The focus is invariably on marital arrangements, where men by adopting more humble and (so-called) feminine roles (kitchen work, cleaning, etc.) while on tour (Metcalf 1998, 114; Siddiqi 2012; A. Khan 2018) lead to "more egalitarian relationships between women and men" (Metcalf 1998, 115), or at least "encourage positive and cooperative relations between husband and wife" (Siddiqi 2012, 177).

7   *Khwaja sira*, once used to designate the sometimes powerful (British-designated "eunuch") figures of the Mughal courts, became increasingly used by community members and by society at large since the late 2000s, entering official parlance of identity recognition with rights projects (Khan 2019). Numerous nomenclatures continue to circulate, contingent on region and subject position, including *hijra*, *moorat*, and *khadra* and *fakir* as used particularly in the south (Kasmani 2012; Pamment 2019a), *bugga* in Balochistan (Naqvi and Mujtaba 1997), and *khusra* in the Punjab. The Maulana's use of *"khusra"* instead of the official terms *"khwaja sira"* and more recently "transgender," discursively separates these communities from rights developments.

8   The public page on which this video was initially posted, has been modified. Transcript with the author.

9   As above, transcript with the author.

10  Mehak explains how she performs in dance functions in far northern regions of Khyber Pakhtunkhwa, locations that have witnessed extreme violence toward *khwaja sira* people, yet she claims she is treated respectfully (Shutter super star 2019).

REFERENCES

Abbott, Nicholas. 2020. "'In That One the *Ālif* Is Missing': Eunuchs and the Politics of Masculinity in Early Colonial North India." *Journal of the Economic and Social History of the Orient* 63, nos. 1–2: 73–116.

Attar, Shaykh Fariduddin [n.a., Urdu trans.]. 1997. *Tazkirat-ul-Auliya*. Lahore: Al-Farooq Book Foundation.

Baloch, Akhtar Hussain. 2015. *Teesri Jins* [*Third Gender*]. Lahore: Fiction House.

Bhattacharya, Sayan. 2019. "The Transgender Nation and Its Margins: The Many Lives of the Law." *South Asia Multidisciplinary Academic Journal* 20: 1–19.

Bhatti Fruit Farm. 2018. "Mehak Malik tableegh k ly logo ko jmaa krty hoy." YouTube. https://www.youtube.com/watch?v=ANjPuvbNSGc.

Boone, Jon. 2016. "Pakistan Transgender Leader Calls for End to Culture of 'Gurus.'" *The Guardian*. December 25. https://www.theguardian.com/society/2016/dec/25/pakistan-transgender-leader-culture-of-gu#rus—nadeem-kashish.

CCTV Pakistan. 2019. "Almas Bobi Famous Transgender Change His Life. Exclusive Interview." YouTube. October 8. https://www.youtube.com/watch?v=_moAYzor1dY.

Dutta, Aniruddha. 2013. "Legible Identities and Legitimate Citizens: The Globalization of Transgender and Subjects of HIV Prevention in Eastern India." *International Feminist Journal of Politics* 15, no. 4: 494–514.

Hamzić, Vanja. 2019. "The Dera Paradigm: Homecoming of the Gendered Other." *EthnoScripts* 21, no. 1: 34–57.

Hossain, Adnan, Claire Pamment, and Jeff Roy. *Badhai: Hijra-Khwaja Sira-Trans Performance across Borders in South Asia*. London: Methuen Drama, 2023.

Ilaahi, Maulana Aashiq. n.d. "Six Fundamentals." In *Faza'il-e-A'maal: Revised Translation of Tablighi Nisaab*. https://archive.org/stream/Fazail_amal_in_englishByGulamRasool/fazail_amal_complete. Accessed April 8, 2022.

Jaffer, Amen. 2017. "Spiritualising Marginality: Sufi Concepts and the Politics of Identity in Pakistan." *Society and Culture in South Asia* 3, no. 2: 175–97.

Jagiella, Layla. 2021. *Among the Eunuchs: A Muslim Transgender Journey*. London: Hurst.

Jameel, Mehlab. 2017. "Thoughts?" Facebook. December 24, 2017.

Kasmani, Omar. 2012. "Of Discontinuity and Difference: Gender and Embodiment among Fakirs of Sehwan Sharif." *Oriente Moderno* 92, no. 2: 439–57.

Kasmani, Omar. 2021. "Futuring Trans* in Pakistan: Timely Reflections." *TSQ: Transgender Studies Quarterly* 8, no. 1: 96–112.

Kasmani, Omar. 2022. *Queer Companions: Religion, Public Intimacy, and Saintly Affects in Pakistan*. Durham, NC: Duke University Press.

Kasmani, Omar, Nasima Selim, Hansjörg Dilger, and Dominik Mattes. 2020. "Introduction: Elsewhere Affects and the Politics of Engagement across Religious Life-Worlds." *Religion and Society* 11, no. 1: 92–104.

Khan, Abeera. 2020. "Queer Secularity." *Lambda Nordica* 25, no. 1: 133–39.

Khan, Arsalan. 2018. "Pious Masculinity, Ethical Reflexivity, and Moral Order in an Islamic Piety Movement in Pakistan." *Anthropological Quarterly* 91, no. 1: 53–77.

Khan, Darakhshan. 2020a. "Intention as the Bridge between the Ideal and Contingent: Rabea Basri and the Women of the Tablighi Jama'at." *ReOrient* 5, no. 2: 183–97. doi: 10.13169/reorient.5.2.0183.

Khan, Darakhshan. 2020b. "Praying in the Kitchen: The Tablighi Jama'at and Female Piety." In *Food, Faith, and Gender in South Asia: The Cultural Politics of Women's Food Practices*, edited by Usha Sanyal and Nita Kumar, 201–16. London: Bloomsbury Academic.

Khan, Faris. 2014. "Khwaja Sira: Culture, Identity Politics, and 'Transgender' Activism in Pakistan." PhD diss., Syracuse University. June, 2014. https://surface.syr.edu/cgi/viewcontent.cgi?article=1056&context=etd.

Khan, Faris. 2019. "Institutionalizing an Ambiguous Category: 'Khwaja Sira' Activism, the State, and Sex/Gender Regulation in Pakistan." *Anthropological Quarterly* 92, no. 4: 1135–71.

Khan, Shahnaz. 2016. "What Is in a Name? Khwaja Sara, Hijra, and Eunuchs in Pakistan." *Indian Journal of Gender Studies* 23, no. 2: 218–42.

Mahmood, Saba. 2012. *Politics of Piety: The Islamic Revival and the Feminist Subject*. Princeton, NJ: Princeton University Press.

Marhaba Official. 2017. "Ek Khwaja Sara Ne Tablighi Jamat Main Kasy Hisa Lya By Maulana Tariq Jameel (New Bayan)." YouTube. https://www.youtube.com/watch?v=-6jHHTVKrGw.

Marmon, Shaun Elizabeth. 1995. *Eunuchs and Sacred Boundaries in Islamic Society*. New York: Oxford University Press.

Masud, Muhammad Khalid, ed. 2000. *Travellers in Faith: Studies of the Tablīghī Jamāʿat as a Transnational Islamic Movement for Faith Renewal*. Boston: Brill.

Mehak Malik. 2018. "Zayada sy zayada sher kary please." Facebook. October 1. https://www.facebook.com/669638046572997/videos/1902338786528223.

Mehak Malik. 2020. "Mehak Malik Recite Holy Quran and Naat Rasool Maqbool (S. A. W) Best Tik Tok Video|2K20|." YouTube. May 19. https://www.youtube.com/watch?v=ct26wBhKw8Q.

@mehakmalikofficial578. 2020. "Reply to alibhattiofficial578." TikTok. December 6. https://www.tiktok.com/@mehakmalikofficial578/video/6903302159731838209.

Metcalf, Barbara D. 1990. *Perfecting Women: Maulana Ashraf 'Ali Thanawi's Bihishti Zewar: A Partial Translation with Commentary*. Berkeley: University of California Press.

Metcalf, Barbara D. 1995. "Islam and Women: The Case of the Tablighi Jama'at." *Stanford Humanities Review: Contested Polities, Religious Disciplines and Structures of Modernity* 5, no. 1: 51–59.

Metcalf, Barbara D. 1998. "Women and Men in a Contemporary Pietist Movement: The Case of the Tablighi Jama'at." In *Appropriating Gender: Women's Activism and Politicized Religion in South Asia*, edited by Patricia Jeffery and Amrita Basu, 107–21. New York: Routledge.

Metcalf, Barbara D. 2002. *"Traditionalist" Islamic Activism: Deoband, Tablighis, and Talibs*. Leiden: ISIM.

Naqvi, Noman, and Hasan Mujtaba. 1997. "Two Baluchi Baggas, a Sindhi Zenana and the Status of Hijras in Contemporary Pakistan." In *Islamic Homosexualities: Culture, History and Literature*, edited by Stephen O. Murray and Will Roscoe, 262–66. New York: NYU Press.

National Assembly of Pakistan. 2018. Transgender Persons (Protection of Rights) Act. www.na.gov.pk/uploads/documents/1526547582_234.pdf.

Nisar, Muhammad Azfar. 2018. "(Un)Becoming a Man: Legal Consciousness of the Third Gender Category in Pakistan." *Gender and Society* 32, no. 1: 59–81.

Pak Tea House. 2019. "Almas Bobby Is Shah Jee now." Facebook. March 27. https://www.facebook.com/PakTeaHouseBlog1/videos/566367033866152.

Pamment, Claire. 2010. "Hijraism: Jostling for a Third Space in Pakistani Politics." *TDR: The Drama Review* 54, no. 2: 29–50.

Pamment, Claire. 2019a. "Performing Piety in Pakistan's Transgender Rights Movement." *Transgender Studies Quarterly* 6, no. 3: 297–314.

Pamment, Claire. 2019b. "The Hijra Clap in Neoliberal Hands: Performing Trans Activism in Pakistan." *TDR: The Drama Review* 63, no. 1: 141–51.

Pamment. Claire. 2022. "Staging 'Fake' *Khwaja Siras*: The Limits of Impersonation" In *Mimetic Desires: Impersonation and Guising across South Asia*, edited by Pamela Lothspeich and Harshita Mruthinti Kamath, 148–168. Honolulu: University of Hawai'i Press.

Puar, Jasbir. 2007. *Terrorist Assemblages: Homonationalism in Queer Times*. Durham, NC: Duke University Press.

Redding, Jeffrey, A. 2019. "The Pakistan Transgender Persons (Protection of Rights) Act of 2018 and Its Impact on the Law of Gender in Pakistan." *Australian Journal of Asian Law* 20, no. 1: 8: 1–11.

Reddy, Gayatri. 2005. *With Respect to Sex: Negotiating Hijra Identity in South India*. Chicago: University of Chicago Press.

Saria, Vaibhav. 2019. "Begging for Change: Hijras, Law, and Nationalism." *Contributions to Indian Sociology* 53, no. 1: 133–57.

Shaheen Studio. 2018. "Mehak Malik Islamic New—Message All Friends." YouTube. August 25. https://www.youtube.com/watch?v=Wc4sMOWrzWs.

Shakeel, Rubban. 2019. "Why Did Almas Bobby Change Her Appearance?" YouTube. December 8. www.youtube.com/watch?v=u1pDTSUAH04.

Shroff, Sara. 2021. "Operationalizing the 'New' Pakistani Transgender Citizen: Legal Gendered Grammars and Trans Frames of Feeling." In *Gender, Sexuality, Decolonization: South Asia in the World Perspective*, edited by Ahonaa Roy, 260–82. Abingdon: Routledge.

Shutter super star. 2019. "Mehak Malik Meeting with Molana Tariq Jameel Mehak Malik Tariq Jameel YouTube." YouTube. January 5. https://www.youtube.com/watch?v=XysnZvaJDJI.

Siddiqi, Bulbul. 2012. "Reconfiguring the Gender Relation: The Case of the Tablighi Jama'at in Bangladesh." *Culture and Religion* 13, no. 2: 177–92.

Sikand, Yoginder. 2002. *The Origins and Development of the Tablighi Jama'at, 1920–2000: A Cross-Country Comparative Study*. Hyderabad: Orient Longman.

Some Fun. 2018. "Mehak Malik Islamic biyan in Masjid." YouTube. October 20. https://www.youtube.com/watch?v=Hpz7r8bJCBk.

Stryker, Susan. 2019. "General Editor's Introduction." *Transgender Studies Quarterly* 6, no. 3: 279–80.

Taj, Hunia. 2020. "Top 10 Pakistani TikTokers—Young Emerging Talent." *Incpak*. July 16. https://www.incpak.com/entertainment/top-10-pakistani-tiktokers/.

TNM. 2018. "LGBTQIA+ Community Condemns Trans Activist Laxmi Narayan Tripathi's Ram Temple Comment." November 24. https://www.thenewsminute.com/article/lgbtqia-community-condemns-trans-activist-laxmi-narayan-tripathis-ram-temple-comment-92152.

Upadhyay, Nishant. 2020. "Hindu Nation and Its Queers: Caste, Islamophobia, and De/Coloniality in India." *Interventions: International Journal in Postcolonial Studies* 22, no. 4: 464–80.

van Nieuwkerk, Karin. 2013. *Performing Piety: Singers and Actors in Egypt's Islamic Revival.* Austin: University of Texas Press.

Wasif, Sehrish. 2017. "Transgender Preacher Defies Dysphoria: Amir Khusro Speaks about Journey from Heera Mandi to Tablighi Jamaat." *The Express Tribune.* December 10. https://tribune.com.pk/story/1580402/1-transgender-preacher-defies-dysphoria.

Young, Nikki. 2017. "Queer Studies and Religion: Methodologies of Freedom." *The Scholar and Feminist Online* 14, no. 2. https://sfonline.barnard.edu/queer-studies-and-religion-methodologies-of-freedom/.

Zafar Production. 2017. "Mehak Malik Islami Msg All Frinds. New Show 2017 Rec by Zafar Production." YouTube. October 20, 2018. https://www.youtube.com/watch?v=Hpz7r8bJCBk.

Abdullah Qureshi

# 10

# A Queer History of Pakistani Art
## Anwar Saeed and Other Ways of Love

It happens all the time in heaven,
And some day
It will begin to happen
Again on earth—
That men and women who are married,
And men and men who are
Lovers,
And women and women
Who give each other
Light,
Often get down on their knees
And while so tenderly
Holding their lovers hand,
With tears in their eyes
Will sincerely speak, saying,
My dear,
How can I be more loving to you;
How can I be more kind?
—Hafiz, 1320–1389

In their article, *Queer Theory and Permanent War,* Maya Mikdashi and Jasbir K. Puar open with the question, "Can queer theory be recognizable as such when it emerges from elsewhere?" (Mikdashi and Puar 2016, 215). They go on to discuss how the United States, and by extension the West (Europe, Australia, Canada, and New Zealand), "remains foundational to queer theory and method, regardless of the location, area, archive, or geopolitical history" (Mikdashi and Puar 2016, 215). In other words, making a case for the potential "different contexts" have "to push conversations in queer theory in surprising directions precisely because they disturb the *taken for granted* background picture of queer theory as American studies" (Mikdashi and Puar 2016, 221). While Mikdashi and Puar were speaking specifically from an anthropological point of view, I feel many of the same criticisms apply to queer representations and queer theory in contemporary art and its history. In October 2020, I moderated a panel discussion titled *Queerness Elsewhere* that brought together three creative practitioners from Pakistan within the larger context of my ongoing doctoral project, "Mythological Migrations: Imagining Queer Muslim Utopias." Hadi Rehman, one of the panelists, asked and commented, "Elsewhere of what? I live in Pakistan and deal with my own set of issues; my place is here and now" (Rehman, Shakar, Sajid, and Qureshi 2020). They explained that they actively choose to distance themselves from a Western discourse and instead respond to their surroundings and context in Pakistan. The statement is powerful for two reasons: one, in its explicit rejection of dominant frameworks of approaching gender and sexuality; and two, pointing toward an active queer discourse in Pakistan that situates itself parallel to the Western canon. With the aim of tracing one such genealogy, I look toward the Pakistani artist Anwar Saeed's work. Born in 1956, over the last four decades, Saeed has explored homoerotic subject matter, in particular, same-sex desire and its intersections with the sociopolitical and spiritual from Pakistani and South Asian perspectives. By following Saeed's artistic trajectory and oeuvre, in this chapter, through the lens of his practice, I propose expanding how we theoretically understand and read *queer* frameworks within contemporary art and, thus, trouble the existing dominant discourse and field.

From the onset, I wish to establish my use of *queer,* which is often understood as an umbrella term for the LGBTIQ+ (lesbian, gay, bisexual, trans, intersex, and queer) communities; taking this as a given, I am more interested in evoking queerness' political history and how, as an ever-evolving and fluid concept, it resists definition. It encompasses how we understand nonheteronormative identities, frameworks, and existences. Drawing on the ideas of José Esteban Muñoz, I see queerness as an "ideality" that is "imbued with potentiality"—one that can be "distilled from the past and used to imagine a future" (Muñoz 2009, 1). When it comes to Pakistan with the exclusion of derogatory terms, *gay* and *queer* do not exist in Urdu or Punjabi.[1] There is, however, a formal and seldom-used term for homosexual, *humjins-parast*, which translates as *same-sex worshipper*—but can also be understood as same-sex believer, follower, or promoter. While it might be that we do not find literal translations of *gay* and *queer,* it is not to say that there aren't any long histories of homoerotic and queer expression in both Urdu and Punjabi traditions. One example is the legend of Sultan Mahmud of Ghazna and his servant-lover, Ayaz, an incredibly celebrated topic in the late medieval and early modern periods of Urdu literature (Kugle 2020, 30). Or Madho Lal Hussain—the unified remembrance and celebration of the Sufi saint and poet Shah Hussain (1538–1599) and his lover, Madho Lal, whose death anniversary is celebrated annually with song and dance at their shrine in Lahore. As Scott Kugle has observed, a systematic attack on such homoerotic imagery can be witnessed as part of colonial governance. The British authorities, Kugle mentions, commissioned selected "Urdu poets and critics [who], drawing on what had been less-than-dominant homophobic elements in Islamic tradition, excised the homoerotic Mahmud from their literary tradition" (Kugle 2020, 37). However, despite the onslaught of colonialism, and its weaponizing of conservative elements in Islamic society, forms of queerness continue to be expressed and remain culturally visible. As these histories come to be revisited from a contemporary standpoint, they continue to be ascribed with new meanings that open up decolonial potentialities toward rethinking queerness outside Western traditions.

BACKGROUND

In recent years, there have been several public conversations on queer issues in Pakistan. In 2019, a first conference focusing exclusively on queerness was organized at the Lahore University of Management Sciences, titled "Queer Futures: Politics, Aesthetics, Sexualities." Reflecting on her visit, Anjali Arondekar, the keynote speaker, mentions a student referring to the conference as *musafir sex conference* (Arondekar 2020, 2). She writes: "That playful, throwaway, yet resplendent figuration, *musafir sex* stayed with me, proffering a sightline for an alternate and potentially radical historical orientation: *musafir* as traveler, guest, visitor, itinerant (in Arabic,

Hindi, Persian, Urdu, and even Romanian, Turkish and more—though spelt as *misafir*), coupled with the cruising, moving body of sex, more precisely, queer sex, summoned a geo/epistemology, a challenge to the historical imagination that surely merited further exploration. What would it mean to conjure *musafir* sex as historical object, to conjure it through a hermeneutic of protean and playful translation?" (Arondekar 2020, 2).

Thinking of *musafir* as traveler, I am reminded of a song by Kishore Kumar, *musafir hoon yaro, na ghar hai, na thikana*, which translates as *I am a traveller, I have no home or place*. In many ways, the lyrics of this 1972 Bollywood song speak of wanderlust and a refusal to settle. Building upon this cultural use of the word *musafir* and recontextualizing it to queerness, and in particular cruising, as Arondekar points out, we are indeed presented with the idea of seeing the queer figure as fluid, and not one who is out of place, rather one who exists outside of place. Understanding *musafir* as *visitor* changes our reading and the potential implication, especially if looked at from the lens of dominant queer discourses as *foreign*. Could it be that the comment *musafir sex conference* had a dual meaning and was also intended as a tongue-in-cheek critique of a congregation of international (including diasporic) folks coming in to flirt with the local—people, ideas, and terrain—and then moving on? We may never honestly know. But we know that in these histories that have always existed—of Sultan Mahmud and Ayaz, Madho Lal, and Shah Hussain—and *musafir* as a framework, we might open a pathway to assess and think about contemporary art locally. Coming to Saeed's work and looking at the symbolically loaded use of historical references in his paintings, positioned in dialogue with images that emerge from his immediate surroundings or experiences, it would not be amiss to say that like a *musafir*, he moves between the past and present, fusing earthly and celestial realms, resulting in a world where, like the term *humjins-parast*, sexuality and spirituality collide.

ENCOUNTERING SAEED

*A Queer Arrival*

My first encounter with Saeed's work coincides with my *arrival* at queerness. I had just moved back to Pakistan after doing six years of art school in London. Though I had *come out* to myself and a small group of friends, I struggled to reconcile my sexuality with my religious and cultural identi-

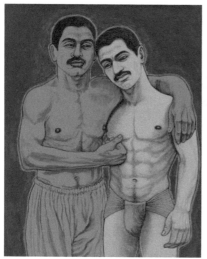 

FIG. 10.1. *Parallel II*, Anwar Saeed, 2006–7, acrylic paint, charcoal, and graphite on paper, 28 × 18 inches.

ties because the term *gay* carried shame. In 2013, I started teaching critical and contextual studies to foundation year students at the Pakistan Institute of Fashion Design in Lahore. Our second class involved a field trip to *Return of the Native*, a group exhibition at Rohtas II Gallery, organized as part of the inaugural Lahore Literary Festival. The show included two diptychs from *Other Ways of Love* by Saeed. Created in 2006–7, the series is dark and macabre, and includes a total of four artworks, where each is presented in sets of two. As examples, I discuss two paintings from the larger body of work. Painted in hues of green, the characters have a gentle glow around them, but the overall tone is melancholy. In one of the paintings (see figure 10.1), we see two muscular men holding each other. The *langot*, an undergarment made of a single piece of fabric, tells us that one of them is a *pahelwaan* (wrestler), while the other man is playing with his nipple. Next to this image, we see a man injecting himself with a syringe—presumably, with steroids, considering their prevalent use in bodybuilding cultures. The other image (see figure 10.2) is similarly structured with two characters in the left image and a single model on the right. Here, we see a man embracing a winged figure, an angel; the man is holding a knife and about to stab the celestial being, who is wearing jeans. This is potentially

 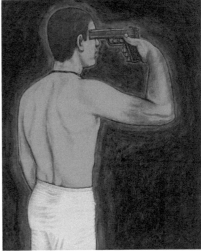

FIG. 10.2. *Other Ways of Love I*, Anwar Saeed, 2010, acrylic paint, charcoal, and graphite on paper, 28 × 18 inches.

a reference to the story of the Prophet Lot. As per one interpretation in the Islamic tradition, it is believed that Lot's people wanted to commit sodomy against angels disguised as men.[2] Next to this, we see the back of a man, who is holding a gun as if he is about to shoot himself. If we are to read this through the tale of Lot, then it can also be deduced that in presenting this act of potential self-annihilation, Saeed is drawing attention to and evoking the historical and religious burden of sin and shame associated with same-sex desire. From the artist's personal perspective, the works examine the forbidden nature of such love in his context, particularly addressing the burden and violence of discretion and secrecy imposed on such relationships.

Following the gallery visit, I encouraged the students to respond to Saeed's paintings in our class discussion. At first, a deep silence fell throughout the room, followed by awkward glances and sniggering. Slowly, responses and remarks started to pour in—a few of them pointing out *"yeh ghalat kaam kar rahay hain,"* meaning that they are doing wrong things. Some drew parallels between homosexuality and drug use—that both are *bad* for us, and thus, forbidden in Islam. One shouted, "They are gay," while others laughed as if the word was derogatory. A few mustered up the courage to say that it is okay to be gay and that perhaps the paintings are talking about the lonely and depressive state of homosexual existence in Pakistan. I asked about the man holding the gun—and among the most disturbing responses was that since homosexuality is a sin, people who practice it should kill themselves. I want to say that these responses shocked me; sadly, they did not. On a personal level, as a queer individual, I wanted to protect my own identity, and at the same time, not deny it. As an instructor, I was conscious of where I was teaching—at a federally chartered higher education institute in Pakistan and engaging with a diverse student body. The institutional rules forbade me to discuss or promote *controversial* subject matter. I was also aware and conscious that some among the students were yet to discover queerness and the impact of this conversation on them. With this in mind, at the time, I carefully crafted my questions, comments, and responses such that my words did not take an outright pro-LGBTIQ+ stance, but nonetheless created a space for tolerance and acceptance.

Legally, homosexuality remains criminalized in Pakistan under Section 377 of the Pakistani Penal Code, 1860, which forbids "carnal intercourse against the order of nature with any man, woman or animal."[3] And though the trans movement has seen some advancement in recent years,[4] by and large, culturally and socially, the LGBTIQ+ community continues to face many challenges in their day-to-day lives. Still, in light of its own homoerotic and queer histories, it is not ironic that upon returning from London, it was in Pakistan that my queerness started to make sense to me. Struggling to identify with white gay and queer cultures, it was in Lahore at a private gathering hosted by NAZ (a nongovernmental organization working in LGBTIQ+ health, policy, and advocacy in Pakistan) that, for the first time, I felt part of a community. In December 2015, this gathering brought together a cross-generational congregation of gay, lesbian, trans men and women, and *khawaja siras.* As a group, it cut across the intersections of gender, sexuality, class, ethnicity, and geography. Despite the diversity in the room, it is essential to acknowledge that there were (and remain) some members of the community who are more vulnerable and at risk of persecution in Pakistan. For instance, despite legal progress, the trans and *khawaja sira* communities remain marginalized and at risk of violence. At the same time, however, at that moment, it was powerful to witness the radical potential of a community coming together in celebration, solidarity, and allyship. That simply by being in a room as a collective of people, who otherwise are denied existence or recognition in a society, it becomes possible for them to define themselves—and thus form and add to discourses that so far do not exist.

In our various conversations, conducted informally between 2017 and 2020, Saeed has categorically emphasized that he does not want his personal life to be discussed—instead, that his work should be read based on what it is saying, visually, symbolically, and metaphorically. Challenging Western readings of *gay* and *queer* terminologies as postindustrial foreign subcultural identities, Saeed forefronts nonheteronormative desires from local perspectives (Ataullah 2015, 73). Based on what we know about the mostly absent or minimal existence of the LGBTIQ+ community on the legal and social fronts in Pakistan, I want to interrogate the spaces Saeed references. With local narratives about Sultan Mahmud, Ayaz, and Madho Lal Hussain, we know that there are historical instances of homoerotic and homosocial celebration, but how does this continue into our present? Speaking to Ali Mehdi Zaidi, a lifelong friend of Saeed, we begin to find some answers. Zaidi and Saeed were colleagues at the NCA (National College of Arts), Lahore, from 1987 to 1988. During this time, they would often go on field trips together to draw and photograph in parks and various public spaces; it was here that they saw many scenes of intimacy playing out, in broad daylight. In an interview I conducted in 2019, Zaidi recounts, "Men would be lying there with their legs intermingled, there were times you could see stains of ejaculation on their *shalwars* (trousers), and that is when the penny dropped that we are totally messed up in our understanding of sexuality."[5] Elaborating further in an email correspondence in 2021, Zaidi explained, "Because the long-standing caste and class system, both, render sexuality invisible. The poor are invisible for whatever they do because they aren't important enough to be seen or acknowledged. The rich and their sexuality is invisible too, the thick veil of the upper class renders it so. Truly messed up are the ones in the middle, visible to both the extremes and burdened by the collective prejudice."[6] At the end of the 1980s, Zaidi moved to the United Kingdom; however, Saeed stayed on in Lahore, and to him, navigating encounters in public parks and on the daily commute by the river went beyond art-making, and became a part of life. With this background in mind, looking at the breadth of Saeed's practice, we can further expand the reading of Saeed's work, where in addition to an intricate play between sexuality, desire, and spirituality, it has also been about journeying toward a more decolonized sexuality that is rooted in working-class experiences. Here, as Zaidi notes, though in some instances displays of sexuality take place in public, in most cases, it remains private due to a range of factors. Hence, as I move forward into Saeed's world, I do so with caution. In discussing and analyzing the themes of his work, I am careful and conscious of not betraying a space that so far has been deliberately elusive.

## SAEED'S WORLD

*A Visual Dialogue with History*

Saeed's career began in the late 1970s, shortly after he graduated from the NCA. Apart from one year abroad, where he went to the Royal College of Arts in London on a British Council scholarship from 1984 to 1985, and few years before that in Islamabad, he has mostly lived and worked in Lahore. Since the 1980s, his work has been regularly exhibited in Lahore, Islamabad, and Karachi, and included in major national and international surveys on contemporary art from Pakistan.[7] Subsequently, various local art critics and writers have also reviewed Saeed's work, celebrating the art for its formal and technical command, and in most cases, cautiously skirted around his nonheteronormative gaze. The late 1970s and 1980s were repressive times for Pakistan. The democratically elected government of Zulfikar Ali Bhutto was overthrown, and an Islamic military rule was imposed on the country under General Zia-ul-Haq from 1977 to 1988, causing a ripple effect politically, socially, and culturally in the years and decades to follow. This period also marks a politically charged beginning for artists in Pakistan. In reaction to the oppressive policies of the time and heavy censorship of art and media, a secret Women Artist's Manifesto was signed, and artists began addressing critical subject matter through visual art and activism (Hashmi 2003, 8). In this earlier period of Saeed's artistic trajectory, his work was primarily read as autobiographical and a depiction of anguish and pain, as observed in articles by Salima Hashmi (1986) and the human rights activist I. A. Rehman (1988). Apart from the fact that Jean Genet, the French novelist, playwright, and political activist who dealt with themes of homosexuality and criminality, is often cited as a significant influence in Saeed's work, direct gay or queer references to his work in art reviews are minimal. By the 1990s, however, questions about Saeed's exploration of sexuality, or lack thereof, started appearing in reviews. Aasim Akhtar noted the absence of female figures in Saeed's paintings and contextualized it as a "fault" (Akhtar 1991). Similarly, in another review, Samina Choonara (1995) writes that "only in some places where the feminine form makes an appearance does he make himself open to metaphors," continuing to comment that Saeed "veers dangerously close not only to the literary but to the literal parts in his work. Potentially, to dodge such questions and comments, Saeed is attributed to have said, "although all art is autobiographical, it need not be reduced to confessional" (Choonara 1995).

However, at the turn of the millennium, we see Saeed's shift, where his public exhibitions become bolder in addressing explicit homoerotic themes and sexuality. Reflecting on this period, Saeed situates this change in a near-death experience. In 1999, while Saeed was visiting the artist Zahoor ul Akhlaq (1941–1999), who was a mentor to him, an assassin broke in and opened fire. The tragic incident led to Akhlaq and his daughter's death and injured Saeed. For a period of time, Saeed lost mobility in his right and drawing hand (Ataullah 2009, 56). During his rehabilitation, he had been reading *I, Pierre Seel, Deported Homosexual*—initially published in French, a gay Holocaust survivor's memoir. The heart-wrenching account of pain, torture, and suffering had a profound impact on Saeed, resulting in him making drawings, paintings, and collages on the very pages of Seel's autobiography. Titled *A Book of Imaginary Companions* (2008), the images created are perhaps Saeed's most erotic to date. At the time, Saeed's decision to address aspects of sexuality more directly in painting was also noted in Pakistan, but not always with comfort. For instance, in a scathing review, and questioning the confessional nature in the artist's work, Naqvi found the explicitness vulgar and framed it as Western import (Naqvi 2002). On the whole, in the article, Naqvi's views on art-making and what constitutes authentic homoerotic representation within the subcontinental culture are rigid, limiting, and romanticize the hidden existence of same-sex desire and intimacies in Sufi, Persian, and South Asian cultures. However, the images Saeed creates, and the experiences that he shares within them, are not to be judged but rather witnessed; his paintings, and the complex narratives that unfold there, open a personal world—and by extension, a history of nonheteronormative desire in the Pakistani and South Asian spheres.

Visually, Saeed's work has often been contextualized within the South Asian traditions of storytelling, where Saeed himself has acknowledged narrative-building as a strategy (Saeed and Akhtar 2005, 33–34) and his paintings have been described as having "a beginning, a middle, and end" (Naqvi 1998, 593). However, because Saeed develops his painting in multiple series, I feel a linear reading of his work would be counterintuitive. Though each of his paintings is very much a complete work in its own right, I feel seeing them in relation to one another in a way that feeds into

FIG. 10.3. *The Punishment Orders*, Anwar Saeed, 1995, mixed media on chipboard, 48 × 96 inches. The artwork was retitled by the artist as *Every Supper Is the Last Supper* by the artist in 2012.

and builds image to image is essential—and, ultimately, allows us a better sense of the tales Saeed is weaving. Another thing worth noting is that all of Saeed's paintings depict the night, where he illuminates his characters with moonlight. Where the moon is physically absent, the picture still maintains a dark palette. In contrast to his position that aspires to depict homoerotic desires from a localized perspective, throughout his painting, but especially in the earlier decades, there is ongoing juxtapositioning of Western art historical references, especially from the Renaissance period, with South Asian imagery. This process of combining different traditions of visual representation can also be seen in late Mughal painting: for example, in *Jahangir's Dream* (c. 1600), alongside the image of Emperor Jahangir (1569–1627) and the King of Persia, Abbas Shah (1571–1629), we see winged cherubs taken from European paintings. Similarly, Saeed actively engages the visual approach, deliberately putting disparate conventions of representation in dialogue with one another. For instance, in the 1995 painting *The Punishment Orders* (see figure 10.3), Saeed recreates *The Last Supper* by Leonardo da Vinci as well as more recent works (see figure 10.4). In the former image, Saeed works with Da Vinci's iconic biblical painting, recreating the composition with his characters, replacing the twelve racially

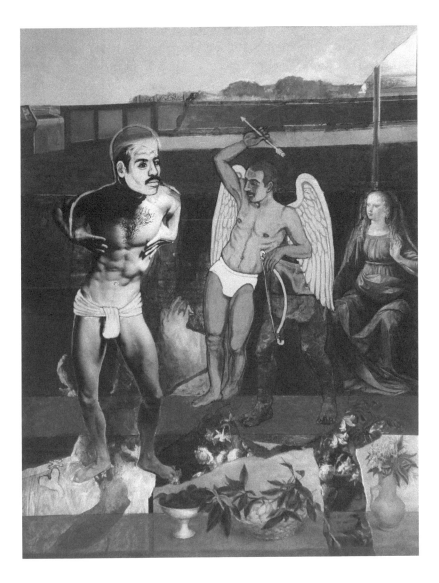

FIG. 10.4. *Our Lady of the Unfulfilled Desires* (detail), Anwar Saeed, 2016, acrylic, felt pen, and collage on paper, 12×16 inches.

white men with brown characters, adding an angel and *Buraq*, an equine creature that took the Prophet Muhammad to heaven. In Saeed's version, one of the men is holding a black cat, often considered an unlucky symbol in South Asian superstitions. Another is smoking marijuana, while a couple plays games, such as juggling or making shapes with thread. In the center, a man is holding a symbolic staff and the man on his right is holding a knife.

Similar to the original painting, there is food on the table, but items such as fish and fruit replace the bread. A musical instrument on the table, which read in relation to the ominous title, *The Punishment Orders*, perhaps points toward a celebration coming to a halt. Further analyzing this in the context of the deliberate structuring of *The Last Supper*, which tells us a Christian legend of betrayal, it would not be unfair to say that Saeed is telling us a similar story and pointing toward a backstabber in the mix. In the latter work, figure 10.4, while engaging references from Renaissance paintings, Saeed takes a different approach and incorporates the images as collages alongside painted areas. Various torn images of still life are scattered across the bottom of the image; the figure of Mary from Da Vinci's *The Annunciation* (circa 1472) sits to the right of the frame. Like the original biblical story, Saeed's version also involves an angel. However, he seems distracted by another man in the picture, whose presumably white body from a pornographic magazine is superimposed with a painted head and is made hairier and adorned in a *langot*, so it reads as South Asian.

As is illustrated in both these paintings, Saeed's work actively engages specific Western art histories rooted in Christianity. On some level, this influence can be attributed to his early training at the NCA, where a lot of the curriculum, to date, focuses on dominant art historical movements in Europe and North America. However, considering Saeed's avid relationship with poetry and literature, it can also be deduced that Saeed's decision to incorporate, or in other words, converse with art from the Renaissance period, is also a draw to the hidden meanings and mysteries discussed around such works, where often the tension between the artist, the state, and church is extensively discussed. For Saeed then as an artist whose thinking and lived experience was heavily shaped during the repressive dictatorship of General Zia-ul-Haq, as much as it is a deliberate strategy, to speak in the hidden meanings of visual metaphors can also be seen as emerging from a place of need at the time. For example, during this period, Saeed exhibited a series of works, which included a painting titled *Birds Flying against Window*, where the image depicts a window from a dark interior space. The light from the exterior casts a strong shadow, and

FIG. 10.5. *Sharing Dreams, Boys Hostel*, Anwar Saeed, 1978, pencil on paper, 23 × 33 inches.

beyond the glass barrier, we see flying birds against the open sky. Speaking about this, he states, "It showed the contrast between the inner desire for peace, beauty, and affection and the turbulence of the outer world, where people were being persecuted and executed" (Mustafa 1993). This approach is drastically different from drawings made in private as studies, which depict scenes of friends—lounging or sleeping together in the same bed (see figs. 10.5 and 10.6). In contrast to the paintings, these drawings are direct in portraying the characters and their activities, and most likely were not intended for public display. It is a relatively recent decision by the artist to upload these images on his personal social media profile. Stripped of the metaphors that accompany a Saeed painting, the drawings offer insight into Saeed's process. They are revealing of his gaze, which more than anything, seems to crave contact and intimacy.

FIG. 10.6. *Looking at Two as One II, Soofi Arshad and Athar Rasool, Boys Hostel,* Anwar Saeed, 1978, pencil on paper, 23 × 33 inches.

CONCLUSION

*Saeed's World beyond Saeed*

At the last edition of the Lahore Biennale in 2020, a dedicated section focusing on Saeed's work was part of the main exhibition program. For many, this was also their first exposure to Saeed's work in a comprehensive manner. Though Saeed has exhibited nationally, the public reach of contemporary art galleries is limited compared with art festivals. As a result, the exhibition at the biennale was important in not only celebrating Saeed's practice, but also igniting a larger conversation on queer pasts, presents, and futures. In an age where information and discourses are rapidly shared on social media, parallel to other investigations and conversations into queerness, it is inevitable for the LGBTIQ+ community to see their history reflected in Saeed's work; in many ways, Saeed's work was always intended for this moment, where the stories that he created and diligently recorded would one day become the bridge into a past, allowing others to imagine their futures. Commenting on Saeed's work, Akhtar writes, "by capturing the present, Anwar instinctively knows that the record would ultimately deliver a past—cumulative stories of love, friendship, desire, and their aftermath" (Saeed and Akhtar 2005, 32). Discussing the relationship between the images that Saeed paints and where they come from, he states: "I can never think of my work, my expression, as separate or distanced from my life because I believe they grow out of each other. In my view, the only purpose of art is to communicate, and we want to communicate is what we are" (Saeed and Akhtar 2005, 35). Based on this statement by Saeed and his practice in general, if we reconnect with the question I began this text with, regarding notions of queerness *elsewhere*, perhaps the inquiry of two seemingly oppositional positions becomes redundant. In many ways, his situation of South Asian bodies, engaged in homoerotic interactions, in dialogue—at times confronting and reworking—dominant art historical references can be seen as a way to disrupt multiple canons at the same time. Extending the quoted poem by Hafiz in the epigraph, what Saeed's work shows us is that as *it happens all the time in heaven*, where men and men are lovers, whether we see it or not, and whether we define or not, on earth it has also been happening all the time and everywhere.

NOTES

1   It is important to note that there are other regional languages in Pakistan, including, but not limited to, Sindhi, Balochi, and Pashto. However, given the scope of this essay as it pertains to the artist Anwar Saeed, who has spent most of his time in Lahore, I mention Urdu and Punjabi as the two widely spoken languages in the city.
2   Quran 54:37.
3   Pakistani Penal Code, 1860, "Section 377."
4   See Transgender Person (Protection of Rights) Act 2018, which was passed by the Pakistani Senate in March 2018, passed in the National Assembly on May 8, 2018, and passed into law on May 18, 2018, by the president.
5   Ali Mehdi Zaidi (artist). Interview by author, London, October 29, 2019.
6   Ali Mehdi Zaidi, e-mail message to author, June 15, 2021.
7   Select exhibitions include 2009, *Hanging Fire: Contemporary Art from Pakistan*, Asia Society, New York; 2007, Inaugural exhibition, National Art Gallery, Islamabad, Pakistan; 2005, *Beyond Borders: Art of Pakistan*, National Gallery of Modern Art, Mumbai, India; 2002, *Threads, Dreams, Desires: Contemporary Art from Pakistan*, Harris Museum and Art Gallery, Preston, England; 2000, Pakistan: *Another Vision*, Brunei Gallery, SOAS, London.

REFERENCES

Akhtar, Aasim. 1991. "Unbearable Lightness of Being." *Herald Pakistan.* November 10.
Arondekar, Anjali. 2020. "The Sex of History, or Object/Matters." *History Workshop Journal* 89: 207–13. doi: 10.1093/hwj/dbz053.
Ataullah, Naazish. 2009. "Conflicts and Resolution in the Narrative." In *Hanging Fire: Contemporary Art from Pakistan,* edited by Salima Hashmi, 51–58. New Haven, CT: Yale University Press.
Ataullah, Naazish. 2015. "Of Whispers and Secret Callings: On Anwar Saeed and Lahore." In *The Eye Still Seeks: Pakistani Contemporary Art,* edited by Salima Hashmi, 71–82. London: Penguin Studio.
Choonara, Samina. 1995. "Between the Sensual and Spiritual." *Herald Pakistan.* May 14.
Hashmi, Salima. 1986. "Art as Autobiography." *The Star* (Islamabad). November 13.
Hashmi, Salima. 2003. *Unveiling the Visible Lives and Works of Women Artists of Pakistan.* Islamabad: ActionAid Pakistan.
Kugle, Scott. 2020. "Sultan Mahmud's Makeover: Colonial Homophobia and the Persian-Urdu Literary Tradition." In *Queering India: Same-Sex Love and Eroticism in Indian Culture and Society,* 30–46. New York: Routledge.
Mikdashi, Maya, and Jasbir K. Puar. 2016. "Queer Theory and Permanent War." *GLQ: A Journal of Lesbian and Gay Studies* 22, no. 2: 215–22. April 1. https://doi.org/10.1215/10642684-3428747.

Muñoz, José Esteban. 2009. "Introduction: Feeling Utopia." In *Cruising Utopia: The Then and There of Queer Futurity*, 1–18. New York: NYU Press.

Mustafa, Anisa. 1993. "The Language of Art Shouldn't Be Limited—Anwar Saeed." *Weekend Post*. March 19.

Naqvi, Akbar. 2002. "Banal Confessions." *Herald Pakistan*. May 12.

Naqvi, Akbar. 1998. *Image and Identity: Fifty Years of Painting and Sculpture in Pakistan*. Karachi: Oxford University Press.

Rehman, Hadi, Begum Taara Shakar, Umair Sajid, and Abdullah Qureshi. 2020. "Queerness Elsewhere." Proceedings of "Mythological Migrations: Chapter 2: The Darkroom," artistic component of DoA diss., Aalto University, Finland.

Rehman, I. A. 1988. "Art Born of Pain." *Herald Pakistan*. January 10.

Saeed, Anwar, and Aasim Akhtar. 2005. "Presence and Absence." In *Beyond Borders: Art of Pakistan*, 31–37. Mumbai: National Gallery of Modern Art.

Ahmed Afzal  11

# Beyond Hooking Up

Tales from Grindr in Pakistan

Although I had been familiar with social networking apps, it was only during the summer of 2012 on a three month-long trip to Pakistan that I created a profile on the Grindr app on my iPhone. I did so primarily to connect with other gay men in Pakistan. I wondered if this digital engagement would assuage some of the isolation and the loneliness I, as a gay male, experienced during family visits to Pakistan. I had come out as gay while in college in the United States in the late 1980s and the early 1990s. Just as I completed my undergraduate education in 1992, eagerly anticipating life as an openly gay male in the United States, family pressure led to my reluctant return to Pakistan.

Once in Pakistan, vulnerable and fearful of public disclosure, I went back into the closet. At my workplace, a progressive social sciences research institute in Islamabad, I found myself working alongside a few LGBTQI+ men and women. None of them were out publicly, much less to one another. The fact that I was selectively open at work about my sexuality and had attended a progressive liberal arts college likely played a part in these colleagues coming out to me. Yet, these friendships, much as they were meaningful, did not fill the vacuum of a gay community or provide a sense of belonging that I was seeking at the time. In the absence of an LGBTQI+ community and organizations in Pakistan, HIV/AIDS activism and research on male sexual health (Afzal 1995; 2005) provided the closest outlets to legitimate my queerness.

Despite the absence of LGBTQI+ organizations, men have sought to pursue long-term same-sex relationships, particularly in metropolitan cities such as Karachi and Lahore. Through anecdotal accounts, I learned of gay couples, including men who were married to women but were also in same-sex sexual relationships. These possibilities and arrangements notwithstanding, I was unable to imagine a life for myself as an openly gay man in Pakistan. Family pressure to marry started to become oppressive. Instances of casual homophobia became increasingly intolerable. I began to pursue educational opportunities abroad.

The opportunity to do so arose in 1998 when I was accepted into a doctoral program in cultural anthropology in the United States. Much more than anything else, I felt tremendous relief. I was grateful for the opportunity to escape a closeted life in Pakistan. My doctoral research on South Asian Muslims in the United States, and subsequently a challenging and long-drawn-out U.S. immigration application process and the demands of building a professional life, kept me in the United States for years, making trips to Pakistan less frequent.

It had been more than decade when I visited Pakistan in 2012, a trip necessitated more by my father's serious illness than a desire to return to Pakistan. I was anxious about the trip, memories of my closeted life in Pakistan coming to sharp relief. And so, I turned to Grindr. I hoped that it would ease some of my anxiety and loneliness and connect me to other gay men. At the time, I did not realize the profound sense of belonging these Grindr connections would provide, and just how much I had been craving friendships that were grounded culturally in shared queer life stories and experiences.

My trip to Pakistan in 2012 coincided with the completion of a decade-long research project on South Asian Muslims in the United States (Afzal 2015) and I was looking to develop a new research project. The trip, and particularly my interactions with men on Grindr, stimulated an interest in exploring the relationship between new technologies, everyday life, and constructions of sexuality in an increasingly globalized Pakistan. Grindr represented a unique and promising field site for ethnographic research. Given the increasing entrenchment of neoliberal consumption in urban Pakistan and the growing ubiquity of smartphones, I wanted to explore the ways that new media technologies such as smartphones were becoming incorporated into everyday life and in refashioning selfhood. Having previously written about men who have sex with men in Pakistan but disavow gay self-labeling (Afzal 2005; 2016) and gay South Asian Muslim Americans (Afzal 2014; 2015; 2020), I was keen to understand how digitally mediated engagements on social networking apps were impacting constructions of sexuality and same-sex sexual desires, intimacies, and relationships among men in urban Pakistan.

The research presented in this chapter uses ethnographic data that was collected during the summers of 2016, 2017, and 2022, and the winter of 2019–20 in the cities of Islamabad, Rawalpindi, and Lahore. The research was approved after a full review by the Institutional Review Board at California State University, Fullerton. I created a profile on Grindr where I disclosed my identity as a researcher who was studying the uses of the Grindr app among men in Pakistan. I also posted my face pictures on my profile. I used the Grindr app and existing personal contacts to identify and communicate with potential interlocutors. I interviewed and collected detailed life histories of thirty-five men and interacted with more than two hundred men on Grindr.

Given the sensitivities associated with research on homosexuality in Pakistan, I did not use voice, video, or digital recordings. Instead, I hand wrote the answers to interview questions. In keeping with ethical considerations and standard protocol in social science research and to ensure the anonymity of interlocutors, I do not use real names and have also altered certain identifying characteristics. The interviews and my conversations with my interlocutors, both face-to-face and in chats on Grindr, were primarily in English, or a mix of English and Urdu to approximate the linguistic and speech patterns used by my interlocutors and to accommodate wide-ranging levels of English speaking and writing fluency. Following the interviews, sometimes spread over the course of several face-to-face meetings and lasting several hours, I socialized informally with many interlocutors, acquiring deeper insights into their lives. In the process, I built several enduring friendships that have provided a deeper and meaningful sense of belonging to Pakistan. As the research gained momentum, I began to look forward to visits to Pakistan, anxieties associated with prior visits turning into eager anticipation.

In this chapter, I refer to fragments from my interactions with three Grindr users who resided in the cities of Islamabad, Rawalpindi, and Lahore in Pakistan as case studies of digitally mediated engagements and the ongoing refashioning of sexuality among gay and bisexual men in urban Pakistan. I argue that Grindr's usage in Pakistan creates opportunities for casual sexual encounters or hooking up and demonstrates the construction of a cosmopolitan gay identity, as evidenced by the participation of my interlocutors on a social networking app targeting gay, bisexual, trans, and queer men, and the appropriations of Western epistemologies of sexual orientation (e.g., gay and bisexual) and sex roles (e.g., top, bottom, and versatile).

Such appropriations notwithstanding, Grindr's usage in Pakistan illuminates a culturally configured queer sexuality. A majority of the men included in my research profess profound sadness and regret over their inability to be "truthful" about being gay in all spheres of life due to familial, religious, and societal mores that negatively assess homosexuality. Many are married or plan to marry a woman. Others express their desire to immigrate to the West, bolstered by the possibility of sexual freedom that many men see as being elusive in Pakistan. Given these real-life considerations, participation on Grindr allows men who have sex with men to explore their sexuality and construct identity as "gay" or "bisexual" even as this refashioning of sexual identity remains constrained by familial, societal, and religious contexts. Moreover, Grindr provides a significant space to negotiate obligations to adhere to societal heteronorms on the one hand and the desire to imagine and experience same-sex sexual intimacies on the other.

GRINDR STUDIES

Grindr is a mobile social networking app that connects adult gay, bisexual, trans, and queer men older than eighteen with other men based on geographical proximity. When a user logs into Grindr they are provided with a grid of other users. The grid consists of small boxes showing scaled-down versions of user profile pictures. This grid shows men in order of location, with the top profile being the user's own, and others become more geographically distant the farther the user moves down the grid. Users can scroll through the grid and view the profiles of other men, but can only access a limited number of profiles unless they pay a subscription fee (Bonner-Thompson 2017, 2).

Tapping a user's picture takes one to the user's profile. The profile provides a biographical sketch of the user based on a multitude of attributes and characteristics such as height and weight, ethnicity (e.g., Asian, Black, Latino, Middle Eastern, Mixed, Native American, White, South Asian, Other), body type (e.g., toned, average, large, muscular, slim, stocky), sexual position (e.g., top, versatile top, versatile, versatile bottom, bottom), and relationship status (e.g., committed, dating, engaged, exclusive, married, open relationship, partnered, single). One can also choose what they are looking for (e.g., chat, dates, friends, networking, relationship, or right now). Users can also identify themselves by their "tribes" such as bear, clean-cut, daddy, discreet, geek, jock, leather, otter, poz (HIV positive), rugged, trans, or twink. One can also select their gender (e.g., man, cisman, transman, nonbinary, nonconforming, queer, crossdresser), the pronouns that they use (e.g., he/him/his, she/her/hers, they/them/theirs), and their sexual health status, notably HIV status and last test date.

By the year 2018, Grindr had an estimated 27 million users in 192 countries, making it among the most popular and widely subscribed social networking apps for gay, bisexual, trans, and queer men globally.[1] As noted on the "About" page on Grindr.com: "Since launching in 2009, Grindr has quickly grown into the world's largest social networking app for gay, bi, trans, and queer people. With millions of daily users spanning almost every country in every corner of the planet, Grindr brings you zero feet away from connecting to a community that grows stronger every day."[2] Reflecting its global popularity, Grindr is among the most subscribed social networking apps for gay and bisexual men, and men who have sex with men in urban Pakistan.

During the last decade, the increasing ubiquity of smartphones coupled with the popularity of mobile social networking apps globally have contributed to bourgeoning multidisciplinary scholarship on the subject. Research on Grindr has proliferated leading to the emergence of what historian and communication studies scholar Andrew DJ Shield has termed "Grindr Studies" (Shield 2019, 31), that is, "research on gay men's digital cultures since 2010 when dating and networking platforms largely moved to mobile phones and utilized geo-locative technologies to connect (mainly) men to other men within their immediate proximity" (Shield 2019, 7–8). Research has focused on the uses and gratifications of Grindr, self-presentation and identity construction on Grindr, and public health-centered studies that measure the safety and the risks, particularly HIV and STIs, associated with sexual encounters initiated on social networking apps.[3]

Studies have also analyzed representational practices, notably, profile pictures, as a significant facet of the affective experience of Grindr. Cultural geographer Carl Bonner-Thompson (2017) emphasizes that digital bodies on Grindr are produced to be desired to be touched by other men. Bonner-Thompson argues that "the ways men display, expose and place their bodies in online profile pictures, reveals the production of two forms of masculinity, i.e., hypersexualized masculinity and lifestyle masculinity" (1611). Hypersexualized masculinity is produced through profile pictures that focus on the body and particularly exposed flesh and skin. On the other hand, profile pictures of a user at a beach, a hiking trail, a bar or a restaurant, historic sites, and other public places situate the user within particular lifestyles and geographies and illuminate a lifestyle masculinity. Emphasizing the interpretive meanings associated with profile pictures, media and communication studies scholars Kath Albury and Paul Byron (2016) in their study of Grindr app users in Australia found that men did not seek profile pictures "for purposes of arousal, but relied heavily on their interpretation of other users' images in order to navigate the layered in-app space where multiple goals, e.g., sex, friendship, chat, or in worst-case scenarios, exploitation, or deception, might co-exist" (Albury and Byron, 5).

Critiquing pictorial images on Grindr, multimedia artist Tom Penny (2014) suggests that profile pictures on Grindr depict faces and bodies, notably, torso, penis, and buttocks "under the glass of screens . . . [and] perpetuate reductive stereotypes fetishized and consumed by a narcissistic homosexual market" (Penny 2014, 107). In Penny's analysis: "Bodies presented under glass surfaces become manipulable, non-visceral, gaze-oriented visual bodies, for consumption as objects by narcissists through the personal screen [of smartphones]. The commanding fingers of these users rub numb, as if calloused, upon the surface of visual bodies" (Penny 2014, 108).

Despite the increasing ubiquity of smartphones globally and the emergence of Grindr studies, little scholarly attention has been paid to the uses of smartphone-based mobile social networking apps in non-Western countries, especially Muslim societies. A few multidisciplinary studies have begun to explore Grindr users in East and Southeast Asia. These include communication studies scholar Jonathan Ong's (2017) study of the uses of Grindr by gay and bisexual men in the Philippines to construct cosmopolitan identities, sociologist Ming Wei Ang and colleagues' (2021) study of racialized sexual desires and preferences among Grindr users in

Singapore, communication studies scholars Shangwei Wu and Daniel Trottier's (2021) study of structures of sexual desire on online dating platforms among men in China, and epidemiologist Kevin M. Weiss and colleagues' (2017) study of Grindr users and sexual health in Southeast Asia.

Researcher Santos Saraiva and colleagues' (2020) study of constructions of masculinity and heteronormativity among Grindr users in Brazil and psychologist Carlos Hermosa-Bosano and colleagues' (2021) study of socialization and discrimination faced by ethnic minority men on Grindr in Ecuador represent some of the scholarship on Grindr users in South America. Historian and communication studies scholar Andrew DJ Shield's (2019) ethnographic study of the uses of Grindr in practices of cultural adaptation among new immigrants and refugees from countries in the Global South in Denmark is another exception. The research presented in this chapter adds to this scholarship through an ethnographic study of Grindr in urban Pakistan.

### TALES FROM GRINDR IN PAKISTAN

For my interlocutors, Grindr provides a significant digital space to connect with other men who are sexually interested in men. It is a connectivity that transcends educational achievement, professional affiliations, class and socioeconomic status, age, and marital status. Based on my conversations with Grindr users and participation observation on the Grindr app since 2016, I found that Grindr users in Pakistan represent a wide spectrum of educational, professional, and socioeconomic backgrounds; ages; and Pakistani ethnolinguistic groups. Grindr users include men who have completed high school, as well as those with an undergraduate or a graduate education. Administrative officers in the public and the private sectors, teachers, engineers, bankers, marketing executives, entrepreneurs, doctors, local politicians, theater actors, college-going students, expatriate Pakistanis, foreign tourists, and blue-collar workers employed in the service industries illustrate the wide breadth of professional backgrounds. Although the majority of my interlocutors belonged to the Punjabi ethno-linguistic group, primarily due to my fieldwork in cities in Punjab, interlocutors also included Sindhi, Balochi, and Pukhtun ethnolinguistic groups who resided in cities in Punjab for either work or higher education. Ages varied from the early twenties to the early fifties and included single and married men.

The majority of my interlocutors were Sunni Muslims and a few were Shia Muslims. However, Islam and especially the presumed tensions between reconciling queer sexuality with faith were seldom brought up during chats on Grindr. It would appear that the absence of conversations about Islam had much to do with a desire to imagine and construct a particular cosmopolitan queer identity that was premised on silences around religion. It might also well be the case that the omission of religion in chats is due to expectations of social interactions on Grindr that tend to focus on "the production of [sexual] encounters as soon as possible, leading to fast sexual gratification and without any relationship follow-up" (Licoppe et al. 2016, 2548). Toward this end, chats often begin with "location," "role," and "pic" to readily ascertain the viability of a hook-up based on geographical proximity ("location"), sexual role compatibility ("role"), and physical attraction ("pic"). Given these parameters, chats generally avoid potentially contentious topics such as religion that might subvert the structure of a chat that is geared toward a casual sexual encounter.

Below, I elaborate on three interlocutors to demonstrate the range of backgrounds, experiences, and sexualities of Grindr users in Pakistan that belie generalizations. Imran, one of the first men with whom I connected on Grindr in July 2016, was a twenty-seven-year-old professional who worked as an engineer at a government agency. Imran lived with his widowed mother and a younger sister in a middle-class residential locality in Islamabad. Fawad, another interlocutor, was twenty-five years old in 2017 when he responded to my Grindr post about my research. Fawad had completed his high school education and worked as a server at a fast-food restaurant. He lived with his maternal uncle's family in a mixed-use, working-class neighborhood in the inner city in Rawalpindi. A third interlocutor, Adeel, was a thirty-year-old student pursuing a graduate degree at a public university in Islamabad. Adeel lived in an apartment with two other male students. Adeel came from an affluent upper-class, land-owning family that had built its fortunes in agriculture and farming in a small city in Punjab.

HOOKING UP

Much of the scholarship on the uses and the gratifications of Grindr has found that sex-seeking is a major motive for Grindr users (e.g., Gudelunas 2012; Miller 2015; Whitefield et al. 2017), giving credence to conceptions of Grindr as a "hook-up app" (Wortham 2013), a "modern-day gay bar" (Miller 2015), a space for "digital cruising" (Brubaker et al. 2016), and a "meat market" (Bonner-Thompson 2017). Other uses of Grindr include socializing, seeking friendship, talking to strangers, social networking, and building community (Race 2015).

For many, but not all, of my interlocutors, Grindr creates opportunities for hooking up or casual sexual encounters. Imran, Fawad, and Adeel readily acknowledged that they had used Grindr to find potential casual sexual partners. Imran was not out to family, friends, or colleagues. The only people who knew about his sexual attraction to other men were those with whom he had interacted on Grindr. Imran had sought out Grindr as a way to connect with other men looking for discrete casual sexual encounters and friendship. Living with his family, Imran lacked the privacy needed for casual sexual encounters. It was only when his mother and sister were away to see relatives in Karachi that Imran would invite men over for casual sex. Vacations abroad, more recently to Florida in 2019, had provided other significant opportunities for sex with men. "It is really the only time when I can meet other men. It is one of the main reasons for these vacations," he shared when we met in person at a restaurant in Islamabad.

For men such as Imran, as well as a significant number of other interlocutors included in my research, the availability of private space is an important factor in whether or not to continue a chat on Grindr, especially if the intention is primarily to hook up. In addition to "location," "role," and "pic," chats often began with the word "host?" or "place?" "Host" referred to whether an individual could host a meeting in real time either at home or at a hotel. It sought to ascertain the availability of a private place and the viability of meeting in real time. An affirmative response contributed to a greater investment in the chat. The lack of a private place to meet in person often led to a quick end to the chat.

The availability of a safe private place also relates to the negotiations of perceived stigma associated with hook-ups and promiscuity (Ahlm 2017). A study of Grindr users in Chicago and Upstate New York found that "there was . . . a tension between wishing to be perceived positively by other nearby attractive Grindr users they wanted to meet, and avoiding negative consequences of stigma from those outside this group" (Blackwell et al. 2015, 1133–34). Given such stigma, sociologist Jody Ahlm suggests that privacy is central to the construction of "respectable promiscuity," enabling Grindr users to "enact stigmatized sexual practices, manage sexual reputations, and give meaning to their sexual practices" (Ahlm 2017, 364).

Fawad had also sought out Grindr primarily for casual sexual encounters with other men. Fawad and I met at a café during a weekday early evening when it was less busy and when we would be assured privacy to chat freely. Initially a little nervous, Fawad became increasingly comfortable as our conversation went on and narrated a memorable weekend trip to Murree, a mountain resort town an hour's drive from Islamabad. Fawad had met a thirty-something Pakistani Canadian on Grindr who was visiting from Toronto. Their chats led to a date at a café and soon afterward a weekend trip to Murree. Speaking about the weekend in Murree, Fawad shared: "I live with my relatives and I told them that I was going to Murree with some friends. They didn't suspect anything. We rented a car and drove to Murree where we checked into a hotel. We had sex for hours—I don't think we came out of our room the first day we were there. I was so happy. I didn't want to come back. After we returned, we didn't really have a place to get together again so we just chatted on Grindr. Then he left for Canada. I haven't heard from him . . . still, I'll never forget him."

Hook-ups and meaningful connections are upended not only by the absence of privacy and the transience of hook-ups, but also by the very real risk of being outed, harassed, and threatened online, and the potential for blackmail and sexual and/or physical abuse during face-to-face meetings (Albury and Byron 2016, 7). The risks are potentially severe, especially given the criminalization of homosexuality in Pakistan and that Grindr along with other apps such as Tinder have been banned by the Pakistan government since 2019. Grindr is accessible by using a virtual private network, or VPN, an encrypted connection over the internet from a device to a network. Khalid, a thirty-five-year-old high school teacher in Lahore, whom I met in winter of 2019, described a horrifying experience that had left him violated and traumatized. Khalid had met a man on Grindr who invited him to his place and assured him that he lived alone. When Khalid arrived, he found four young men at the house. Khalid was in tears as he recounted: "I didn't quite have time to react before they locked the front door and held me to the ground. They raped me. I was crying, literally begging them to let me leave. They took my money and threatened to out me if I told anyone about what had happened. Homosexuality is a crime in Pakistan. It was not like I could have gone to the police and reported the incident. I felt so helpless . . . and so humiliated. I couldn't do anything about it." Despite the devastating risks and the vulnerabilities associated with hook-ups on Grindr, several interlocutors, including Khalid, persist in participating in Grindr because of its potential to affirm queerness that is elusive in mainstream Pakistani society.

BEYOND HOOKING UP

Despite the primacy of hook-ups, for my Pakistani interlocutors such as Imran, Fawad, and Adeel, Grindr is more than simply a platform for hooking up. Rather, for my interlocutors, access to and participation in apps such as Grindr represent sites for negotiating invisibility in mainstream public life. Given the paucity of meeting places such as LGBTQI+ clubs and organizations, and legal conceptions of homosexuality as a crime in Pakistan, Grindr is among the only online venues that provide opportunities for sociality centered on same-sex eroticism and intimacies that is elusive in majoritarian public spheres. Noting the importance of online platforms, the United Nations Office for the Coordination of Humanitarian Affairs Report asserts that the internet is contributing to a sense of growing solidarity among gay men in Pakistan.[4]

Participation in digitally mediated platforms enables not only queer sociality but also the construction of a cosmopolitan sexual identity as evidenced from the appropriation of a Western language of queer sex roles (e.g., top, bottom, versatile) and self-identification as gay. On his Grindr profile, Imran had selected "versatile" and his repertoire of sexual activities included making out, kissing, and topping and bottoming. Fawad, on the other hand, had selected "versatile top" as his preferred sex role, and "discreet" as his tribe. When I asked Fawad about his repertoire of sexual activities, he admitted that he found bottoming or penetrative sex to be painful and that he enjoyed topping more. Recalling a passion-filled encounter with a man whom he had met on Grindr, Fawad shared: "We lay in bed, making out for hours. Sexual intercourse is fine but I love kissing and mutual masturbation. That's what turns me on the most." More recently, he had expanded his sexual repertoire to include analingus or rimming. "I didn't know if I would like it. I hadn't tried it before. Then I met a guy who introduced me to it." Such expansions in sexual repertoire may well be due to greater exposure and an openness to new sexual practices, as also noted by sociologist Hector Carrillo (2017) in his study of Mexican gay male immigrants in San Diego. Unlike Imran and Fawad, Adeel was evasive or perhaps a little shy about discussing sexual activities publicly, saying only, "I like everything but I am a top."

Despite appropriation of Western vocabularies of sex roles in fashioning a cosmopolitan sexual identity and self-identification as "gay," many of my interlocutors were either married or had reconciled to getting married in the future. I asked Imran if he wished to be in a relationship with another man. "No, anything more than a hook-up is not an option for me," he replied. "You see, I am the only son. I don't have a father. It is just my mother, younger sister, and me. It is going to fall on me to take care of them."

"But you could do that and still have a relationship with a man, no?" I had interjected.

Imran didn't agree, telling me: "No. Not at all. I cannot imagine bringing a man home to my mom. Living on my own is not an option for me. My family expects me to get married to a woman and to have a family. That's what I see in my future."

"What about your attraction to other men?" I asked.

Imran explained: "Well, I hope I'll meet other men who are in my situation. My mother will always live with me so it would have to be someone who is discreet and has a private place where we can meet; or we will meet when my mother and sister are out of town."

"But what if you don't find someone like that? And even if you did, would it be enough to just have sex with someone sporadically? Don't you want more from a relationship?" I asked, pressing the issue.

"Well . . . it'll have to be enough," Imran answered quietly before changing the topic of our conversation.

Fawad, the twenty-five-year-old server at a fast-food restaurant, shared Imran's assertions about the inevitability of marriage. I met Fawad for coffee at a local café in Rawalpindi in the summer of 2017. When I asked him if he was gay, Fawad answered without skipping a beat. "Yes, I would say I am gay. Sure." He paused before continuing: "You know, I'm married. I got married two years ago to a distant relative's daughter. She lives in London. We had an arranged marriage. Her family came to Pakistan and we got married during their trip. She has gone back to London."

"I also have a one-year-old son," Fawad continued laughingly, perhaps noting my undisguised surprise at this significant disclosure. Fawad added: "Although we didn't plan it, she got pregnant right after our marriage. My son is in London with his mother. I haven't met him as yet. I am waiting for my visa to come through so I can join her and our son."

"Does anyone in your family know that you are gay?" I asked.

"No! Of course not!" Fawad answered, appearing positively horrified at the mere thought of his family or relatives finding out about his relationships with other men. He continued: "I live with my relatives here. They would throw me out of the house if they knew. They wouldn't react well at all."

Despite the enormity of the consequences, Fawad had met several men online. He was open with me and talked freely about his sexual liaisons. In fact, among all interlocutors, Fawad was perhaps among the most open and even eager to share his sexual experiences with me. "I'll meet other guys when I am in London," he said to me, having reconciled his attraction to men with his identity as a married man with a young son.

Adeel and I met regularly, often at an upscale mall in Islamabad. We would sometimes spend hours just window shopping, before sitting down to eat at the food court. Much like Imran and Fawad, Adeel also self-identified as gay. Adeel, confident in his assertion, said to me: "I'm not out to my family but it's not like I am scared to tell them. It's just that now is not the right time." Unlike Imran and Fawad, Adeel did not plan to marry a woman and was instead hoping to move abroad. "The ideal situation would be if I could go abroad," Adeel said to me. "I feel like I could really only be open abroad, perhaps in the United States."

The desire to leave Pakistan and to go abroad recurred as a common theme in my interviews and in my conversations with interlocutors on the Grindr app. Indeed, the pursuit for sexual freedom through relocation abroad might well be characterized as a type of "sexual migration," i.e., migration that is "motivated fully or partially, by the sexuality of those who migrate" (Carrillo 2017, 4). Adeel had resisted family pressure thus far to marry, and expressed that an "ideal situation" for him would be if he could go abroad. Although Fawad was married and had a young child, he hoped reunification with his wife and son in London would provide him with opportunities to meet other men like him. Familial obligations to family precluded Imran from moving abroad. Yet, as noted in his narrative, vacations abroad provided a significant opportunity for Imran to meet men.

Many of my interlocutors imagine Europe and the United States as places that will allow them greater freedom to express themselves sexually and to assert their queerness publicly. For many of these men, engagements with wider queer communities on social networking platforms such as Grindr, Facebook, Instagram, TikTok, and Twitter have allowed them to imagine a life beyond the heteronormative tradition and family-bound confines of Pakistan. Many also reference LGBTQI+-themed television shows such as *Modern Family* and *Schitt's Creek* and films such as *Brokeback Mountain, God's Own Country,* and *Love, Simon* that are available to stream on platforms such as Netflix and YouTube as aspirational narratives. Significantly, in espousing the idealization of the West, none of my interlocutors spoke about the prevalence of homophobia, racism, and Islamophobia in mainstream Western society as well as within certain segments of the LGBTQI+ communities in the West. The often-harsh reality and challenges to building a life in a new country are also obscured by the prospect of sexual freedom that, for many, remain elusive in Pakistan.

CONCLUSION

More than two decades have passed since I left Pakistan in 1998 to attend graduate school in the United States. Much has changed in Pakistan during the ensuing years as evidenced by the variegated engagements of my interlocutors with mobile social networking platforms and global queer communities, practices, and discourses. Yet, for all the ongoing transformations, and the generational differences between myself and many of my younger interlocutors, their narratives resonated deeply with me. The fears, the vulnerabilities, and the compromises that characterize the compartmentalized lives of my interlocutors felt sadly familiar and heartbreaking. Although my life in the United States had presented its own set of challenges, oppressions, and struggles as a racialized new immigrant and as a gay, Muslim person of color in a post-9/11 America, I had been able to escape a life of subterfuge. This was unlike many of my interlocutors, who appeared to have reconciled themselves to queer futures that are inevitably and devastatingly circumscribed by familial, cultural, and religious expectations and norms.

The fragments of my conversations with Grindr users beg a reconsideration of pervasive scholarly approaches to homosexuality in Pakistan, including my own pre-Grindr-era research. My prior research had focused on men who had sex with men in Pakistan but disavowed self-labeling as gay or even bisexual (Afzal 2005; 2016). As I had argued in this pre-Grindr-era research, the sexual experiences of my interlocutors fit into a more traditional sexual scheme characterized by taxonomies based on active and passive sex roles, a disavowal of Western vocabularies of sexual orientation, and limited engagement with global queer communities, practices, and discourses.

The traditional sexual scheme based on active and passive sex roles only partially represented the constructions of sexuality among my interlocutors who had profiles on Grindr and were engaged with global queer discourses, practices, and communities. In contemporary Pakistan, the global flows of media, technologies, ideologies, and capital are contributing to the emergence of Westernized gay communities that, quite significantly, also accommodate a wide spectrum of culturally configured queer identities. As I have discussed in this chapter, most of my interlocutors such as Imran, Fawad, and Adeel self-identified as gay and were active participants on online gay social networking apps such as Grindr. Their appropriation of a language of sex roles and self-identification as top, versatile, or bottom demonstrates engagements with global queer communities and a cosmopolitan queer self-positioning in digitally mediated spaces such as Grindr.

Despite these digital engagements, marriage and adherence to societal heteronorms seemed inevitable given broader familial, cultural, and religious contexts in Pakistan. Participation on mobile dating apps provides important insights into the complex relationship between globalization, digital media technologies, and the construction of cosmopolitan queer sexualities in urban Pakistan. Significantly, ongoing engagements with Grindr in Pakistan disrupt common misunderstandings of contemporary South Asian Muslim cultures as inherently intolerant of same-sex sexual desires, intimacies, and relationships and instead illuminate digitally mediated spaces for the accommodation of same-sex sexual intimacies.

NOTES

The field research in Pakistan was made possible through an International Travel Grant and a Junior/Senior Faculty Intramural Grant from California State University, Fullerton. Parts of this chapter have been presented at the virtual annual conference on South Asia in October 2021, the annual meetings of the American Anthropological Association in Baltimore in November 2021 and in Seattle in November 2022, and the annual meeting of the Association for Asian Studies in Honolulu in March 2022.

1 https://www.datingsitesreviews.com/staticpages/index.php?page=grindr-statistics-facts-history. Accessed on February 1, 2021.

2   https://www.grindr.com/about/. Accessed on March 27, 2018.
3   For studies on the uses and the gratifications of Grindr, see Brubaker et al. 2016; Chan 2017; Gudelunas 2012; Johnson et al. 2017; Miller 2015; Race 2015; van de Wiele and Tong 2014. For studies on self-presentation and identity construction on Grindr, see Albury and Bryon 2016; Bonner-Thompson 2017; Licoppe et al. 2016; Moller and Peterson 2018; Ong 2017; Penny 2014; Shield 2019. For public health-centered studies that measure the safety and the risks, particularly HIV and STIs, associated with sexual encounters initiated on social networking, see Cruess et al. 2017; Heijman et al. 2016; Holloway et al. 2015; Jandovitz et al. 2012; Rendina et al. 2014; Weiss et al. 2017; Whitefield et al. 2017; Winetrobe et al. 2014; Zou and Fan 2017.
4   https://www.thenewhumanitarian.org/feature/2005/05/10/focus-gay-rights. November 3, 2015.

REFERENCES

Afzal, Ahmed. 1995. "Public Policy Limitations: The Individual, the Family and AIDS in Pakistan." *Development: Journal of the Society for International Development* 2: 61–63.

Afzal, Ahmed. 2005. "Family Planning and Male Friendships: *Saathi* Condom and Male Same Sex-Sexual Desire in Pakistan." In *Culture and the Condom*, edited by K. Anijar and T. DaoJensen, 177–205. New York: Peter Lang.

Afzal, Ahmed. 2014. "'Being Gay Has Been a Curse for Me': Gay Muslim Americans, Narrative, and Negotiations of Belonging in the Muslim *Ummah*." *Journal of Language and Sexuality* 3, no. 1: 60–86. doi: 10.1075/jls.3.1.04afz.

Afzal, Ahmed. 2015. *Lone Star Muslims: Transnational Lives and the South Asian Experience in Texas*. New York: NYU Press.

Afzal, Ahmed. 2016. "Islam, Marriage, and *Yaari*: Making Meaning of Male Same-Sex Sexual Relationships in Pakistan." In *Cultural Politics of Gender and Sexuality in Contemporary Asia*, edited by Tiantian Zheng, 187–204. Honolulu: University of Hawai'i Press.

Afzal, Ahmed. 2020. "'I Want a Yaar': Gay South Asian Muslim Americans and Transnational Same-Sex Sexual Cultures." In *Gender, Sexuality, Decolonization: South Asia in the World Perspective*, edited by Ahonaa Roy, 137–59. Abingdon: Routledge.

Ahlm, Jody. 2017. "Respectable Promiscuity: Digital Cruising in an Era of Queer Liberalism." *Sexualities* 20, no. 3: 364–79.

Albury, Kath, and Paul Byron. 2016. "Safe on My Phone? Same-Sex Attracted Young People's Negotiations of Intimacy, Visibility, and Risk on Digital Hook-Up Apps." *Social Media + Society*. October 17.

Ang, Ming Wei, Justin Ching Keng Tan, and Chen Lou. 2021. "Navigating Sexual Racism in the Sexual Field: Compensation for and Disavowal of Marginality by Racial Minority Grindr Users in Singapore." *Journal of Computer-Mediated Communication*, 26, no. 3: 129–47.

Blackwell, Courtney, Jeremy Birnholtz, and Charles Abbott. 2015. "Seeing and Being Seen: Co-Situation and Impression Formation Using Grindr, a Location-Aware Gay Dating App." *New Media and Society* 17, no. 7: 1117–36.

Bonner-Thompson, Carl. 2017. "'The Meat Market': Production and Regulation of Masculinities on the Grindr Grid in Newcastle-upon-Tyne, UK." *Gender, Place and Culture* 24, no. 11. http://dx.doi.org/10.1080/0966369X.2017.1356270.

Brubaker, Jed R., Mike Ananny, and Kate Crawford. 2016. "Departing Glances: A Sociotechnical Account of 'Leaving' Grindr.'" *New Media and Society* 18, no. 3: 373–90.

Carrillo, Hector. 2017. *Pathways of Desire: The Sexual Migration of Mexican Gay Men*. Chicago: University of Chicago Press.

Chan, Lik Sam. 2017. "The Role of Gay Identity Confusion and Outness in Sex-Seeking on Mobile Dating Apps among Men Who Have Sex with Men: A Conditional Process Analysis." *Journal of Homosexuality* 64, no. 5: 622–37.

Cruess, Dean G., Kaylee E. Burnham, David J. Finitsis, Cherry Chuncey, Tamar Grebler, Brett M. Goshe, Lauren Strainge, Moira O. Kalichman, and Seth C. Kalichman. 2017. "Online Partner Seeking and Sexual Risk among HIV+ Gay and Bisexual Men: A Dialectical Perspective." *Archives of Sexual Behavior* 46: 1079–87.

Gudelunas, David. 2012. "There's an App for That: The Uses and Gratifications of Online Social Networks for Gay Men." *Sexuality and Culture* 16: 347–65.

Heijman, Titia, Ineke Stolte, Ronald Geskus, Amy Matser, Udi Davidovich, Maria Xiridou, and Maarten Schim van der Loeff. 2016. "Does Online Dating Lead to Higher Sexual Risk Behavior? A Cross-Sectional Study among MSM in Amsterdam, the Netherlands." *Bio Medical Central Infectious Diseases* 6, no. 28: 1–13.

Hermosa-Bosano, Carlos, Paula Hidalgo-Andrade, and Clara Paz. 2021. "Geosocial Networking Apps Use among Sexual Minority Men in Ecuador: An Exploratory Study." *Archives of Sexual Behavior* 50, no. 7: 2995–3009.

Holloway, Ian W., Craig A. Pulsipher, Jeremy Gibbs, Anamika Barman-Adhikari, and Eric Rice. 2015. "Network Influences on the Sexual Risk Behaviors of Gay, Bisexual, and Other Men Who Have Sex with Men Using Geosocial Networking Applications." *AIDS Behavior* 19: S112–S122.

Jandovitz, Raphael J., Chi-Hong Tseng, Matthew Weissman, Michael Yamer, Brett Mendenhall, Kathryn Rogers, Rosemary Venigas, Pamina M. Gorbach, Cathy J. Reback, and Steven Shoptaw. 2012. "Epidemiology, Sexual Risk Behavior, and HIV Prevention Practices of Men Who Have Sex with Men Using Grindr in Los Angeles, California." *Journal of Urban Health* 90, no. 4: 729–39.

Johnson, Kristine, M. Olguta Vilceanu, and Manuel C. Pontes. 2017. "Uses of Online Dating Websites and Dating Apps: Findings and Implications for LGB Populations." *Journal of Marketing Development and Competitiveness* 11, no. 3: 60–66.

Lasén, Amparo. 2004. "Affective Technologies—Emotions and Mobile Phones." *Receiver* 11. https://www.academia.edu/472410/Affective_Technologies_Emotions_and_Mobile_Phones.

Licoppe, Christian, Carole Anne Riviere, and Julien Morel. 2016. "Grindr Casual Hook-Ups as Interactional Achievements." *New Media and Society* 18, no. 11: 2540–58.

Miller, Brandon. 2015. "'They're the Modern-Day Gay Bar': Exploring the Uses and Gratifications of Social Networks for Men Who Have Sex with Men." *Computers in Human Behavior* 51: 476–82.

Moller, Kristian, and Michael Nebeling Petersen. 2018. "Bleeding Boundaries: Domesticating Gay Hook-Up Apps." In *Mediated Intimacies: Connectivities, Relationalities, and Proximities*, edited by Rikke Andreassen, Michael Nabeling Peterson, Katherine Harrison, and Tobias Raun, 208–23. London: Routledge.

Ong, Jonathan Corpus. 2017. "Queer Cosmopolitanism in the Disaster Zone: 'My Grindr became the United Nations.'" *International Communication Gazette* 79, nos. 6–7: 656–73.

Penny, Tom. 2014. "Bodies under Glass: Gay Dating Apps and the Affect-Image." *Media International Australia* 153: 107–17.

Race, Kane. 2015. "Speculative Pragmatism and Intimate Arrangements: Online Hook-Up Devices in Gay Life." *Culture, Health, and Sexuality* 1: 496–511.

Rendina, H. Jonathan, Ruben H. Jimenez, Christian Grov, Ana Ventuneac, and Jeffrey T. Parsons. 2014. "Patterns of Lifetime and Recent HIV Testing among Men Who Have Sex with Men in New York City Who Use Grindr." *AIDS Behavior* 18: 41–49.

Saraiva, Luiz Alex Silva, Leonardo Tadeu dos Santos, and Jefferson Rodrigues Pereira. 2020. "Heteronormativity, Masculinity and Prejudice in Mobile Apps: The Case of Grindr in a Brazilian City." *Brazilian Business Review* (Portuguese ed.) 17, no. 1: 114–31.

Shield, Andrew. 2019. *Immigrants on Grindr: Race, Sexuality and Belonging Online*. New York: Palgrave Macmillan.

Tziallas, E. 2015. "Gamified Eroticism: Gay Male 'Social Networking' Applications and Self-Pornography." *Sexuality and Culture* 19: 759–75. https://doi.org/10.1007/s12119-015-9288-z. May 9.

van de Wiele, Chad, and Stephanie Tom Tong. 2014. "Breaking Boundaries: The Uses and Gratifications of Grindr." *UBIComp'14*, September 13–17.

Weiss, Kevin M., Kai J. Jonas, and Thomas E. Guadamuz. 2017. "Playing and Never Testing: Human Immunodeficiency Virus and Sexually Transmitted Infection among App-Using MSM in Southeast Asia." *Sexually Transmitted Diseases* 44, no. 7: 406–11.

Whitefield, Darren L., Shanna K. Kattari, N. Eugene Wallas, and Alia Al-Tayyib. 2017. "American Grindr, Scruff, and on the Hunt: Predictors of Condomless Anal Sex, Internet Use, and Mobile Application Use among Men Who Have Sex with Men." *Journal of Men's Health* 11, no. 3: 775–84.

Winetrobe, Hailey, Eric Rice, Jose Bauermeister, Robin Petering, and Ian W. Holloway. 2014. "Associations of Unprotected Anal Intercourse with Grindr-Met Partners among Grindr-Using Young Men Who Have Sex with Men in Los Angeles." *AIDS Care* 26, no. 10: 1303–8.

Wortham, Jenna. 2013. "How Grindr Is Changing the Way We Connect." *New York Times*. March 10. http//bits.blogs.nytimes.com/2013/03/10/how-grindr-is-changing-the-way-we-all-connect.

Wu, Shangwei, and Daniel Trottier. 2021. "Constructing Sexual Fields: Chinese Gay Men's Dating Practices among Pluralized Dating Apps." *Social Media + Society* 7, no. 2: 1–14.

Zou, Huachun, and Song Fan. 2017. "Characteristics of Men Who Have Sex with Men Who Use Smartphone Geosocial Networking Applications and Implications for HIV Intervention: A Systematic Review and Meta-Analysis." *Archives of Sexual Behavior* 6: 855–94.

Nida Mehboob  12

How I Like It

FIGS. 12.1, 12.2, 12.3, 12.4, 12.5. 00:44–00:58.

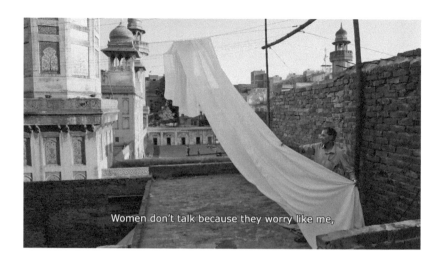

FIGS. 12.6, 12.7, 12.8, 12.9. 01:20–01:35.

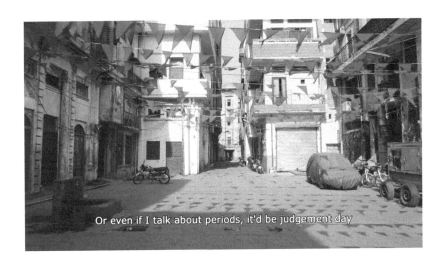

FIGS. 12.10, 12.11, 12.12. 01:47–2:00.

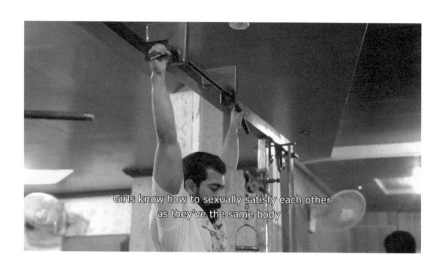

You do it calmly and slowly;
you can go for up to six hours if you want.

FIGS. 12.13, 12.14, 12.15, 12.16. 04:35–5:00.

*In my first actual swinging,*

FIGS. 12.17, 12.18, 12.19, 12.20. 06:35–7:20.

FIGS. 12.21, 12.22, 12.23. 10:44–11:03.

Gayatri Reddy

13

# Queer *Desi* Formations

## Marking the Boundaries of Cultural Belonging in Chicago

This essay is a reflection on fieldwork in Chicago among gay/queer-identified *desi* men twenty years ago—in the early 2000s—focusing on their articulated desires for a "community." As such, it serves as a historical text, contextualizing more contemporary queer *desi* aspirations, desires, and formations in Chicago. The term *desi* refers to one who is from the land/country (*des*), a native. In the United States, *desi* is used as a coded and affect-laden term of reference—self and other—for people from South Asia, including Pakistan. In that sense, the term accommodates the more capacious understanding of nation/place in the asterisk that is sometimes used in the text of this volume—Pak*stan—a transnational understanding that not only troubles the boundedness of the nation/area studies, but also signals an affective configuration of subjectivity and desire. In this essay, I argue that *desi* gay men's desire for community at the turn of the century in Chicago signaled a social formation whose contours were crystallized through engagements with normativity. By heeding Roderick Ferguson's call to place normativity front and center, to "address [it] as an object of inquiry and critique" (2003, 148), it explores past productions and regulations of ethnic, racial, gender, sexual, and class normativity—the contours of queer and racial becoming—among *desis*. And through engagements with *other* queer orientations in Chicago, captured in this essay by one iconic Pakistani figure, it gestures toward alternative queer futures and the possibilities for crafting a different kind of "brown commons" (Muñoz 2020).

"What *is* it about the *desi* queer community in this city?" Ganesh, a self-identified queer, cosmopolitan, Hindu, upper-caste/class man, who had recently moved to Chicago, asked me irritatedly.[1] "It's bizarre! This is the only major city that I have been in, that doesn't seem to really *have* a community." When pressed, he said, "All these other cities—New York, and San Francisco, DC and even Delhi...all of them have a functioning *desi* queer group, they have an actual organization, they have a space where they have regular meetings, the members of the group hang out together, they are there for each other, you know...a real community. Here though, there is nothing! I know there have got to be lots of queer *desis* in Chicago. Where are they?" For Ganesh and several other queer *desi* men I spoke to in Chicago at the time, there appeared to be some understanding of what a community was supposed to be and do for you: it was a space, a place, a social formation whose members one could rely on for company, and for a sense of "feeling comfortable, at home," a "family" as many stated. And just as clearly this ideal community didn't seem to exist in Chicago. Using Ganesh's quest for community as a springboard for further reflection, this essay tentatively speculates on what this romance of (and with) community reveals about intersections of sexuality, ethnicity, and class for these queer *desi* men and provides a platform to explore the radical potential of queer politics.

I originally began this project by asking how these nonheteronormative subjects—*desi* gay/queer men—negotiate the articulation of self and belonging, when family and home, ethnicity, and culture are implicitly constructed to privilege heterosexuality, and at the same time brown bodies reveal themselves as always already racialized/brown—"forever foreign"—in the public arenas/narratives of (white) gay cosmopolitanism in the United States. When visibility and accompanying constructions of sexual and racial difference, in all their manifold, protean, quotidian forms in the United States, acquire a somewhat heightened valence, how do *desi* queers articulate and negotiate their subject position?

In exploring these issues in Chicago, a narrative of frustration repeatedly emerged, as echoed in Ganesh's lament: frustration at the perceived lack of community, the lack of a family or support system where one could "talk about these things...talk about our troubles and help each other." When probed, invariably, the next comment—and attribution for why community did not exist in Chicago—would center on Sangat, the only self-identified South Asian gay organization or space in Chicago at the time, and on one visible, almost iconic figure in this organization: the Pakistani diasporic figure of Iftikhar Nasim, or Ifti, who appeared to embody, literally and figuratively, some of the boundaries marking cultural belonging within the *desi* queer space of Chicago.[2]

Sangat was originally founded in 1986 by "Ma Viru" as Ifti affectionately referred to Virendra Joshi. As Vikas tells the story, in the 1970s, he was so tired of seeing only white people in Chicago bars (and the occasional black man) that he placed an advertisement in the local rag, calling for *desi* gay men who were interested in meeting. Two individuals responded to his advertisement, and over the course of that year, they started a hotline and would meet occasionally. It was only the following year, when Ifti "officially" joined the group, that the organization began to "get a public profile" as Ifti told me. The organizations' name was changed—from Trikone-Chicago (as a derivative of Trikone-San Francisco) to Sangat—a name that Ifti suggested and one that, somewhat ironically, means coming together as a group or community. It was at this point that Sangat socials were regularized, often being held at Ifti's house, and it was Ifti who regularly organized and marched under the organization's name in the annual Gay Pride Parade. As some *desi* gay men I spoke with stated, "Arre, Sangat *is* Ifti," a comment that was corroborated by a glance at the erstwhile Sangat website: other than a long-defunct posting about meetings at Big Chicks, a bar in Uptown, the only information on the site were links to Ifti's poetry/publications.

Ifti was a Pakistani-born openly gay man who described himself as "a poet . . . a working class, struggling artist and activist." He migrated to the United States in 1969, and moved to Chicago in 1974, having abandoned graduate school in Detroit. He worked for several years as a car salesman but quit his job to devote himself to his writing, both his journalism (as a reporter for a local Urdu newspaper) and, more important, his poetry.[3] He was known—in both Pakistan and the United States—for his poetry, having published the acclaimed book *Narmaan* in 1994. In the early 2000s, Ifti was a well-known and recognizable figure within the Pakistani and queer community in Chicago, having been inducted into the Chicago Gay and Lesbian Hall of Fame in 1996. His visibility, even notoriety, stemmed at least in part from his flamboyance and his penchant for fur jackets, flashy jewelry, and colorful—visible—drag clothing, as can be seen on the cover of his books of poems: it has a picture of him in a bright orange *salwar-kameez*, with a blonde wig and lots of jewelry, looking directly, and coyly, at the camera.

I met Ifti shortly after I moved to Chicago. I was at Big Chicks with some friends when I saw this South Asian man sashay into the bar in his fur coat; it was winter. He dramatically threw off his coat and revealed a pink, sequined *kameez* over his designer jeans. He was clearly comfortable, physically and socially, in this space and circulated among the patrons of the bar, greeting people familiarly as he walked by. It wasn't until months later that I met Ifti again for a Sangat social at his house, and over the years had several conversations with him about his life, his art, his experiences with Sangat, his political activism, and his growing disenchantment with U.S. and Pakistani politics and the state of activism. In his mid-fifties at the time, Ifti appeared thoroughly frustrated with the younger generation of *desi* men in Chicago, whom he felt "only want to party and don't want to do any of the work that got us this far . . . got us our rights and all. . . . They want to have their cake—or I should say *laddoo*—and eat it too," he added half-joking but with a note of bitterness or resignation in his voice. This positioning is, of course, in contrast to the ways many other middle-class gay men saw and articulated their own predicament.

As Mohan, one of my interviewees stated, "I attended some of the Sangat meetings when I first moved here way back when, but they were just not for me. I didn't feel comfortable there. I just don't like all this drag-wag stuff, and frankly, I always felt as though I was being checked out . . . you know, for sex. I didn't like that." This was reiterated by Akhil, who said, "Those Sangat meetings?! I didn't want to go back there. Ifti is always so over the top—with his dressing up, his jewelry, the way he and his friends talk and the way he looks at you . . . like you are just a piece of meat, you know. He is very rude and just crude in his manner. I didn't like it, so I left after attending just one social." Rajiv, a young, professional, Indian doctor—a "nice Indian stereotype" as he once referred to himself—told me that he had heard "wild stories" about Ifti, stories that "really did not make me want to go for any of those meetings or meet the man." Ruminating on his life, he said, "When I was a kid, I always dreamed about growing up, meeting this nice woman, getting married, having those 2.5 kids, having a professional job. . . . Now, of course, I dream of meeting this nice *man*, getting married, I already have the house and the job, and I still want those 2.5 kids. . . ." On another occasion, he said: "I feel like I am a good role model for the *desi* gay community. . . . I'm a good representation of the gay community to other people, you know. I'm a doctor, very professional, very respectable. . . . I'm conservative in my dress and in my mannerisms and everything, my lifestyle. . . . I'm a good role model for the *desi* community to see... we aren't just a bunch of fags or whatever, you know...." Professional, middle-class, "family-oriented," somewhat "socially conservative" and "not flamboyant," Rajiv is in many ways the model of what Lisa Duggan has recently termed "new homonormativity,"[4] a model that is in some ways the antithesis of Ifti.

It seemed to be a similar distaste for Ifti's "over the top[ness]," all that "drag-wag stuff" that alienated these men from Sangat meetings. Mohan described the one meeting he attended: "I was going for the first time, so I didn't really know anyone. I mostly stood in a corner and watched everything. It was really just not my scene!... There were about ten people, all men of course, and they were all helping this one individual, Ifti, put on make-up, and dressing him up and then playing Bollywood songs and dancing around him... like Krishna, or I should say, Radha and her *gopis*.... And this went on for hours! That's just not what I'm interested in doing." For many of these (younger) men like Mohan and Akhil, sexual difference and "being gay" was not necessarily mediated by cross-gender-identified performances, an understanding that perhaps encodes class-specific constructions of gender and sexuality in the subcontinent. As Mohan stated: "You can be more masculine, you can be more feminine, whatever. But you don't *have* to be feminine." For Ifti, it seemed that his understanding and enactment of gayness was indelibly linked to a specific kind of gender performativity, a cross-gender identification, performance, and understanding of desire and pleasure. Moreover, it was a pleasure linked to mythology and, more often, the performance of femininity in Hindi melodramas, as well as tied to an urban, burlesque dance tradition associated in part with the stigmatized and transgressive figures of *hijra* and *khwajasira* in India/Pakistan.[5]

Others recounted similar experiences and expressed outrage at this overt emphasis on sexual practice, the explicitly sexual language, the overly rigid and dichotomous understanding of sexual desire and its corporeal enactments, and an overly familiar body language that was "just crude" and at variance with their own desires/practices. Further, it appeared to be naked sexual desire for other *desi* men that alienated them. Recall Akhil's quote: "It is the way [Ifti] looks at you... like you are just a piece of meat." To be sure, it could very well be the candid nature of such desire, the lack of any masquerade or need to dissemble it that was discomfiting. However, as many of these men indicated to me based on their own relationship histories, and their observations of patterns of *desi* desire, overwhelmingly, their own object of sexual desire was white men, a pattern that is explicitly referenced in the few studies exploring this issue (cf. Groetzinger 2004). This could be interpreted in terms of the relative number and availability of sexual partners, white and *desi*, but coupled with the preponderance of *desi*-white partnerships, this pattern could perhaps symbolize a broader construction of desire and racialized identity, a construction that Ifti appeared to trouble.

Ifti was explicitly sexual in his encounters and interactions with *desi* men—in his language usage, in his corporeal performances, in his articulated desires; he is also, simultaneously, in a committed and long-term relationship with Prem, an Indian cab driver. They have lived together for years, and troubled as the relationship may be, as Ifti matter-of-factly stated, "We will probably be together until the end." Although increasingly worried about old age and the infirmities of his body, Ifti had no desire to get married to Prem in order to cement their relationship, noting, "We don't need the permission of the government to be what we are to each other!"

How do we understand these tensions and the issues, emotions, and politics at play at that time? What were the particular nodes of in/visibility that structured ways of seeing and acting in the world, the forms of racial, ethnic, sexual, and class nomination that were invoked in the service of articulating subjectivity? In the diasporic context, how did forms of race, class, gender, and sexual privilege produce and reproduce South Asian understandings of self and other in the lives of these *desi* queer men in Chicago? Here, I want to highlight two issues implicated in the production (and regulation) of subjectivity: one, the historical formations that highlighted *the visibility of "culture" and the invisibility of race* in *desi* frameworks of social understanding. And two, the ways in which this class-cultural understanding articulated with and refracted understandings of sexuality with deep, resonating effects for uncovering (and occluding) the *intersections* of these domains and the possibilities for a transformational coalition politics that critiques the structures/modes of normative power.

REGULATIONS OF NORMATIVITY

*Migration and Its Class-Cultural Productions*
I locate these *desi* configurations within at least two (related) contexts: first, within the context of U.S. state regulations and its history of racial and class surveillance and regulation; and second, within and through diasporic South Asians' own understandings of themselves as a culturally

different category in America, a framing that necessarily invokes the logic of "model minority" class identification with its attendant celebrations of neoliberal, multicultural "diversity" and its inherent divisions between "culture" and political-economy in America.[6]

As scholars have noted, U.S. immigration has literally crafted the nation and its inhabitants by including (and excluding) particular immigrant racial, ethnic, gender, and class segments. These exclusions at the border also structure and reproduce exclusions *within* the nation and immigrant (social) body. In other words, understanding U.S. border regulation allows us to better understand what Robert Chang (1999) has referred to as the "figurative border"—the configurations and subsequent regulations of race, sexuality, and class that marginalized "minority" groups within the U.S. employ to police their own communities (Luibheid 2002, xix; cf. Lowe 1996; Lubheid and Chávez 2020; Reddy 2011). Given this argument, I offer an abbreviated history of South Asian immigration to the United States.

From the turn of the nineteenth century until the 1920s, South Asian migrants were largely men—rural farmers from the Punjab and itinerant lascars and peddlers from Bangladesh and other places (Bald 2013; Bald et al. 2013; Jensen 1988; Leonard 1994; Mazumdar 1989; Melendy 1977; Prashad 2012). Until 1900, these individuals—categorized in the census and the law as "East Indians" or "Hindoos"—numbered merely 2,050. But after 1904, there was a new influx of immigrants, and by the end of that decade there were as many as ten thousand East Indians or "Asian Indians" as they were now termed in the United States. The majority of these early immigrants were engaged in agricultural labor or were itinerant peddlers of "exotic" goods; they were largely uneducated, with the median schooling in 1940 being 3.4 years, with only 3 percent of the population being "professionals" at this time (Hing 1993; Visweswaran 1997). Following, as they did, the waves of Chinese and Japanese immigrants at the turn of the century and the subsequent outbreak of World War I, Indians not only were subjected to "Yellow Peril" racism directed at these other groups of immigrants, but in fact began to be especially targeted by groups such as the Asian Exclusion League, which called for the termination of Indian immigration. Hostility against the Asian Indians quickly translated into legislative and legal exclusion, with the declaration of the Alien Land Act of 1913, which excluded Indians from land ownership; the Asiatic (or Racial) Barred Zone Act of 1917, which temporarily stopped all immigration from Asia (except from Japan); and finally the Supreme Court ruling in the Bhagat Singh Thind case of 1923, which conclusively "resolved" the contradictory decisions on the racial identity of Asian Indians by ruling that whatever their scientific categorization, they were nonwhite in "common understanding," and on this basis, were therefore ineligible for citizenship. Prior to this ruling, from the turn of the century to 1923, sixty-nine South Asian individuals were naturalized as citizens on the grounds that they were members of the "Aryan race," and as such of white or Caucasian origin.[7] As scholars have pointed out, in this early phase of South Asian immigration therefore, until the early 1920s, the model of citizenship was a racial one: laying claim to whiteness was a necessary step to claiming citizenship, even though theoretically, after 1870 when blacks gained the right to citizenship, blackness could have been the grounds for such claims.[8]

Following the passage of these exclusionary acts and legal rulings in the 1920s, South Asian immigration to the United States for the next four decades slowed to a trickle. It wasn't until 1965, when the new immigration act (known as the Hart-Celler Act or INS Act of 1965) reversed the discriminatory patterns and initiated preferential admission of Asian immigrants "with needed skills" that a second phase of South Asian immigration was initiated. These new immigrants were highly educated, urban, economically successful, middle-class professionals from different regions of the subcontinent (Jensen 1988; Prashad 2012). In contrast to the primarily single, lower-class, and male-biased immigration of the previous phase, which resulted in a significant number of Punjabi-Mexican marriages following the Thind Supreme Court ruling (Leonard 1994), the new immigrants were able to make use of the new allowances (and categories) of immigration, namely, those of "professional and technical worker" and the "family reunification program," and by 1985 these two categories accounted for 98 percent of immigration from the subcontinent (Koshy and Radhakrishnan 2008). Consequently, in the space of just a few decades, according to the 2010 U.S. Census, South Asians are currently the fastest growing Asian American immigrant group, with a "uniquely balanced gender ratio" and a radically transformed class character, surpassing the Japanese to emerge as the most affluent minority population in the United States.

Highly educated, urban, and middle-class, this wave of immigrants—namely, the post-1965 generation that constitutes the bulk of the South Asian community in present-day America—quickly emerged as a model minority whose public profile, as Ajantha Subramanium notes, "fits neatly into the logic of American multiculturalism" (2000, 107). South Asians perceive themselves and are perceived as hard-working, not lazy; they are family-oriented, a model predicated on marriage and the (heterosexual) family as the immigrant unit of choice; they have distinct, easily commodifiable cultural traditions and practices; and their political conservatism supports their solidly middle-class material interests (and vice versa). Most important, they define themselves in these terms by emphasizing their class and ethnic location, *claiming an identity unmarked by race*.[9] The rhetoric of a color-blind meritocracy—a rhetoric that allows for South Asian employability to be read as the product and proof of hard work rather than the demand for skilled labor that resulted in immigration reform—simultaneously affirms the value of South Asian achievements while coding these successes as fundamentally American. Further, such rhetoric, as Koshy and others note, necessarily positions South Asians—and their achievements—against those of other minorities. In this context, it is interesting to note the point that Vijay Prashad, Claire Kim, and others make: that the model minority myth was resurrected at precisely the same time as the underclass myth was gaining ascendance in America. Both these myths were predicated on a culturalist argument: that it was the *culture* of these social formations, Asian American and African American, respectively—emphasizing the virtues of hard work, frugality, and family values and not history or class—that accounted for *both* the financial success of Asian Americans *and* the poverty of African Americans in contemporary America.

Through this logic, we see, in Claire Kim's words, the "American racial order: Blacks are confirmed as the pathological underclass; [Asian-Americans] as the hardworking model minority; Whites as neutral enforcers of colorblind justice" (2000, 11). As one, or perhaps *the* exemplar of such Asian American model minority success, South Asians are solicited to think of themselves as "value-added Americans.... As long as there are other minorities to wear the sign of race, we have the alibi of ethnicity," Koshy notes (1998, 307). And ethnicity, in the matrix of power relations in contemporary multicultural America, is indexed not so much by race (either whiteness as in the earlier phase of immigration or blackness as in the U.K. diasporic context), but by "cultural difference." Subsequently, "the racialization of South Asians (like that of other Asian Americans) was fundamentally shaped ... by their positioning as an *intermediary* in the racial hierarchy" (Koshy 1998, 311; emphasis added), a positioning that contributed to the invisibility of blackness (and the corresponding reformulation of race) in South Asian articulations of identity and difference in America.[10]

With this shift—from a racial to a cultural model of citizenship—South Asian subjectivity in America was recast in cultural terms, terms that necessarily articulate and secure both class and, implicitly, heterosexual privilege, while eliding any and all referents of race. It is culture now that is the definitive characteristic of immigrant identity and which secures articulations of belonging in multicultural America. Indeed, as "whiteness became a structure of identification and an institution of assimilation" in the years following large-scale Western European immigration, Roderick Ferguson reminds us, the invention of ethnicity in fact *"depended* on the designation of culture as a socially constructed [rather than a biologically determined] domain of difference" (2003, 56). A domain, moreover, whose regulation became the litmus test for normative compliance, and through which the supposedly universal properties and ideals of citizenship were accessed.

And as several scholars have pointed out in this context, the idea of culture that operates within this multicultural terrain is often, if not always, overly essentialist, static, unitary, and bounded (Lowe 1996; George 1997; Prashad 2000; Duggan 2003; Rudrappa 2004). Further, it often operates by members of the socially oppressed community themselves regulating the forms of "their" own culture, often actively "disallowing fluidity or dissent" (Mathew and Prashad 2000, 524).[11] As Radhakrishnan points out, "In the diasporean [*sic*] context of the United States, ethnicity is often forced to take on the discourse of authenticity just to protect and maintain its space and history ... [an authenticity whereby the issue is not merely] ... 'being Indian' in some natural, self-evident way ... but cultivating 'Indian-ness' self-consciously" (1996, 224). In other words, the goal is being *authentically* South Asian, a pursuit that often results in defining a singular ethnic culture.[12]

Not only is there tremendous pressure to conform to such a singular culture—a culture that is predicated on a superior work ethic and on strong (heterosexual) family or kinship bonds, the very criteria by which these immigrants are "allowed" to enter the United States—but any threat to these values, such as that constituted by the so-called choice of homosexuality in America, is then vilified by the heteronormative *desi* majority as the embodiment of immoral Western modernity. As the anthropologist Karen Leonard states, "Most South Asian parents view homosexuality as a chosen lifestyle or identity, an undesirable indulgence of individual freedom in the United States" (1992, 148). Commenting on this tension in his life, Rakesh, one of the young, middle-class men I interviewed, said, "I was always made to feel as if I was betraying my Indian culture; as if being gay meant I was automatically choosing some kind of immoral life." "Indian culture," in this context, with its attendant regulations of sexuality and class, constitutes an important node of identification to help forestall the cultural degeneracy and moral depravity of (potential) "Westernization" (Maira 2002; 2016). In multicultural America, Sharmila Rudrappa notes, "Being ethnic [is what] makes one a good American" (2004, 169), but I would add it requires an assemblage that is "appropriately" ethnic, signifying a normative regulation of sexual, economic, and gendered domains: in effect, averring that South Asians are, in Rudrappa's words, "oriented and committed to marriage, value immediate and extended family, have good child socialization practices... [are bound to] traditional gender norms... have a strong work ethic... [and value] thrift" (ibid.), all cultural values that, incidentally, are seamlessly sutured to a capitalist and neoliberal ideology (cf. Duggan 2003; Ferguson 2003; 2019).

Any threat to culture defined in these narrow, bounded terms is thereby a threat not just to South Asian identity, but also to model citizenship in America. For instance, in the now well-known story of the banning of SALGA—the South Asian Lesbian and Gay Association—from marching in the annual Indian Independence Day Parades in New York City, the Federation of Indians in America (FIA) marshaled culture to its defense: such organizations, it stated, are "out of place" and "antinational" in the context of "traditional Indian culture" and thereby should not be able to march in this important Indian parade because they do not reflect the reality or tradition of Indian communities.[13] Cultural identity, in this context, is articulated through normative regulations of class and sexuality (and nation), regulations that simultaneously secure middle-class and heterosexual privilege in configurations of authentic immigrant identity and claims to citizenship. As such, "in the updated version of the American Dream, underwritten by corporate and popular multiculturalism, ethnically diverse subjects aspire to success in a system that purports to reward the capitalist virtues of hard work, striving, and success in all alike.... Within the new multiculturalism, 'white' serves only as a modifier of ethnicity, and simultaneously, nonwhite capital-compatible ethnicities are promised incorporation into the American Dream" (Koshy 1998, 194). In striving toward this "value-added" American Dream, South Asians are determined to "occupy a place that is simultaneously privileged *and* unmarked: a place of invisibility" (George 1997, 46), an invisibility that is secured on the basis of specific forms of sexual, ethnic, racial, and class nomination/ex-nomination.

To return to Ifti and queer *desi* desire in Chicago, one could argue that these representations exemplified this homonormative formation and its transgressive foil in the early 2000s; they revealed two different ways of seeing *desi* ethnic, erotic, and gender configurations, two perspectives that represented and marked different class-cultural understandings of sexuality and ethnicity.[14] Fracturing the monolithic *desi* immigrant narrative, the first perspective (exemplified in this story by Ifti) incorporates an explicit recognition of racialization in the image of (and in solidarity with) blackness, visibility, and working-class culture. In his presentation of body and self, Ifti offers himself to be read as a red thread—as gender-transgressive, as non-middle-class, and above all, as a flamboyantly *visible* ethnically different man. His visibility calls attention to *desi* queerness, but more important, his performance also potentially *defines*, to some extent, the public contours of *desi* queerness, a queerness that can be interpreted as "rude and just crude" in Akhil's words. Ifti's apparent crudeness in this context is exemplified by his often coarse, direct, expletive-filled, and overtly sexual style of speech, his sartorial choices, his penchant for class-specific burlesque performances, and his desire for brown as opposed to white bodies—his general "over-the-top-ness" as Akhil and Mohan noted. Despite his long-term residence in the United States, his idiomatic English, his strong Pakistani accent, his nonnormative professional occupation as a car salesman, his evident comfort with Bollywood culture—all mark his identity as insufficiently middle-class and inappropriately ethnic, calling his cultural citizenship as American into question.

It is perhaps not surprising, then, that narratives of *desi* queer-identified men at that time repeatedly invoked Ifti to disavow those attributes of cultural identity and transgressive gayness. These homonormative sets of articulations and identifications, insofar as they even acknowledge a racialized positioning, are premised on whiteness, with its attendant (un) markings of privilege and invisibility. Recall here Lisa Duggan's definition of "new homonormativity" as "a politics that does not contest dominant heteronormative assumptions and institutions, but upholds and sustains them, while promising the possibility of a demobilized gay constituency and a privatized, depoliticized gay culture anchored in domesticity and consumption" (2003, 50). In this sense, as Roderick Ferguson argues, this is "part of a genealogy in which minoritized subjects demand and aspire to recognition by the liberal capitalist state.... [T]he assertion of gay identity ceases to suggest an alienation from, but rather an intersection with heterosexual normativity.... As a category, [ethnicity] preserves and expresses difference by regulating it so that one can still claim the supposed universal properties of citizenship" (2003, 59).

One of my interviewees summed up the situation in these words: "I was just beginning to come to terms with who I was, and [when I saw Ifti], I thought 'I'm not like *that*!' So, it made me question everything—my gayness, my Indian-ness, everything... so I stopped going to those meetings." "That"—in terms of Ifti's public visibility, his disdain for state-sanctioned forms of legitimacy, his racialized construction of desire, and his transgressions of *desi* conformity—could, no doubt, be read as an overdetermined foil to formulations (and regulations) of *desi* queerness and collective identity in Chicago at that time. But then again, as Ganesh, the queer activist in the opening vignette of this section noted, answering his own question about the lack of community, "I guess Ifti *is* the community here, huh?!," highlighting not only Ifti's iconic status as both individual *and* community, but also the nodes and regulations of South Asian visibility and difference, and perhaps more important, the possibilities for their transgression. To give Ifti a voice here, I quote one of his poems, titled "Why Children Did Not Knock at My Door on Halloween This Year," written in 2001:

> Thirty-one years as a law-abiding citizen I am still a foreigner. Foreigner with a crude face and features of a terrorist. My color—two shades darker than an average white man is not accepted anymore.
>
> My café ole color, once I was so proud of, is a guilt trip for me now. My ethnicity has become a crime.

In equating ethnicity with crime, a brown body, as symbol of guilt, with the monstrous visage of a terrorist in this 9/11 context, Ifti is highlighting the racializing practices of the state, implicitly enjoining us to see differently and, by that token, not become docile, well-assimilated—and easily governable—subjects. Rather, he is calling for a recognition of the racialization and implicit sexualization in the production of what Jasbir Puar and Amit Rai have termed the contemporary "Monster-Terrorist-Fag" (2002, 117)—a post-9/11 social formation that draws on nineteenth-century images of sexual and racial perversion that are inscribed onto (potential) terrorist bodies today. As a "hypervisible icon" produced by racialized and sexualized discourses/practices, Ifti is simultaneously sexual deviant (the monster-fag) *and* the racialized terrorist or the "ghost that haunts the machine of war," in Puar and Rai's words (2002, 117). He is one alternative to the multicultural, assimilated citizen-subjects who contribute to their normalization by their refusal in many ways to see their location as classed and raced subjects subject to a regulatory and ultimately minoritizing regime.

Particularly after 9/11, a watershed moment that, in Ifti's vision, "affected all of us, from Pakistan, from Bangladesh, from India... all of us, really," he was frustrated and angry, both at the "fucking government that sees us all only as terrorists" and at the *desi* community that he believes was insufficiently politicized or active in its efforts to combat the forms of profiling, the mandatory registrations, the deportments, the violence directed at South Asians in general and Muslims in particular. Not only was he a vocal critic of the state's response to this crisis, but soon after the start of the Iraq War, it was Ifti, along with a few Indian Muslim organizations and the Chicago Anti-Bashing Network, who called for and organized a well-attended antiwar rally on Devon Street, the South Asian neighborhood in Chicago, one of the first-ever antiwar rallies in that neighborhood. He subsequently joined forces with several antiwar groups in the city, and through petitions and his journalistic work for an Urdu newspaper repeatedly called for political mobilization against state-sponsored violence and discrimination directed at Muslim, and especially Pakistani, communities. Interestingly, Ifti noted that it was after 9/11 that he felt more comfortable as a gay man within the Pakistani community, because, as he stated, "My activism and my speaking out and all the things I did in the past for the gay community... now the Pakistani community recognizes that I have all this knowledge and contacts, and know about organizing and all... so they respect me more and they come to me to ask how to do all these things."[15]

Clearly, not only does such identification—in terms of the religious imaginary and politicohistorical context in the Indian subcontinent as well as in the United States— indelibly and differentially shape the process of racialization (and politicization), resulting in different retrenchments of religious nationalism, cultural difference, and imperatives to visibilize and invisibilize oneself differently, but perhaps by that same token, it also allows for patterns of solidarity (vis-à-vis the state) across sexual and geopolitical lines that were not always bridgeable prior to 9/11. Perhaps, in this sense and this sense alone, Ifti provides an alternative stance that allows us to see these differences, and in so doing provides the space for a coalitional politics in and for contemporary America, a space that allows for different conceptualizations of community and a (queer) politics of strategic solidarity.[16]

I return briefly here to the issue I began with—Ganesh's quest for (queer) community in Chicago. On the one hand, the homonormative formations outlined above lend themselves almost seamlessly to such an interpretation: these individuals can be seen as docile subjects, deeply implicated in sustaining their position as willing subjects of capital and the state. On the other hand, in this securitized era, when visibility and brownness have acquired such a heightened valence, what meanings can we draw from the desire these men express for community, a desire that seemingly flies in the face of the invisibility they have sought these many years? Following the disastrous achievements in the war on terror and the debacle that was the post-Katrina relief effort, there appeared to be a growing awareness of class and racial rifts in America and a realization that despite wealth or status, the color of one's skin is enough to mark an individual as suspicious. As Mohan, the homonormative doctor, said in this context, "I guess it's pretty obvious that 'George Bush doesn't care about black people'[17] . . . or any people of color for that matter! Maybe it's time we all started realizing that and doing something about it." Even as I recognize the fraught parameters of community when translated into state governance and development discourses—especially when overly romanticized or reified, or both—I argue that it is by showing how communities are constituted and regulated by both the state (in the United States and South Asia) and informal social control—in this particular case, using Ifti as the foil—that we can perhaps reclaim the quest for community and see its radicalizing potential. It is in this sense that Ganesh's (and others') desire for community was revealing—and hopeful—for revitalizing a movement with normative power as its object of critique, a movement capable of addressing the complex "racial, gender, sexual and class differences that obtain their distinction through engagements with normativity" (Ferguson 2003, 148).[18]

Drawing on Alberto Melucci's contention that social communities and movements are, in a sense, "prophets of the present" (1996, 1), the perceived lack of a *desi* gay community and movement in Chicago was perhaps just as prophetic: an invisibility that revealed the dynamics of late capitalism, the politics of multiculturalism, the "karma of brown folk" as well as the queer and radical possibilities of subalternity in contemporary America. In this sense, Ifti was both literally and figuratively an aberration in brown (cf. Ferguson 2003), an aberration that potentially revealed the imbrication of capital with yearnings for community and troubled the easy translation of race into ethnic or cultural difference. By this token, Ifti made visible some of the "figurative borders" of *desi* identity and governmentality, highlighting possibilities for crafting sites of and for collective mobilization, a space for political community. While accepting Miranda Joseph's admonition that "it is crucial not to know in advance where the practice of community might offer effective resistance and where it might be an unredeemable site of cooptation, hegemony, and oppressive reiteration of norms" (2002, xxv), I suggest that *desi* queer men's quest for community in the early 2000s, in conjunction with the disruptive social formation represented by Ifti's discourse/practices, together not merely provided a platform for the recognition and celebration of differences (as warranted by a multicultural society) but, more important, created the possibility for this goal of recognition to serve a political project. Such a quest doesn't curtail so much as expand the grounds and scope for reconceptualizing understandings of desire, subjectivity, community, and the possibilities of cross-border coalition work. To give Ifti the last word, in an interview with Kareem Khubchandani in 2009, two years before he passed away, he said: "Honey . . . life went on before you cyber age queens came into existence. We paved your way to walk on to the cyber age" (saada.org/tides/article/paving-the-way-for-cyber-queens). Indeed. Rest in power, Ifti Nasim!

NOTES

I gratefully acknowledge the Social Science Research Council and the UIC Institute for the Humanities for fellowship support on this project, Kareem Khubchandani for connecting me to this project, Omar Kasmani for his enthusiastic support, Anna Romina Guevarra for the many generative conversations about community engagement, as well as more colleagues than I can name, at UIC and elsewhere, for their useful comments on earlier versions of this chapter. Most of all, my utmost gratitude to the late Ifti Nasim and all other interviewees in Chicago for generously opening their lives to me.

1   All individuals/names invoked in this essay are pseudonyms, except for Iftikhar Nasim, who wanted me to use his real name.
2   Sadly, Ifti passed away unexpectedly and too early in 2011. Today, there is a vibrant organization in Chicago—Trikone, whose leaders acknowledge and honor Nasim and his legacy (see Khubchandani 2020).
3   Ifti was also an aficionado of Hindustani classical and Sufi music, hosting *mehfils* and *mushairas* at his house for visiting poets/musicians when he was disinvited from gatherings with other Pakistanis.
4   As Lisa Duggan defines the term—"a politics that does not contest dominant heteronormative assumptions and institutions, but upholds and sustains them,

while promising the possibility of a demobilized gay constituency and a privatized, depoliticized gay culture anchored in domesticity and consumption" (2003, 50).

5   Ifti indicated a great deal of respect for *hijras* and *khwajasiras* for refusing respectability politics and putting themselves "out there," serving as a "good model for all gays" to emulate. Here, note Faris Khan's (2019) analysis of *khwajasira* activism in Pakistan and the play/politics of ambiguity rather than confrontation.

6   Recall Duggan: "Neoliberalism, a late 20th c. incarnation of Liberalism, organizes material and political life in terms of race, gender, and sexuality as well as economic class and nationality, or ethnicity and religion. But the categories through which Liberalism (and thus also neoliberalism) classifies human activity and relationships *actively obscure* the connections among these organizing terms" (2003, 3; emphasis added.).

7   After this ruling, forty-three of these individuals had their citizenship annulled (Mazumdar 1989, 50).

8   See George (1997), Koshy and Radhakrishnan (2008), and Reddy (2011) for a nuancing of this South Asian claim to whiteness.

9   Roderick Ferguson notes: "As contemporary globalization polarized minority communities economically, it produced the social conditions whereby class differences could help establish the normative status of racial subjects" (2004, 148).

10  This positioning—as an intermediary—doesn't necessarily help us understand what it means to *become* an Asian/Asian American in the United States. But it highlights the unique and fraught location Asians occupy in the U.S. racial landscape.

11  In American criminal courts, Asian Americans have been the most successful in using the "cultural defense" plea—the argument that the "defendant's cultural background should excuse crime, mitigate responsibility, or reduce the penalty for criminal behavior" (Reddy 2002, 667; Volpp 1994).

12  By invoking the referent of authenticity, I recognize this is privileging an originary and singular homeland and cultural identity, a notion that has been soundly—and rightly—critiqued in formulations of culture, nation, and invocations of the diaspora. However, in the transnational context, it remains one (among other) canvas against/through which *desis* configure their ethnicity and is repeatedly invoked in narratives of self, other, and cultural difference in multicultural America.

13  Following public protest, in 2000 SALGA was allowed to participate in the parade, galvanizing debate about the politics of solidarity as well as participation in an event that "promotes an increasingly unitary, Hindu-right representation of India" (Shah 2001, 2; cf. Shah 2014).

14  To be sure, this could be seen as an overly Manichean dichotomy that didn't capture the experiences of everyone in the *desi* queer community.

15  The events of 9/11 and its subsequent visibilization of differences in the United States—nation and religion—marked these as fault lines that fed into narratives

of American Orientalism with its historical fixation on religious difference. It also signaled negotiations of religious nationalism and differently commodified (and commodifiable) images in South Asia with its own history of religious violence against Muslims, calling for a differently oriented analysis of geopolitics with queer studies (Arondekar and Patel 2016).

16 While acknowledging a certain racialized positioning, this perspective simultaneously invisibilizes women and especially lesbian/queer women. Further, I do not mean to suggest that Ifti provided the solution, an unproblematic radical voice that questions all forms of normative power; he is, in fact, fundamentally contradictory. I am merely suggesting that what Ifti represents highlights fissures that artificially divide culture from economy, race from sexuality, class from gender, and, in the context of this volume, area/ethnic studies from queer studies, rather than recognizing their deep implication with/in one another.

17 George Bush was the president of the United States at the time, and this phrase is a reference to the oft-cited phrase by the popular musician Kanye West in response to the Bush-orchestrated Katrina relief efforts.

18 Here, Khubchandani's (2020) analysis of *desi* "ishtyle" in gay nightlife spaces—in Chicago and Bangalore—and the possibilities they provide for negotiating and resisting normativity, for imagining queer futures otherwise, is pertinent.

REFERENCES

Arondekar, Anjali, and Geeta Patel. 2016. "Area Impossible: Notes toward an Introduction." GLQ: *A Journal of Lesbian and Gay Studies* 22, no. 2: 151–71.

Bald, Vivek. 2013. *Bengali Harlem and the Lost Histories of South Asian America*. Cambridge, MA: Harvard University Press.

Bald, Vivek, Miabi Chatterji, Sujani Reddy, and Manu Vimalassery, eds. 2013. *The Sun Never Sets: South Asian Migrants in an Age of U.S. Power*. New York: NYU Press.

Chang, Robert. 1999. *Disoriented: Asian Americans, Law, and the Nation-State*. New York: NYU Press.

Duggan, Lisa. 2003. *The Twilight of Equality? Neoliberalism, Cultural Politics, and the Attack on Democracy*. Boston: Beacon Press.

Ferguson, Roderick. 2003. *Aberrations in Black*. Minneapolis: University of Minnesota Press.

Ferguson, Roderick A. 2019. *One-Dimensional Queer*. Medford, OR: Polity.

George, Rosemary M. 1997. "'From Expatriate Aristocrat to Immigrant Nobody': South Asian Racial Strategies in the Southern Californian Context." *Diaspora: A Journal of Transnational Studies* 6, no. 1: 30–61.

Groetzinger, Linda. 2004. "Attitudes and Behaviors of South Asian Men in Chicago: Culturally Contextualizing Health Risk." PhD thesis, University of Illinois, Chicago.

Hing, Bill O. 1993. *Making and Remaking Asian America through Immigration Policy, 1850–1990*. Stanford, CA: Stanford University Press.

Jensen, Joan M. 1988. *Passage from India: Asian Indian Immigrants in North America*. New Haven, CT: Yale University Press.

Joseph, Miranda. 2002. *Against the Romance of Community*. Minneapolis: University of Minnesota Press.

Khan, Faris. 2019. "Translucent Citizenship: Khwajasira Activism and Alternatives to Dissent in Pakistan, *South Asia Multidisciplinary Journal*, May 4: 1–23. https://journals.openedition.org/samaj/5034.

Khubchandani, Kareem. 2020. *Ishtyle: Accenting Gay Indian Nightlife*. Ann Arbor: University of Michigan Press.

Kim, Claire Jean. 2000. *Bitter Fruit: The Politics of Black-Korean Conflict in New York City*. New Haven, CT: Yale University Press.

Koshy, Susan. 1998. "Category Crisis: South Asian Americans and Questions of Race and Ethnicity." *Diaspora: A Journal of Transnational Studies* 7, no. 3: 285–320.

Koshy, Susan, and R. Radhakrishnan. 2008. *Transnational South Asians: The Making of a Neo-Diaspora*. New Delhi: Oxford University Press.

Kurien, Prema. 2004. "Multiculturalism and Ethnic Nationalism: The Development of an American Hinduism." *Social Problems* 51, no. 3: 362–85.

Leonard, Karen. 1992. *Making Ethnic Choices: California's Punjabi Mexican Americans*. Philadelphia: Temple University Press.

Lowe, Lisa. 1996. *Immigrant Acts: On Asian American Cultural Politics*. Durham, NC: Duke University Press.

Luibheid, Eithne. 2002. *Entry Denied: Controlling Sexuality at the Border*. Minneapolis: University of Minnesota Press.

Luibhéid, Eithne, and Karma R. Chávez, eds. 2020. *Queer and Trans Migrations: Dynamics of Illegalization, Detention, and Deportation*. Urbana-Champaign: University of Illinois Press.

Maira, Sunaina. 2002. *Desis in the House: Indian American Youth Culture in NYC*. Philadelphia: Temple University Press.

Maira, Sunaina. 2016. *The 9/11 Generation: Youth, Rights, and Solidarity in the War on Terror*. New York: NYU Press.

Mathew, Biju, and Vijay Prashad. 2000. "Protean Forms of Yankee Hindutva." *Ethnic and Racial Studies* 23, no. 3: 516–34.

Mazumdar, Sucheta. 1989. "Racist Responses to Racism: The Aryan Myth and South Asians in the United States." *South Asia Bulletin* 9, no. 1: 47–55.

Melendy, Howard Brett. 1977. *Asians in America: Filipinos, Koreans, and East Indians*. Boston: Twayne Publishers.

Melucci, Alberto. 1996. *Challenging Codes: Collective Action in the Information Age*. Cambridge: Cambridge University Press.

Muñoz, Jose Esteban. 2020. *The Sense of Brown*. Durham, NC: Duke University Press.

Nasim, Ifti. 2000. *Myrmecophile*. Bloomington, IN: Xlibris.

Prashad, Vijay. 2000. *The Karma of Brown Folk*. Minneapolis: University of Minnesota Press.

Prashad. Vijay. 2012. *Uncle Swami: South Asians in American Today*. New York: New Press.

Puar, Jasbir K., and Amit Rai. 2002. "Monster, Terrorist, Fag: The War on Terrorism and the Production of Docile Patriots." *Social Text* 20, no. 3: 117–48.

Radhakrishnan, Rajagopalan. 1996. *Diasporic Mediations: Between Home and Location*. Minneapolis: University of Minnesota Press.

Reddy, Chandan. 2011. *Freedom with Violence: Race, Sexuality, and the US State*. Durham, NC: Duke University Press.

Reddy, Sita. 2002. "Temporarily Insane: Pathologising Cultural Difference in American Criminal Courts." *Sociology of Health and Illness* 24, no. 5: 667–87.

Rudrappa, Sharmila. 2004. *Ethnic Routes to Becoming American: Indian Immigrants and the Cultures of Citizenship*. New Brunswick, NJ: Rutgers University Press.

Shah, Svati. 2001. "Out and Out Radical." *SAMAR Magazine*, Fall/Winter. https://static1.squarespace.com/static/618858de1b94642aba159141/t/61d869cf31b4de336940714a/1641572815991/Out+and+Out+Radical+_+Samar+Magazine.pdf.

Shah, Svati. 2014. "Queering Critiques of Neoliberalism in India." *Antipode: A Radical Journal of Geography*, August: 1–17.

Subramanian, Ajantha. 2000. "Indians in North Carolina: Race, Class, and Culture in the Making of Immigrant Identity." *Comparative Studies in South Asia, Africa, and the Middle East* 20, nos. 1–2: 105–13.

Visweswaran, Kamala. 1997. "Diaspora by Design: Flexible Citizenship and the South Asian Diaspora in U.S. Racial Formations." *Diaspora: A Journal of Transnational Studies* 6, no. 1: 5–29.

Volpp, Leti. 1994. "(Mis)Identifying Culture: Asian Women and the Cultural Defense." *Harvard Women's Law Journal* 17: 57–101.

Jeffrey A. Redding      14

## Queer in a Time of Kashmir

Pakistan is a queer land. Fragmented, resolute, messy, and proud, Pakistan resists both easy cartography and simple sexuality. Noncontiguous at inception, its western wing and eastern wing (now Bangladesh) bifurcated by thousands of kilometers of Indian territory, Pakistan remains constellated with India. More than seventy-five years have passed since Partition, yet desire binds these two South Asian powers, rivals, and snippy lovers. Kashmir is a key object of this queer desire.

The antagonistic desire for Kashmir is one of the most prominent legacies of the Partition of colonial India. Moreover, Kashmir's present predicament is a consequence of the paradigm of national choice that the British inaugurated for contemporary South Asia even as they were leaving the stage. The year 1947 is often remembered for the imperiousness by which South Asia was carved into awkward bits by British bureaucrats. It also was a time when South Asian princely states—not under the direct rule by the British—were given the consequential opportunity to join Pakistan, or India, or to remain independent (Indian Independence Act, section 2(4)). Kashmir was one of those princely states where the ruler had different interests and ambitions than the state's people as a whole (Rai 2004). The Kashmiri head was at cross-purposes with Kashmiri hearts, and the South Asian conflict over this territory is one consequence of this divergence between Kashmir's historic ruler and its people.

This is both a queer and a tragic state of affairs. Moreover, Kashmir's uncertain political identity and agency provide a parable of South Asian politics more broadly. At the very least, it is not surprising that a geographic region defined by elementary national ambiguity and contestation is also witness to fundamental contestations regarding religious identity—for example, controversies over Ahmadis in Pakistan and love *jihad* in India—and now also gender identity.[1] South Asian discussions concerning transgender rights, like Kashmiri rights, are caught between competing notions of solidarity and sovereignty. Queerness here takes place in a time of Kashmir.

Movements around gender identity and transgender rights in South Asia have been some of the twenty-first century's most unanticipated and remarkable developments. Historically vilified, surveilled, and impoverished by the colonial state (Hinchy 2019), transgender people across the region continued to face steep odds even after independence and the proclamation of fundamental rights by various postcolonial constitutions. Recently, however, several South Asian judicial and legislative bodies have favorably pronounced on the social and political rights of transgender people. Starting in Nepal in 2007 not long after a Maoist insurgency and shortly before a royal abdication (Knight 2014), and then moving to Pakistan in 2009 after the assassination of Benazir Bhutto and the fall of the Musharraf regime (Redding 2018), India too saw widespread discussion of these matters in 2014 as the Hindu nationalist BJP political party was racking up landmark and traumatic electoral successes (*National Legal Services Authority* 2014).

The BJP ballot box successes would lead five years later to an even deeper "state of siege" in the parts of Kashmir under Indian occupation and not presently controlled by Pakistan or China (Zia 2019, 11). Indeed, on August 5, 2019, India's president took steps to abrogate the erstwhile Indian state of Jammu and Kashmir's territorial integrity and (already circumscribed) legal autonomy. On the same day, India's lower house of parliament, the Lok Sabha, passed the Transgender Persons (Protection of Rights) Bill of 2019 after little substantive debate. These two developments—one relating to geography and another to gender—are not just temporally but substantively linked. More broadly, there are overlooked but important attributes linking discussions about territorial and transgender communities.

In this contribution, then, I explore why and how geography and gender are both queer issues regarding Pakistan, and also the uncertain and fraught implications of this queerness. Other contributions to this volume have recognized and argued that queerness is not simply about nonnormative genders and sexualities; rather, queerness is also about nonintuitive understandings and configurations of social and political power. Kashmir's relation to Pakistan and gender alike represents such a configuration. As a result, it is not surprising that recent Pakistani discussions about gender identity and transgender rights embody aspects of the historic conflict over Kashmir, including disputes over the definition and demarcating of sovereignty and community. Queerness in Pakistan takes place on the strange map of South Asia with a conflicted Kashmir at its center.

## QUEER GEOGRAPHY

Geography is typically conceived of conservatively. Allegedly bounded, territory is often seen as knowable, discrete, and objectively measurable. Legal scholar Kal Raustiala captures this traditional view when he notes: "As a governing principle, territoriality is so intuitive that we rarely question it. That states have borders, and that these borders determine the limits of their sovereign domain, is a widely accepted proposition in the modern world" (Raustiala 2009, 5). Conversely, Raustiala also observes how "[t]oday we generally think *noncontiguous* territories ... anomalous and odd" (2009, 9, emphasis added).[2]

The early imagination of Pakistan was certainly strange. As an attempt to accumulate many of South Asia's Muslims into one new state, Pakistan's revolutionary efforts resulted in peculiar arrangements—most notably the creation of two separate eastern and western "wings" (East and West Pakistan).[3] As Faisal Devji describes this bifurcated and weird national space: "Pakistan's was a situation unknown either in the history or theory of nationalism, and the only other example that comes to mind is the short-lived United Arab Republic that brought Egypt and Syria together into an ethnic and ideological state from 1958 to 1961" (Devji 2013, 28). Adding to the complexity of Pakistan's initial imagination was the fact that it was designed to be a fluid space, at least in the sense that princely states were given the legal option of joining Pakistan at a later date. Again, the Kashmir tragedy is perhaps the most well-known consequence of the intentionally mobile boundaries imagined for Pakistan at its inception.

Moreover, the early queer imagination of Pakistan continues to be deeply relevant for present times. In 2020, for example, Pakistan's prime minister issued updated political maps of Pakistan after India's 2019 occupation and bifurcation of its erstwhile State of Jammu and Kashmir (Siddiqui 2020). Not only was the entirety of Kashmir (inclusive of the portions controlled by Pakistan and India both) colored in one unified shade of green, but the Indian-held portion of Kashmir was conspicuously marked with text declaring "DISPUTED TERRITORY—FINAL STATUS TO BE DECIDED IN LINE WITH RELEVANT UNSC RESOLUTIONS." Such resolutions include United Nations Security Council Resolution 47 from 1948 and its declaration that there shall be a "free and impartial [Kashmiri] plebiscite to decide whether the State of Jammu and Kashmir is to accede to India or Pakistan" (United Nations Security Council Resolution 47).

Two offset boxes of enlarged and decontextualized territory also feature in the lower right-hand corner of the updated map. One of these boxes highlights a border dispute—the Sir Creek dispute—involving territory whose demarcations are confused, in part, by murky and shifting water. The other box spotlights a visually baffling territorial dispute involving a small piece of coastal land in the present-day Indian state of Gujrat and requiring far more explanation. This dispute concerns the historic princely state of Junagadh. At Partition, this state represented something of the converse of the Kashmir situation in that the Muslim leadership of this Hindu-majority state attempted to accede to Pakistan. As historian Rakesh Ankit describes this area: "Junagadh could be, and was, understood as a 'mirror-image' of Kashmir or as 'Hyderabad in miniature'" (Ankit 2016, 372; citation omitted).[4]

In its many details, the Junagadh dispute—while only involving "[a] 'little-regarded and 'over-looked patchwork quilt' of 3,300 scattered square miles and [then] 700,000 people ... in the intricate Kathiawar region in Western India" (Ankit 2016, 372; citation omitted)—represents something of South Asia's complex geography writ large. While unconnected by land with present-day Pakistan, Junagadh was itself noncontiguous and also encompassed areas claimed by other sovereigns.[5] In Jinnah's famous words, if Pakistan itself was born "moth-eaten," then its claims on Junagadh could be seen as a gesture toward a similarly "misshapen" state.[6]

Ultimately, the revival of the Junagadh-cum-Kashmir dispute represents the continuing relevance of complex and queer notions of territories and people in postcolonial South Asia. Seemingly objective or scientific categories like "territory" are in fact made and remade and unmade through human decisions.[7] In the cases of Kashmir or Junagadh, these decisions might even be made by powerful individuals like a *maharaja* or *nawab* single-handedly choosing accession for their princely state. Regardless, both Pakistan and India are patchwork assemblages of land and persons, stitched together by ever-shifting and fluid notions of who and what belongs to each. This fluidity results from not only conflicts between these sovereigns but also competing notions about where sovereign authority lies—for example, with the United Nations, a head of state, or ordinary individuals.

To be sure, this fluidity also has important limitations. I will return to this example in more detail below, but recent efforts to strip citizenship from Muslims in India demonstrate how the queerness of geography in South Asia is marked by existential dangers in the contestation between states and individuals over the forging of national community. Moreover, no matter what the relative sovereign, not everyone counts equally. For example, both Pakistan and India claim Kashmir as an integral part of each country respectively and exclusively, but Kashmir's own historic and contemporary identity as "neither Pakistan nor India" rarely comes into full focus.[8]

Similarly, efforts for gender self-identification have received Pakistan's official sanction, but individual transgender voices often turn out to be less important than the competing interests and claims of dominant cismale and cisfemale communities. The following section explains the tensions present in Pakistani transgender rights discussion concerning who counts and who belongs to any particular gender identity. Gender, like geography, Pakistan's patchwork is knitted as much by patriarchy as it is personal choice.

QUEER GENDER

Over the past many years, transgender rights in Pakistan have witnessed numerous ups and downs and have been part of multiple global and local discussions. The present movement can be dated to a Supreme Court petition filed in early 2009 by charismatic lawyers aiming to highlight the multiple official and social abuses that transgender people have experienced in Pakistan. This intervention came shortly after an anti-police riot led by transgender women aggrieved at the arrest and harassment of fellow community members in the northern city of Rawalpindi.[9]

In response to this legal petition, and over the course of the next several years, the Supreme Court issued multiple directives to various governmental actors to take steps to improve the material and political position of transgender citizens of Pakistan. Among other things, these orders attempted to reduce police harassment, increase access to crucial education and employment opportunities, ensure the franchise, and guarantee Islamic inheritance rights for transgender Pakistanis. The latter objective confirms that the Pakistan gender identity and transgender rights discussion has been informed as much by local conditions and aspirations as it has been by global developments.[10]

Further evidencing the multidimensional quality of these queer discussions, the Supreme Court struggled with how to refer to the transgender community members who appeared in front of the court. Over time, the court used a variety of terms and identifications for transgender people, highlighting the court's perception of them as neither cismale or cisfemale. These terms included the now-repudiated and offensive English-language word "eunuch" and also the current politically correct Urdu expression *khwaja sira*. Other aspects of the court's orders included a discussion about whether it benefits transgender persons to use the already-available legal category of disabled persons—suggesting a court (and society) struggling to embrace the demand for gender self-identification.[11]

Nine years after this litigation began, however, Pakistan legislated a groundbreaking act formally recognizing the right to self-identification for the purposes of gender. The Transgender Persons (Protection of Rights) Act, 2018, firmly declared that "[a] transgender person shall have a right to be recognized as per his or her self-perceived gender identity" (Transgender Persons (Protection of Rights) Act, 2018, section 3(1)). However, belying this neat guarantee, the same act defined "transgender person" to multifariously include:

(i) intersex (khusra) with mixture of male and female genital features or congenital ambiguities; or
(ii) eunuch assigned male at birth, but undergoes genital excision or castration; or
(iii) a transgender man, transgender woman, *KhawajaSira* or any person whose gender identity or gender expression differs from the social norms and cultural expectations based on the sex they were assigned at the time of their birth. (Transgender Persons (Protection of Rights) Act, 2018, section 2(n))[12]

While a number of transgender people have benefited from this 2018 legislation, it is only being imperfectly enforced. This reality was recently on vivid display in a 2020 case adjudicated by the Rawalpindi bench of the Lahore High Court, *Syed Amjad Hussain Shah v. Ali Akash alias Asima Bibi and Five Others*.[13] This habeas corpus case was brought by an aggrieved father attempting to halt the relationship his adolescent daughter had formed with an older school teacher (who also happened to live with the family at one point in time).[14] According to the father, the school teacher had legally changed their official gender from female to male, presumably using the provisions of the Transgender Persons (Protection of Rights) Act of 2018. With this legal gender change, the older teacher was able to enter into an officially heterosexual marital union with the father's young daughter.

> In his petition to the Lahore High Court, the father narrated how he, the petitioner having knowledge about the above said illicit relation of [the teacher] with detenue daughter ... immediately removed the detenue daughter from above mentioned [learning] institution but even then [the teacher] secretly connected with detenue daughter and subsequently [the teacher] changed her name from Asma BiBi to Ali Aakash, just for playing fraud with courts of law as well as illegal act and design for in continuation of above said illegal relation with detenue daughter and after changing of named, [the teacher] managed a nikah nama with detenue daughter.... [E]ven in Sharia/Islam a marriage within same sex/gender is not only prohibited but also define [sic] as adultery as well as Gunah [sin]. (*Syed Amjad Hussain Shah v. Ali Aakash Alice [sic] Asma Bibi Etc.*, Writ Petition No. 1421/2020, Lahore High Court, July 11, 2020, Petition, para. 6)

Ultimately, this case was resolved by the Lahore High Court on relatively narrow grounds due to an intervening divorce statement by the teacher and the court's reading of judicial precedent to mandate that the daughter's freedom of movement and residence be respected.[15] That being said, a perusal of judicial records related to this case shows that a gender-determination medical inspection of the teacher was at one point ordered by the Lahore High Court in the process of adjudicating this matter.[16] Further, the final order of the Lahore High Court in this matter appeared to both sidestep and revive the issue of the teacher's gender, ordering

> the National Database & Registration Authority (NADRA) [to] pass a fresh order regarding the change of entry in the column relating to

**gender** made in the [national identity card] relating to Ali Akash alias Asima Bibi... in accordance with the law... including the provisions of the *Transgender Persons (Protection of Rights) Act, 2018*) [*sic*] and after providing fair opportunity of hearing to all the parties concerned. (*Syed Amjad Hussain Shah vs. Ali Akash alias Asima Bibi and Five Others*, W.P. No. 1421 of 2020, Lahore High Court, September 14, 2020, Judgment, para. 13, emphasis in original)

These Lahore High Court actions and statements are both confusing and alarming, however, since the 2018 act appears to contemplate that there should be only one "concerned" party with regards a person's gender identity—namely, the individual who is contemplating their own gender identity.

LINES OF CONFUSION AND CONTROL

*State, Community, and Individual*

In many ways, it is unsurprising that a region of the world where fundamental questions about national belonging have taken center stage would produce some of the most profound legislative declarations about gender choice. The terrain of choice has been rocky in South Asia but the social categories of nationality and gender are traveling this uneven landscape together. The historic choices of princely states created contemporary Pakistan and India. This was as true for voluntary choices as it was for unrecognized or coerced ones; the uncertainty and fluidity of South Asia's borders continues to be impacted by historically imperfect choices. Contemporary gender in Pakistan is also the product of an incomplete regime of self-identification. While self-identification is revolutionary for gender globally, it looks less original for Pakistan when viewed against the ongoing history of nationality and territory in South Asia. Queerness here takes place in a time of Kashmir.

This being the case, there are somewhat different sovereigns relevant for national choice versus gender choice. Or rather, there are always multiple competing sovereigns—the state, the community, and the individual—making claims regarding nationality and gender alike, but nationality and gender discourses currently prioritize these various stakeholders differently. For example, most commentators would agree that the state has an important role to play in defining citizenship, even while problematizing that role. Some commentators would further argue that national communities have interests here—for example, Indigenous communities in Australia (*Love v. Commonwealth of Australia*; *Thoms v. Commonwealth of Australia* 2020) or ethnic Kashmiris regarding Kashmir itself. By way of contrast, few commentators argue that individuals should be able to choose their citizenship, free from restriction by other individuals, national communities, or the state.[17] This latter consensus sits in sharp contrast, however, with discussions concerning gender where individual feeling and self-identification occupies a much larger place in the contemporary conversation.[18]

Indeed, one might say that national and gender communities mobilize different combinations of relevant stakeholders to demarcate the line between member and nonmember. However, these combinations have not proved especially discrete or stable, and nationality rights movements have impacted those pertaining to gender rights, and vice versa. In closing, I aim to illustrate this queerness while also cautioning that it does not provide any clear road to salvation.

Some human rights activists would prefer a more personalized assessment of citizenship and nationality—indeed, something along the lines of the self-identification operationalized by recent transgender rights movements. In South Asia, the benefits of a national self-identification regime emerge, for example, when considering recent efforts to strip citizenship from Muslims in India. The recent National Register of Citizens (NRC) exercise in the Indian state of Assam, in combination with the even more recent national Citizenship Amendment Act (CAA), has posed the real possibility of tens of millions of Indian Muslims being denationalized and rendered stateless (Ahmed 2020). There are evidently many dangers present in allowing states versus individuals to choose and forge (national) community.

Dangers lurk, however, with self-identification. Toward this point, Pakistan was a historically innovative project not only because of its strange territorial imagination but also because it was conceived as a Muslim homeland within South Asia (Devji 2013, 44–45). As a result, not only were princely states invited (however irregularly) to join it but so were individual Muslims. As historian Vazira Zamindar has documented, the "long Partition" of India and Pakistan meant that relatively unencumbered migration from contemporary India to contemporary Pakistan continued until it become much more difficult in the lead-up to and aftermath of the

1965 war between India and Pakistan (Zamindar 2007, 176). Moreover, this regime was largely one where individual nationality could only be chosen with actual physical migration. Despite this history, Hindu nationalists in today's India have accused many contemporary Muslim Indians—despite being well and voluntarily ensconced within India for generations—of harboring sympathies for Pakistan. Hindu nationalists have additionally labeled Muslim residential locales "little Pakistans" and, most recently, have worried about supposed covert Muslim migration from Bangladesh into the eastern Indian state of Assam because of this alleged migration's national security implications.[19]

These discussions are often conspiratorial in tone and indubitably bigoted. They also embody an assumption that neither India's or Pakistan's territory can be easily demarcated. Indeed, in the accusation that "enemy territory" exists where minorities gather to live, there is an admission that territory and nationality are underscored by noncontiguity, fluidity, and personal affinities—even while expressing a great deal of anxiety and loathing over this queerness. In short, Pakistan's alleged archipelago is not accompanied by celebration here.

Moreover, similar anxieties about especially fluid self-identification have been articulated by some transgender individuals in Pakistan. For example, in Pakistan, the Supreme Court's many orders in connection to the original 2009 legal petition concerning transgender rights eventually resulted in a number of efforts to improve the socioeconomic conditions facing transgender Pakistanis. These efforts have included initiatives in Pakistan's public sectors to generate employment for Pakistan's marginalized transgender citizens, many of which have been given shape and force via the formulation of numerical quotas for transgender individuals. In this regard, Pakistan's Sindh province recently announced a 5 percent employment quota for transgender individuals in its police department (Ali 2019), and a 2 percent employment quota in Khyber Pakhtunkhwa's education department has also been debated (Bureau Report 2018).

The question of "who counts" as transgender has become fundamental here. The percentage of educational or employment spots allocated to transgender persons depends (at least roughly) on a determination of the percentage of applicants who are transgender in each province. Reserving too few positions for potential beneficiaries would not achieve the desired result. Reserving too many positions, however, could "incentivize" claiming a transgender status. Indeed, one testament—both promising and fraught—to the capability of these quota schemes to transform transgender welfare in Pakistan has been the emergence of sharp controversies within and without transgender communities in Pakistan about who counts as transgender and should be able to avail transgender quota schemes and, conversely, who does *not* count and should *not* be able to avail (Pamment 2023, 152–53, 161–63). In these contestations, allegations of bad intent and fraud in gender choice and self-identification have proliferated, both within and without transgender communities.

Evidently, states, communities, and individuals battle for control regarding Pakistan's geographies and genders alike. Lines of control and sovereignty are never clear and always doubled-edged. Queerness is both everywhere and always, for better and worse.

CONCLUSION

Geography is theory. The introduction to this volume notes how dominant queer scholarship has long presupposed "there is no geography to theory" before proceeding to argue that "other inheritances and orientations of queer"—such as those found in Pakistan—need greater attention and articulation. With these apt observations in mind, this chapter has demonstrated that Pakistan's queer geographies and queer genders are imbricated and how, in fact, queer geography is queer theory.

This being the case, Pakistan's shifting terrains, borders, and communities are not only enlivening but fraught, and sometimes perilous like quicksand itself. More than seventy-five years have passed since the 1947 Partition, yet South Asia's boundaries and belongings—its geographies and genders—remain uncertain as ever. Kashmir is central to this reality, and theorizations of queerness remiss to historically constructed and contested sovereignties in South Asia are likely to not only exaggerate what is "new" in gender in South Asia, but also overstate what is possible in this queer region. Choice is enlivening but multiple stakeholders disagree about the right choices to be had. In all this plurality, we see how gender and geography—queerness and Kashmir—are not only inseparable and inspirational, but also intractable.

## NOTES

1. For a discussion of how anxieties concerning religious identities in Pakistan can parallel those around gender identities, see Redding (2015b). For a recent discussion of Indian controversies about the ostensible conversion of Hindu women by Muslim men, see Tyagi and Sen (2020).

2. Similarly, historian Sunil Purushotham has characterized the "advent of Pakistan as a territorial entity... an anomalous one" (Purushotham 2020, 158). Of course, there are many noncontiguous parts of contemporary states—Alaska and Hawai'i in the context of the United States, Tasmania in the context of Australia—and then too historic empires. See also Cons (2016) for a discussion of the complexity of the border between India and Bangladesh.

3. Faisal Devji argues that it was the Indian nationalist Congress political party, and not the Muslim League, which was interested in a strict demarcation of Pakistan's borders (and India's too) according to local religious demographies. Devji also argues that Muslim League leader Mohammed Ali Jinnah was fairly pragmatic about (or perhaps even somewhat indifferent to) Pakistan's precise territorial composition (Devji 2013, 24–28).

4. On Hyderabad, see Purushotham (2020); Sherman (2015).

5. Ankit (2016, 403) also emphasizes that Junagadh is significant because of the ways "a complex and layered colonial sovereignty resided in the princely state and its 'sub-states.'"

6. "Speech by Muhammad Jinnah on the Partition of Bengal and the Punjab, May 4, 1947 (FO 371/63533)."

7. Sunil Purushotham makes a similar point when he argues that the "territorial nation states that emerged in the subcontinent after 1947 were products not simply of dividing the Raj, but of a complex and thorough process of territorialization. India and Pakistan (and latterly Bangladesh) had to be *made*" (Purushotham 2020, 195, emphasis in original).

8. Rai (2004, 4) also laments "a venerable tradition of deliberating about Kashmir with Kashmiris left out of the picture."

9. For details of these early events, see Redding (2015a).

10. Here I specifically disagree with the analysis offered by Farhat et al. (2020, 33; citation omitted) and their argument that the 2018 Transgender Rights (Protection of Persons) Act "is likely to be seen as an alien imposition on Pakistani society and might lead to differences and chaos.... The revision of approach and text of the Act in indigenous context is therefore essential."

11. In an order stemming from a Supreme Court hearing on November 20, 2009, the court ordered Pakistan's provincial and federal governments to provide for transgender persons' inheritance rights, franchise rights, and also educational opportunities. Also, the court begins in this order to describe "this class of the society" as suffering from a "gender disorder" (Constitution Petition No. 43 of 2009, 20.11.2009 Order, para. 2). Indeed, on this basis of this understanding

of what it means to be transgender, the court directed the federal and provincial governments to ensure employment opportunities for transgender persons, noting that "[a]s the Government has already ensured the jobs to the disable[d] persons... similar policy can also be adopted for [transgender persons]" (para. 3).

12  See Farhat et al. (2020, 21) for a similar observation about the potential over-inclusiveness of this legislative definition.

13  *Syed Amjad Hussain Shah vs. Ali Akash alias Asima Bibi and Five Others*, W.P. No. 1421 of 2020, Lahore High Court, September 14, 2020, Judgment.

14  This habeas corpus petition was brought using section 491 of the Pakistan Code of Criminal Procedure. Section 491 reads, in part: "Any High Court may, whenever it thinks fit, direct... that a person illegally or improperly detained in public or private custody within such limits be set at liberty" (The Code of Criminal Procedure (Pakistan), section 491).

15  Regarding this, the court wrote: "Mst. Neha Ali... being *sui juris*... is **set at liberty** and permitted to live her life as she pleases within the dictates of law and faith.... Furthermore, the petitioner [father] and his family members are directed not to cause any harassment to Mst. Neha Ali.... It is observed that Mst. Neha Ali... is competent to lead a life of her choice and no restraint can be imposed on her event at the instance of her father or brother" (*Syed Amjad Hussain Shah vs. Ali Akash alias Asima Bibi and Five Others*, W.P. No. 1421 of 2020, Lahore High Court, September 14, 2020, Judgment, para. 10, emphasis in original).

16  See Memo from Office of the Medical Superintendent, District Head Quarters Hospital, Rawalpindi to Assistant Registrar (Writ), Lahore High Court, Rawalpindi Bench, Subject: Constitution of Medical Board, August 5, 2020.

17  For a recent critical take on citizenship's neglect of individuality, see Kochenov (2019).

18  See Knight's (2014) description of the Nepalese Supreme Court's 2007 ruling regarding the recognition of third gender individuals in Nepal and the court's order that government officials had to follow the "self-feeling" of these individuals.

19  Metcalf (2011) has observed how "[i]n the case of Muslims in India, suspicion and disapproval after 9/11 has been further exacerbated by the enduring prejudice that Muslim Indians are 'proto-Pakistanis,' their neighborhoods are 'little Pakistans,' and so forth."

REFERENCES

Ahmed, Farrah. 2020. "Arbitrariness, Subordination and Unequal Citizenship." *Indian Law Review* 4: 121–37.

Ali, Imtiaz. 2019. "In a First, Transgenders to Be Offered 5pc Jobs in Sindh Police: IG." *Dawn*, April 2. https://www.dawn.com/news/1473252.

Ankit, Rakesh Ankit. 2016. "The Accession of Junagadh, 1947–48: Colonial Sovereignty, State Violence and Post-Independence India." *The Indian Economic and Social History Review* 53: 371–404.

Bureau Report. 2018. "Court Summons Edu Dept Officials over Transgender Job Quota." *The News*, March 17. https://www.thenews.com.pk/print/293462-court-summons-edu-dept-officials-over-transgender-job-quota.

The Code of Criminal Procedure (Pakistan).

Cons, Jason. 2016. *Sensitive Space: Fragmented Territory at the India-Bangladesh Border*. Seattle: University of Washington Press.

Constitution Petition No. 43 of 2009, 20.11.2009 Order (Pakistan).

Devji, Faisal. 2013. *Muslim Zion: Pakistan as a Political Idea*. Cambridge, MA: Harvard University Press.

Farhat, Syed Nadeem, Muhammad Daniyal Abdullah, Shafei Moiz Hali, and Hamza Iftikhar. 2020. "Transgender Law in Pakistan: Some Key Issues." *Policy Perspectives* 17: 7–33.

Hinchy, Jessica. 2019. *Governing Gender and Sexuality in Colonial India: The Hijra, c. 1850–1900*. Cambridge: Cambridge University Press.

Indian Independence Act, 1947.

Knight, Kyle. 2014. "The Spark: How Sunil Pant Ignited a Queer Rights Movement in Nepal." *Caravan*. February 28. https://caravanmagazine.in/reportage/spark.

Kochenov, Dimitry. 2019. *Citizenship*. Cambridge, MA: MIT Press.

*Love v. Commonwealth of Australia; Thoms v. Commonwealth of Australia* [2020]. HCA 3.

Memo from Office of the Medical Superintendent, District Headquarters Hospital, Rawalpindi to Assistant Registrar (Writ), Lahore High Court, Rawalpindi Bench, Subject: Constitution of Medical Board, August 5, 2020 (Pakistan).

Metcalf, Barbara D. 2011. "'Traditionalist' Islamic Activism: Deoband and Deobandis, Ten Years Later." *items*. September 6. https://items.ssrc.org/10-years-after-september-11/traditionalist-islamic-activism-deoband-and-deobandis-ten-years-later/.

*National Legal Services Authority v. Union of India* (2014) 5 S.C.C 438.

Pamment, Claire. 2023. "Mediatizing 'Fake' *Khwaja Siras*: The Limits of Impersonation." In *Mimetic Desires: Impersonation and Guising across South Asia*, edited by Harshita Mruthinti Kamath and Pamela Lothspeich, 148–68. Honolulu: University of Hawai'i Press.

Purushotham, Sunil. 2020. "Federating the Raj: Hyderabad, Sovereign Kingship, and Partition." *Modern Asian Studies* 54: 157–98.

Rai, Mridu. 2004. *Hindu Rulers, Muslim Subjects: Islam, Rights, and the History of Kashmir*. Princeton, NJ: Princeton University Press.

Raustiala, Kal. 2009. *Does the Constitution Follow the Flag? The Evolution of Territoriality in American Law*. Oxford: Oxford University Press.

Redding, Jeffrey A. 2015a. "From 'She-Males' to 'Unix': Transgender Rights and the Productive Paradoxes of Pakistani Policing." In *Regimes of Legality: Ethnography of Criminal Cases in South Asia*, edited by Daniela Berti and Devika Bordia, 258–89. New Delhi: Oxford University Press.

Redding, Jeffrey A. 2015b. "Khwaja Siras and State (Dis)Belief." *Tanqeed*. March 15. http://www.tanqeed.org/2015/03/suspect-genders-khwaja-siras-and-state-disbelief-tq-salon/.

Redding, Jeffrey A. 2018. "Transgender Rights in Pakistan?: Global, Colonial, and Islamic Perspectives." In *Human Rights in Translation: Intercultural Pathways*, edited by Michal Jan Rozbicki, 49–75. Lanham, MD: Lexington Books.

Sherman, Taylor C. 2015. *Muslim Belonging in Secular India: Negotiating Citizenship in Postcolonial Hyderabad*. Cambridge: Cambridge University Press.

Siddiqui, Naveed. 2020. "In Landmark Move, PM Imran Unveils 'New Political Map' of Pakistan." *Dawn*, August 4. https://www.dawn.com/news/1572590.

"Speech by Muhammad Jinnah on the Partition of Bengal and the Punjab, May 4, 1947 (FO 371/63533)." Accessed January 20, 2023. https://www.nationalarchives.gov.uk/education/resources/indian-independence/jinnah-partition/.

*Syed Amjad Hussain Shah v. Ali Aakash Alice [sic] Asma Bibi Etc.*, Writ Petition No. 1421/2020, Lahore High Court, July 11, 2020, Petition (Pakistan).

*Syed Amjad Hussain Shah vs. Ali Akash alias Asima Bibi and Five Others*, W.P. No. 1421 of 2020, Lahore High Court, September 14, 2020, Judgment (Pakistan).

Tyagi, Aastha, and Atreyee Sen. 2020. "*Love-Jihad* (Muslim Sexual Seduction) and *Ched-Chad* (Sexual Harassment): Hindu Nationalist Discourses and the Ideal/Deviant Urban Citizen in India." *Gender, Place & Culture: A Journal of Feminist Geography* 27: 104–25.

United Nations Security Council Resolution 47 (adopted April 21, 1948).

Zamindar, Vazira Fazila-Yacoobali. 2007. *The Long Partition and the Making of Modern South Asia: Refugees, Boundaries, Histories*. New York: Columbia University Press.

Zia, Ather. 2019. *Resisting Disappearance: Military Occupation and Women's Activism in Kashmir*. Seattle: University of Washington Press.

Anjali Arondekar

# Afterword

Everywhere *Mehfil*

Show and tell. Search and rescue. A collection on geopolitics and sexuality faces the inevitable question of its relevance. Are its locations new, undeciphered, unfree, shiny fodder for the diversity mill? Are its exemplars adequately queer, inadequately represented, and ultimately translatable? There may be journeys, but at stake are destinations. Are we there yet?

What happens if we eschew such habits of capture, rendition, and circulation? What happens if sexuality is a gathering, a provocation of genres and spaces and tongues, of multilingual encounters and spiritual forays? To transact the geopolitical then is to enter the everywhere *mehfil*, a quotidian coupling of place and pleasure, of form and friction, of call and response. A *mehfil*, after all, is a Hindustani term (gifted through Urdu, Arabic [*mahfil*], and Persian) that summons publics into lives of conversation and proximity, at once a place of frenzied engagement and quiet meditation. From its early invocations as a space of courtly performance to its more recent iterations as assembly, celebration, forum, the *mehfil* has always been a terrain of paradoxical potentiality: infused with secrecy and sexuality, yet decidedly public and performative.[1]

I have returned often to the concept-metaphor of *mehfil* as I imagined a response to this timely and efflorescent collection, *Pakistan Desires*. After all, I encountered many of its interlocutors at one such raucous *mehfil* in Lahore in 2019, otherwise known as the first queer conference to be held in Pakistan. I was there to give a keynote on my work on histories of sexuality and abundance, and found myself surrounded by a cacophony of theories, languages, and affects. While the organizers, Nida, Omar, and Kamran, sustained us with food, inspiration, and schedules, there was a general sense of convivial chaos settling in. Very little was agreed upon, even as more was said and learned each day.[2] Grumblings of elitism (the conference was held at a private, gated university) accompanied celebrations of unions, otherwise impossible in the beleaguered landscape that is contemporary Pakistan. Queer futures were summoned and jettisoned, queer pasts recuperated and corrupted even as the present forged a poetics of the political and the improbable. It was a *mehfil* like no other.

Akin to my experience of the Lahore Conference, this collection too is a riotous, messy, inviting, erudite, and engaging *mehfil*—a staged congeries of voices, visualities, and histories that refuses to settle into any mandated orders of knowledge. From pointed provocations to think between and beyond geo-objects (pace Pak*stan) to renderings of Urdu aesthetics and prose, from cruisy whisperings of desire and dissent to joyous movements of sound and spirit, there is a sense that we are in thrall of an endless *mehfil*. Shall we re/join the action? I think it's time.

I: DOES THE THING EXIST?

Even as I write this, queer ideations of place, as Omar Kasmani writes in his elegant introduction, seem particularly urgent, especially as Pakistan, and indeed South Asia, remains within the stranglehold of rising authoritarianism, communalism, and staggering economic precarity. Pandemic horrors, endlessly corrupt political regimes, and environmental devastation make for futures that are anything but hopeful. What does it mean then to participate in an intellectual gathering of nonrecognition, to summon a space that eschews the subtractive (even extractive) failures and fantasies of such a historical present/presence? How does one exist in an elsewhere outside the grids of visibility tethered to secular and liberal logics of rights and reform? After all, as the contributors variously remind us, we are not here to find Pakistan's queer pasts, or to carve out clear (righteous and rights-infused) pathways to scripted, liberatory futures. Instead, the fourteen chapters in the collection treat queer axiomatically as geopolitical form and lineage, inviting us to think of Pakistan as a shifting, restless, lyrical landscape of time and space.

While the collection is clearly not invested in the evidentiary regimes and conventions of recuperative history, there is a central tension here: geography as fabulation merges with geography as value. Pakistan accrues value, even as Pakistan remains outside the scenes of queer representation. As such, each contribution—especially in the first section—does not merely excavate or summon queerness; rather, each response participates in a materialized dialectic between the registers of (lost) visibility and the hermeneutics of possibility. To be in Pakistan, one must traverse outside of the settled geographies of Pakistan and Euro-American queer studies. For Masood, Quraishi, and Rajani, the thing that does not exist (to recast Masood's words) unfolds in playfully serious fictions, versions of Pak*stan's life story across cross-hatched imaginaries and memoirs of Sufi time and sacral spaces, within and beyond the nation-state. Others like Khan and Tariq turn to counter listening and telling tales/*qissahs* of queer learning that return us to the sounds and sensibilities of trans/histories and feminist revolution. While Patel voyages to the lyrical past to speak of the in-between entanglements of the Urdu poet Miraji and Sappho, Kirk turns to Pakistani cinema as a site of gender undoing and geopolitical critique. As we enter the queer worlds of Pak*stan, vernaculars of history become fiction, as origin stories of queer/trans subjectivities that refuse the seductions of monumentalization.

II: A PLACE DESIRES

A central conceit of this *mehfil* is its plangent commitment to the infrastructure of "desire" as an archive of theoretical entailments that forges the idea of a queer Pak*stan. The turn to desire as an idiom of opening invokes a continuous seeking, a looking for that requires more journeys than destinations. Pakistan is jettisoned as geo-object to make room for Pakistan as subject, rethinking the epistemological value immanent to geopolitics. Each essay demands roaming—literal, figurative, affective; the story of Pakistan is told in a subtlety of archives and genres that demand futures not yet assigned: these are the idioms particular to *Pakistan Desires*. What is at stake is less the well-rehearsed ritual combat of identitarian histories (LGBTQI, etc.) than the assemblage of queer/trans forms that gather only to disperse.

The second half of the collection specifically turns to border crossings (spatial, disciplinary, affective) as porous queer forms that extend histories of sexuality and gender across diasporas, communities, and occupations.

Less focused on archival hermeneutics than the first half, these essays suture Pakistan more with forms of dissent that refuse histories of stigmatization and/or valor. Hamzić and Pamment turn to the varied genealogies of the *khwajasara*, Pakistan's gender-nonconforming collectivities, that spread across divergent Islamic temporalities and ritual practices. Hamzić speaks to the tense and tender ties between *khwajasara* and *hijra* histories to think across partitions of thought and space, while Pamment's detailed ethnographies breathe life into the rich contradictions of *khwajasara* in an Islamic missionary movement, the Tablighi Jamaat. Qureshi, Mehboob, and Afzal combine the demands of aesthetic forms with the exigencies of virtual/visual desire, asking us yet again to think Pakistan outside the mandates of social and/or political realism. One challenge of curating a *mehfil* such as this one is that there will always be guests who rupture the space of invitation. For Reddy and Redding, the uneven burdens of territorial occupation and collective organizing make Pakistan a place forever in abeyance. Racial violence, territorial dispossession, affective estrangement often render gay/trans subjects visible at the very moment of their erasure.

There is of course much more to say here about the singular ambition of this raucous, multilingual, multimedia *mehfil* whose invitation to gather otherwise and elsewhere remains generatively opaque. Simply put, *Pakistan Desires* gives us more provocation than prescription, more content than category, folding us into archives and histories of writerly possibility. Desire here is method, inward to the imaginary territories of Pak\*stan, and outward to the global reaches of its material geographies. For just as no map can be full of straight lines and planes, no *mehfil* can convene without circling back to the unmet and unfinished possibilities of all who gather.

NOTES

1   Multiple genealogies of the *mehfil* can be traced across periods, fields, and geographies. For an etymology, see Edward Lane's excerpt in *An Arabic-English Lexicon* (1863). A select sampling of readings around the *mehfil* as a place of gathering, from courtesans in Mughal courts to urban music halls in colonial Bombay, are Katherine Brown (2006), Tejaswani Niranjana (2019), and Daniel Majchrowicz (2020). I thank Geeta Patel, Amina Mulla, and Shiraz Ansari for their assistance on the rich histories of the term.

2   For more on my meditations on the Lahore Conference, see Arondekar (2020).

## REFERENCES

Arondekar, Anjali. 2020. "The Sex of History, or Object/Matters." *History Workshop Journal.* Spring: 1–7.

Brown, Katherine. 2006. "If Music Be the Food of Love: Masculinity and Eroticism in the Mughal 'Mehfil.'" In *Love in South Asia: A Cultural History,* edited by Francesca Orsini, 61–86. Cambridge: Cambridge University Press.

Lane, Edward. 1863. *An Arabic-English Lexicon.* London: Williams and Norgate. http://www.perseus.tufts.edu/hopper/text?doc=Perseus%3Atext%3A2002.02.00 20%3Aroot%3DHfl%3Aentry%3DHf%7Eluh. Accessed AU: INSERT DATE.

Majchrowicz, Daniel. 2020. "Malika Begum's *Mehfil:* The Lost Legacy of Women's Travel Writing in Urdu." *South Asia: Journal of South Asian Studies* 43, no. 5: 860–78.

Niranjana, Tejaswani. 2019. "Mehfil (Performance): The Spaces of Music." In *Musicophilia in Mumbai: Performing Subjects and the Metropolitan Unconscious.* Durham, NC: Duke University Press, 2019.

*Contributors*

AHMED AFZAL is an associate professor of anthropology and collaborating faculty in the Department of Asian American Studies at California State University, Fullerton. Afzal has taught at Colgate University, State University of New York at Purchase, and California State University, Stanislaus. Afzal's research focuses on globalization, urbanism, and everyday life; gender and sexuality; anthropology of mass and digital media; transnational communities; South Asian Americans and Muslim Americans; and new immigrant experiences with special emphasis on the United States and contemporary Pakistan. He is the author of *Lone Star Muslims: Transnational Lives and the South Asian Experience in Texas.*

ASAD ALVI is a PhD student in comparative literature at the University of Texas at Austin. They read and write on the intersections of gender and sexuality studies, translation theory, Urdu and Sindhi languages, and Islam. Their work has appeared in the international translation(s) journal *Words beyond Borders* and in *We Will Be Shelter: An Anthology of Contemporary Feminist Poetry, Uprooted: An Anthology of Gender and Illness,* and *The World That Belongs to Us: An Anthology of Queer Poetry from South Asia.* In 2016, Alvi became the youngest recipient of the Nasrin Bhatti Poetry Prize.

ANJALI ARONDEKAR is a professor of feminist studies and the founding codirector of the Center for South Asian Studies at the University of

California, Santa Cruz. Her research engages the poetics and politics of sexuality, colonialism, and historiography, with a focus on South Asia and the broader Indian Ocean world. She is coeditor (with Geeta Patel) of *Area Impossible: The Geopolitics of Queer Studies*, and the author of two monographs: *For the Record: On Sexuality and the Colonial Archive in India* and *Abundance: Sexuality's History*.

VANJA HAMZIĆ is a reader in law, history, and anthropology at SOAS University of London and a former residential member at the Institute for Advanced Study at Princeton. His work seeks to shed new light on how gender-nonconforming communities have braved the turbulent tides of colonialism, slavery, and other forms of oppression and how, in turn, they have developed and abided by multiple formations of insurrectionary knowledge. He is coauthor, with Ziba Mir-Hosseini, of *Control and Sexuality: The Revival of Zina Laws in Muslim Contexts* and author of *Sexual and Gender Diversity in the Muslim World: History, Law, and Vernacular Knowledge*.

OMAR KASMANI is a postdoctoral research associate in cultural anthropology at the Collaborative Research Center 1171 *Affective Societies* at Freie Universität, Berlin. His work is situated across the study of contemporary Islamic life-worlds and queer and affect theory, and queries critical notions of intimacy and postmigrant be/longing. He is the author of *Queer Companions: Religion, Public Intimacy, and Saintly Affects in Pakistan*. His new book project brings personal memoir to bear on an affective geography of postmigrant Berlin.

PASHA M. KHAN is an associate professor and chair in Urdu language and culture at the Institute of Islamic Studies at McGill University in Montreal. He is interested in the narrative *qissah* genre and storytelling in languages such as Urdu-Hindi, Punjabi, and Persian, as well as South Asian literature more broadly. He is the author of *The Broken Spell: Indian Storytelling and the Romance Genre in Persian and Urdu*, among other writings. He is also the creator of two online digital archives: the N. M. Rashed Archive, showcasing McGill University's collection of documents formerly in the possession of the Urdu poet Noon Meem Rashed; and the Saathi Montreal Archive, making available documents and photographs from the collection of the Saathis, a queer South Asian group active in Montreal during the 1990s.

GWENDOLYN S. KIRK is the South and Southeast Asian Librarian at Indiana University, Bloomington. She is a linguistic anthropologist whose research centers on Punjabi cinema, language ideologies, and popular culture in Pakistan. Her current book project addresses questions of language variety, aesthetics, film production, and performance and explores the theoretical flows and exchanges between linguistic anthropology, sociolinguistics, and cultural/cinematic/literary studies. Some of her other research projects have focused on semantics in performative genres of South Asian literature, on linkages between global politics and South Asian librarianship, and on the cinema and television of Pakistan.

SYEDA MOMINA MASOOD is a writer and currently a film and media studies PhD student at the University of Pittsburgh. Her research interests include South Asian cinemas, specifically Pakistani film and Indian film history, spectatorship and cinephilia, and queer Muslim womanhood. Her academic work has appeared and/or is forthcoming in *BioScope*, *Feminist Review*, and *Global Cult Cinemas*, and her essays have appeared in *minor literature[s]*, *Kohl*, *Halal If You Hear Me*, and *DAWN*, among others. She tweets at @momina711.

NIDA MEHBOOB is a photographer and filmmaker based in Lahore, Pakistan. Her documentary work has received several grants and fellowships, including the Magnum Foundation's Social Justice Grant. In 2020, she was selected for the Berlinale Talents and was artist-in-residence at the Academy of Arts, Berlin. She is interested in themes of social injustice, including religious and sexual persecution in Pakistan. Her most recent work is the photobook *A Survival Guide for Ahmadi Muslims of Pakistan*.

CLAIRE PAMMENT is an associate professor of world theater and gender, sexuality, and women's studies, and director of the Gender, Sexuality, and Women's Studies Program at William and Mary. She works in areas of Pakistani theater and performance, foregrounding practices marginalized at the intersections of class, gender, sexuality, and/or religion. Her collaborative work with *khwaja sira*-trans communities includes the devised theater *Teesri Dhun* and the short film *Vadhai*. She is the author of *Comic Performance in Pakistan: The Bhānd* and *Badhai: Hijra-Khwaja Sira-Trans Performances across Borders in South Asia*, collaboratively authored with Adnan Hossain and Jeff Roy.

GEETA PATEL is a professor at the University of Virginia. Her first book, *Lyrical Movements, Historical Hauntings*, explores the queer semiotics of Urdu modernism through the lyric, biography, and historical conditions of production of the poet Miraji. Her next book, *Risky Bodies and*

*Techno-Intimacy*, brings haphazard science to media, aesthetics, sexuality, and finance. She translates voraciously from a roster of languages. Her ongoing ventures include bacteria and genocide, pensions and poetics, physics and literary prose, and nationalism and promissory notes.

NAEL QURAISHI is an artist who lives and works between Rotterdam and Karachi. Having grown up in Pakistan and the United Kingdom, the roots of his practice lie within childhood recollections and memories of space and place. Working mainly with photo and video, Quraishi highlights the lasting effects of individual and collective experience of nostalgia, displacement, and (be)longing. His work has been shown internationally at the Nederlands Fotomuseum, Melkweg Expo Amsterdam, International Pakistan Art Festival, Belfast Exposed Gallery, Unseen Amsterdam, and EYE Film Institute. His graduation work, *The Empty Bench*, won second prize in the 2019 Zilveren Camera Prize for Storytelling.

ABDULLAH QURESHI is a Pakistani-born artist, educator, and cultural producer. Within his practice, he is interested in using painting and collaborative methodologies to address personal histories, traumatic pasts, and childhood memories. Through his ongoing doctoral project, "Mythological Migrations: Imagining Queer Muslim Utopias," he examines formations of queer identity and resistance in Muslim migratory contexts. Qureshi's work has been exhibited internationally and he has held numerous positions at cultural and educational institutions, including the British Council and the National College of Arts, Lahore. He is currently a doctoral candidate, supported by the Kone Foundation, at Aalto University in Finland.

SHAYAN RAJANI is a historian who teaches at LUMS University in Lahore, Pakistan. His research and teaching interests include Mughal history, the history of Sindh and Pakistan, and the study of gender and sexuality. His current book manuscript, *Leaving Legacies: Individual Becoming in Early Modern South Asia*, studies the rise of the individual as an object of concern in Mughal South Asia, and tracks the attendant transformations in family, state, and society. He also researches multilingual and visual retellings of early modern romances and their relationship to gender, sexuality, and the environment.

JEFFREY A. REDDING is a senior fellow at Melbourne Law School. He researches and teaches in the areas of comparative law and religion, Islamic law, legal pluralism, family law, and law and sexuality. He has lectured widely on these topics in North America, Europe, Australia, and

Pakistan, where he has also had the distinction of serving as the first out queer dean and professor of the Shaikh Ahmad Hassan School of Law at the Lahore University of Management Sciences. Jeffrey is the author of *A Secular Need: Islamic Law and State Governance in Contemporary India* and coeditor of the recent groundbreaking collection *Queer and Religious Alliances in Family Law Politics and Beyond*.

GAYATRI REDDY is an associate professor of gender and women's studies and anthropology at the University of Illinois, Chicago. Her research lies at the intersections of sexuality, gender, race, and the politics of subject-formation in India. She is the author of *With Respect to Sex*, an ethnography that problematizes contemporary representations of *hijras*. Her more recent work focuses on the afterlives of "African" (Siddi) migration to India. It explores how Blackness, masculinity, and Muslimness are constituted as intersecting social and political categories, with enduring effects on the lives of Siddis and on contemporary politics of race, citizenship, and religion in India.

SYMA TARIQ is a writer, researcher, and sonic practitioner. Her doctoral research, completed at the Centre for Creative Research into Sound Arts Practice, University of the Arts London, approaches the 1947 Partition as a sonic condition, investigating its discursive and temporal separations through archival modes of knowledge production after colonial erasure. Syma has initiated several collaborative audio projects for artistic contexts, namely, *A Thousand Channels* (Ancestors/Colomboscope), and has contributed to several platforms and publications, including *The Funambulist*, *Radio Al-Hara*, *Vancouver Queer Arts Festival*, and *Listening across Disciplines ii*. She is an arts associate at the British School at Athens.

# Index

activism: decolonial, 50–51; HIV/AIDS, 184–85; human rights, 244; queer and trans, 3–4, 8, 17n6, 50–51, 102, 136–39, 142n12, 146–48, 151–52, 218–19, 229; religious reform and, 146–48, 151–52; rights-oriented, 8; visual arts and, 174–75; Western, 27. *See also* Transgender Persons (Protection of Rights) Act
*adab* (respect), 23–24, 30
*Adab-i latīf* (journal), 106–7
aesthetics: governance and, 104; literary realism and, 109–11; queer and trans, 146–47, 157–58; sacred, 6–7, 146–47, 157–58
affect, 8–10, 15–16; archives and, 11–12; digital, 189; history and, 7, 9–12, 31, 78–79, 121; imbrication and, 12; queerness and, 1–2, 5, 8, 13, 15–16, 35, 38, 78–79; religion and, 7–8; space and, 2–4, 14–16, 216–18, 253–54; subjectivity and, 216–18. *See also* desire; *mehfil*
Agar, Prince, 11–12, 49–62
*Agar's Tale* (*Qissah-i Agar Gul*), 49–62, 62n1
Age of Beloveds, 37–38, 43–44
agency, 66, 73–74, 78–79, 96, 141, 146–47, 149–50, 159, 237

*aghāwāt* (castrated individuals), 130–31, 142n9
Ahlm, Jody, 192–93
Ahmed, Manan, 103–4
Akbar, King, 33, 45n9
Akhlaq, Zahoor ul, 175
Akhtar, Aasim, 174–75, 181
Al-Hamra Cultural Center (Lahore), 94–95
Albury, Kath, 189
Ali, Asad, and Kamran Asdar Ali, *Peoples Histories of Pakistan*, 16–17
Ali, Kamran, 65–66, 78–79
Alien Land Act (US), 222–23
Amin, Kadji, 7, 51
*amrad* (beardless young male desired by older men), 52–57, 59, 62n2
Anand, Shaina, 87
ancestors. *See* history
Andrews, Walter. *See* Age of Beloveds
Ang, Ming Wei, 189–90
*Anjuman-e Punjāb* (Assembly of Punjab), 102
Ankit, Rakesh, 239
Apter, Emily, 108
Arabic, 26, 28, 32, 57–58, 105, 113, 132, 142n2, 157–58, 168–69, 251. *See also* language

archives, 9–12; affective, 11–12; body and, 90–91; colonialism and, 87, 90; construction of, 85–86; destruction of historical records after Partition, 83; family, 12; memory and, 84; politics of, 84–89, 91–92, 95, 110–11, 115n6, 134; queerness and, 12, 102, 114; realism and, 109–10; recuperation of what is forgotten, missing, or absent, 15–16, 85; silence and, 96; sonic, 84, 90–91; time and, 86–90; translation and, 114. *See also* history

area studies, 15–16, 216–17

Arondekar, Anjali, 7, 15–16, 105, 134, 168–69

art, art history, 8–9; queer frameworks within, 166–67, 174–75; South Asian traditions of, 175–78; Western references, 175–79

Ashura, 26, 30

Asia Pacific Transgender Network, 136

Asian Exclusion League, 222–23

Asiatic (or Racial) Barred Zone Act (US), 222–23

Asif, Manan Ahmed, 35

*astana* (Urdu: home, dwelling; Sufi: temple, threshold), 2–3

*asthana* (Sanskrit, act of standing), 2–3

Attar, Shaykh Fariduddin, *Tazkirat-ul Auliya*, 151–52

Aurangābādī, Sirāj, 50

Aurat (Women's) March, 8, 17n7

*Aurat Raj* (dir. Rangeela), 66, 75–78

Azad, Muhammad Hussain, 102

Azoulay, Ariella Aïsha, 87

Babur (Timurid king), 36–38, 40–41

Bada'uni, 'Abd al-Qadir, 131–32

Bahlul the Oceanic, Shaikh, 31–32, 38

Bakhtawar Khan, *Mir'āt al-'ālam*, 132–33

Bano, Iqbal, 12, 94–95

Barani, Żiya' al-Din, 131–32

*baṛhak* (shouted challenges and insults), 72–73

Basri, Rabea, 151–52

BBDO Worldwide (advertising agency), 136

Belcourt, Billy-Ray, 2

belonging, 16–17, 184–85; desire and, 14–15; digital intimacy and, 185–87, 194; gender nonconformity and, 125–26, 129–32, 134–36; language and, 28–30; nation and, 14–15; self and, 216–18; time and, 126–31. *See also* community; kinship

Benjamin, Walter, 111–13

Bhabha, Homi, 105–6

Bhasin, Kamla, 86

Bhatṛhārī (fifth-century BCE grammarian and philosopher), 113

*bhūl gayā* (Urdu: mislay, forget, misplace), 101–2, 110–11

Bhutto, Benazir, 237

Bhutto, Zulfikar Ali, 174–75

Bidil, Qadir Bakhsh, 39–40, 44, 46n33

Bikas, Muhammad Muhsin, 44

BJP, 94, 237

Black studies, 127–28, 140

Bobby, Almas, 147–49

body: as archive, 90–91; desire and, 28–29; digitally mediated, 189; discipline and, 33; failure and, 24–25; gender and, 14, 24–25, 33, 52–53, 67–69, 130–32; intimacy and, 17n5; language and, 23–25, 27–29; Muslimness and, 26; queerness and, 24–26; racialization of, 228–29; sacred and, 26–30, 33; sexualization of, 228–29; time and, 126–28, 138–41

borderlands. *See* space

boundaries. *See* space

Bray, Alan, 41–42

*bugga. See khwaja sira, khwajasara*

burqa, 24–25, 29, 73–74, 76–77

Butalia, Urvashi, 86

Butler, Judith, 67–69

Byron, Paul, 189

canon, canonicity, 5–6, 166–67, 181

capitalism, 198; multiculturalism and, 225–28, 230–31; productivity and, 126–27, 140–41

care, 13–14, 86, 155

Carillo, Hector, 194–95

catamites, 37–38

Chand, Abhai, 35, 39–40, 44. *See also* Hussain, Madho Lal; Sarmad

Chand, Karam, 39–40

Chang, Robert, 222

#ChangeTheClap (campaign), 136–38

Chatterjee, Indrani, 105

264  INDEX

*Chewing Gum* (dir. Angeline Malik), 65–66
Chicago, 14–15, 192–93, 216–21, 227–31, 231n2
Chicago Anti-Bashing Network, 229
Chishti, Nur Ahmad, *Tahqiqat-i Chishti*, 45n2. *See also* Hussain, Madho Lal
Choonara, Samina, 174–75
*Churails* (dir. Asim Abbasi), 65–66
citation, 4–5, 77–78
Citizenship Amendment Act (CCA, India), 94, 244
class, 10–12, 14–15; culture and, 223–28; gender and, 66, 69–70, 77–78, 136–37, 220; homosociality and, 55–56; immigration and, 223–25; language and, 23–24, 28–29; masculinity and, 13–14; normativity and, 226–31; queerness and, 23–24; race and, 221, 223–25, 229–31; sexuality and, 173–74, 220–21, 225–28; transformation and, 51
closet (trope), 43–44
colonialism: anticolonial resistance, 103–4; archives and, 87, 90; decolonialism, 17n6, 50, 127–28, 140–41, 173–74; dislocations of, 42; gender nonconformity and, 127, 133–34; geography and, 12; history and, 50, 83, 90, 97nn2–3, 111–12, 128–29; knowledge production and, 90, 133; laws criminalizing homosexuality, 1; Partition and, 83, 85, 90–91, 96; persuasions of the heart, 104; queerness and, 1, 167–68, 173–74; realism and, 109–11; space and, 12, 42, 88, 107; time and, 87–88, 127–29, 140–41; translation projects and, 102–10; universal pensions and, 104; violence and, 89. *See also* postcolonialism
communism, 7, 87–88, 93–94
community, 172–73, 184–85, 216–18, 228–31; community-based movements, 8, 13; desire and, 14–15, 220–21; digital, 13–14, 188, 191–92; time and, 13. *See also* belonging; kinship
consent, 58–59
conversion. *See* religion
corporeality. *See* body
cosmopolitanism, 13–15, 69, 187, 189–91, 194–95, 198, 217
Criminal Tribes Act, 50. *See also* Section 377

cross-dressing. *See* drag; *See also* gender
cruising, 168–69, 191–92. See also *musafir*
culture, 221–28

Da Vinci, Leonardo, *The Annunciation*, 178; *The Last Supper*, 175–78
Dafa, Monia, 90
Dara Shukoh, *The Mingling of Two Oceans*, 35
*dargah* (shrine), 26, 30
Dargah Quli Khan, *Muraqqaʻ-i Dihlī*, 134–35
Das, Veena, 86
dating apps. *See* Grindr
de Mel, Neloufer, 107–9
*desi*, 14–15, 216–31; ethnicity and, 232n12; queerness and, 227–28; US state regulations and, 221–22. *See also* culture; Nasim, Iftikhar (Ifti)
desire, 8–9, 13–14, 253; belonging and, 14–15; body and, 28–29; community and, 216–18, 220–21, 229–31; digital intimacy and, 185–87, 189–98; filmic, 11–12, 14, 18n10, 66–69, 78–79, 203–15; gender and, 49, 57, 59, 67–69, 78–79; heteronormativity and, 66; hierarchy and, 36–40; history and, 13–14, 31, 50, 60; intimacy, 173–74; in Islam, 17n5; language and, 23–24, 28–29; law and, 40–41, 53; from local perspectives, 7, 173–79, 181; morality and, 108–9; privacy and, 192–94; queerness and, 1–2, 5–7, 12–14, 50–53, 59, 62n6, 66; race and, 189–90, 220–21; refusal and, 13–14; across religions, 44; repression and, 14; reproduction and, 37–38; sacred and, 10–11, 26, 28, 39–40; shame and, 169–72; space and, 2–4, 9–10; in Sufism, 17n5; as taboo, 36–37, 39, 44; time and, 9–11, 140–41; visuality and, 13–14, 178–79; between women, 14, 26, 108–9, 112–13, 203–15. *See also* affect; eroticism
Devji, Faisal, 238
Dhawan, Nikita, 85, 96
diaspora, 12–15, 217–18, 221–22, 225, 232n12, 253–54. See also *desi*
difference, 35–36, 50, 69, 84, 92, 130–32, 137–38, 197, 217, 220, 224–25, 227–31, 232n12, 232n15

INDEX   265

digital, 13–14, 87, 157–58, 184, 187–92, 194–95, 198. *See also* Grindr; TikTok
disability, 241, 247n11
disciplinarity, 5, 7–10, 41, 86, 89–90, 188–90, 253–54; interdisciplinarity, 9–10, 16–17, 110
drag, 23–24, 51, 65–71, 73–75, 77–78, 218–20
Dubrow, Jennifer, 93
Duggan, Lisa, 219–20, 227–28, 231n4, 232n6
Dupatta, 23, 26–27, 29–30, 66–67, 75–76, 156–57
Dutta, Aniruddha, 126–27

ekphrasis, 109–10
El-Rouayheb Khaled, 50, 62n2
English, 2–5, 8–9, 13, 24, 28–29, 102–6, 113, 138–39, 186. *See also* language; translation
epigrams, 100–101
epistemology, epistemes, 2–7, 253; desire and, 51, 114, 187; history and, 84, 89; imperialism and, 89, 134; non-Western, 15–16; queerness and, 114, 168–69, 187
eroticism, 17n5, 37, 62n2; ethnicity and, 227; homoeroticism, 13–14, 167–68, 172–73, 175–77, 181, 194. *See also* desire; Saeed, Anwar
ethics: of difference, 35; gender and, 57–58; of listening, 89–90; of love, 10–11, 35–36, 44; piety and, 156–57; South Asian, 225–26. See also *jawānmardī*
ethnicity, 10–12, 14–15, 223–25, 232n12; gender and, 66, 69, 77–78. *See also* culture; *desi*; race

failure, 10–11, 23–25, 27–29, 106, 115n5, 252
Faiz, Faiz Ahmed, *Hum Dekhenge* (We Shall Witness), 7, 12, 92–96
*fakir*. See *khwaja sira, khwajasara*
*fana'* (Sufi: annihilation), 6–7
Faridi, Khan Bahadur Fazalullah Lutfullah, 133
Farooq, Umar, 153
Faruqi, Shamsur Rahman, 53–54, 60–61
Fatimah, Bibi, 26, 30
Federation of Indians in America (FIA), 226
feminism, 8, 12, 66, 127–28; Islam and, 93; listening, 87–88; unmaking and, 5–7;

Ferguson, Roderick, 216–18, 225, 227–28, 232n9
film: censorship and, 71–72, 80n5; desire and, 14, 18n10, 66–69, 78–79, 203–15; film festivals, 8–9; gender and, 70–74, 77–79; interpretation and, 66; "Muslim Social," 75; performances and, 11–12; queerness and, 65–66; stock identity categories, 80n4; "temporary transvestite film," 67–69, 77–79
*fitnah* (sedition), 57
Foreign and Commonwealth Office (United Kingdom), 83
forgetting, 7, 12, 15–16, 101–2, 108–9. *See also* history
form: colonialism and, 87–88, 102–4, 111, 167–68; drag and, 69; fragments and, 53–54; gender and, 151–52, 157; geopolitics and, 3–4, 252; of knowing, 29; minoritized, 1–3; queerness and, 8–9, 252–54; social, 216–17, 221, 223–31; time and, 87–88, 91–92. *See also* performance; transformation
Forster, E. M., 107
Freeman, Elizabeth, 60, 126–27
future, futurity, 1–4, 7–11, 27–30, 38, 42, 95–96, 111–12, 126–28, 140–41, 181, 252. *See also* under time, temporality

Gay Pride, 218
gender: affirmation surgery, 71–72, 77–79, 80nn5–6; body and, 33, 52–53, 67–69, 130–31; class and, 13–14, 66, 69–70, 77–78, 136–37, 220; crossing, 11–12, 65–66, 73–74, 77–79; desire and, 49, 57, 59, 67–69, 78–79; ethnicity and, 66, 69, 77–78; failure of, 23–24; femininity and, 52, 56–57, 59, 70–71, 75–76; in film, 70–74, 77–78; fixity and, 53, 57–59; fluidity and, 56–58; history and, 86; home and, 58; identity and nonconformity, 5, 8, 11–12, 125–41, 142nn4–5, 146–51, 160nn2–3, 237, 241–46; intersectionality and, 11–12; Islam and, 62n4, 149–52, 157–59, 161n6; language and, 23–24, 66–70, 73, 75–78, 80n10; *maẓlūm aurat* (oppressed woman), 78–79; masculinity and, 13–14, 33, 38, 49–52, 57–59, 62n4, 67–69, 72–77, 189–90; nation and, 73, 75, 243–44;

266  INDEX

normativity, 78–79; performance and, 57–58, 65–70, 73–79, 127, 136–37, 148–59, 220; power and, 77; queerness and, 78–79, 220; religion and, 7, 247n1; sacred and, 10–11, 26–27; space and, 69, 237–38; subjectivity and, 126–38, 141; time and, 140–41, 142nn4–5; transformation and, 51–52, 54–55, 59, 67–69, 71–77; transgressing, 36, 65–67; violence and, 58–59, 66, 70–71, 76–77; women's intimacy and, 26, 29; voice and, 14, 18n9. See also *khwaja sira, khwajasara*; queer, queerness; trans, transgender
Genet, Jean, 174–75
geography. *See* space
geopolitics: affect and, 3–4; form and, 2–4; queerness and, 4–5, 15–16, 229, 232n15, 251–53
Ghalib, 13, 121
*gham* (Urdu: sadness), 13
Global South, 3–5, 12
Gopinath, Gayatri, 2, 66
governmentality, 55–56, 103–5, 107, 110–11, 230–31
Gramsci, Antonio, 104
Grant, Charles, 104
Grindr (app), 13–14, 184–88, 190–91, 197–98; hypersexualized masculinity and, 189; negotiating invisibility with, 194–97; in non-Western countries, 189–90; sex-seeking and, 191–94; stigma and, 192–93
*gurdwara* (Sikh place of worship), 91–92
*guru* (teacher), *guru-chela* (teacher-disciple) lineages, 129–30, 136, 146–57, 159, 160n3

HadžiMuhamedović, Safet, 127
hagiography. *See tazkira*
Hajviri, Syed Ali, 31–32, 38
Hali, Altaf Husain, 103–9, 113, 115n3
Hallaj, Mansur al-, 40–41, 46n34, 93
*Halqa e arbāb e zauq* (circle of men of taste), 106–7
*hamd* (praise of God), 60–61
*hamdardī* (sharing pain), 12
Hamzić, Vanja, 17n5, 127
Hart-Celler Immigration Act (US), 223
Hartman, Saidiya, 59

Hashmi, Salima, 174–75
Hassan, Wail S., 104–5, 108
health initiatives, 8, 184–85, 189–90, 199n3. *See also* HIV/AIDS
hegemony, 104, 111, 126–27, 135–37
Hermosa-Bosano, Carlos, 190
heteronormativity. *See* normativity
heterosociality. *See* sociality
hijras (hijṛā), 50, 62n3, 79n1, 126–29, 133–35, 141, 151–52, 159, 160n3, 220, 232n5. See also *khwaja sira, khwajasara*
Hinchy, Jessica, 132–33
Hinduism, 35, 159, 232n13, 237, 239, 244–45. *See also* religion
history: affect and, 7, 9–12, 15–16, 31, 121; ancestors and, 49–50, 61–62, 126, 134, 141, 173–74; colonialism and, 41–42, 111–12, 128–29; counterfactuals and, 61–62; desire and, 9–10, 13–14, 31, 50, 60; destruction of records, 83–85, 90, 97n2; distemporalization and, 127–28, 135, 141; event and, 95; future and, 111–12; gender and, 86; genre and, 60; imaginative verbal art and, 50; listening and, 86, 90–91; memory and, 13, 84–86, 102; microhistory, 14–15; nation and, 16–17; oral history, 87–89, 96; past and, 31, 41–44, 46n36, 50, 59, 60, 105, 127–30, 181, 252; periodization and, 10–11, 41–42, 44; politics of, 91–92, 94–95; possibility and, 60–61; public, 12; queerness and, 2–5, 7, 11–12, 14–15, 23–24, 42–44, 50, 60, 101–2, 105, 108, 113–14; recuperation and, 15–16, 50, 86, 102; silence and, 96; space and, 2–4, 9–10; time and, 87–89; translation and, 101–2, 110–13; transness and, 42–44, 60. *See also* time, temporality
HIV/AIDS, 8, 184–85
Hoffmann, Anette, 90
Holi (Hindu festival of colors), 34
Holroyd, Colonel, 102
home, 1–2, 12, 25, 58, 101, 107, 118–20, 160n3
homoeroticism. *See* eroticism
homosociality. *See* sociality
*How I Like It* (documentary film), 14
Hudood (Sharia-inspired religious laws), 93
*humjins-parast* (same-sex worshipper), 167–69

Huraira, Abu, 154–56
Hussain, Madho Lal, 31–36, 38–44, 45n2, 167–68

identity, 8–9, 13–16; time and, 125–17
Igwe, Onkyeka, 90–91
*īhām* (allusion), *īhām-i musāwāt* (bivalence of meaning), 60–61
immigration, 190, 194–95; class and, 222–25; to US, 185, 187, 196–97, 218, 222–27
index, indexicality, 77–78, 87, 96, 146–47, 224
interdisciplinarity. *See* disciplinarity
internet. *See* digital
intersectionality, 8–12, 16–17, 86, 140–41, 167, 172–73, 217, 221
intersex, 79n1, 130, 132, 160n2, 167–68, 241–42. *See also* trans, transgender
intimacy, 8–14, 17n5, 67–69, 91–92; digital, 13–14, 185–87, 194, 198; between men, 14, 173–75, 179, 185–87, 194, 198; between women, 24–27, 29–30. *See also* affect; desire
*Ishq-i Haqiqi* (True Love of the Divine). *See* love
*Ishq-i Majazi* (Metaphorical Love). *See* love
Islam: body and, 26; circumambulation and, 38; desire and, 17n5, 40–41, 53; deviance and, 17n4; feminism and, 93; gender and, 62n4, 93, 149–52, 157–59, 161n6; *khwaja sira* and, 13, 126, 128–31, 141, 146–48, 150–59; piety and, 149–59; plurality and, 3–4; poetry and, 103; queerness and, 5–6, 17n2, 26, 159, 191, 197–98. *See also* religion; sacred; Sufism

Jahangir, Emperor, 132, 175–78
Jameel, Maulana Tariq, 150–55, 157
Jameel, Mehlab, 146–47
*Jano Kapatti* (dir. Naseem Hyder Shah), 66, 70–74, 77–79, 80n5
Jatt, Maula, 157–58
*jawānmardī* (youngmanliness, knightly ethical code), 57–58
Jehan, Melody Queen Noor, 65–66
Joseph, Miranda, 230–31
Josh Malihabadi, 13, 121
Joshi, Virendra, 218
Junagadh, 239–40, 247n5
Juzjani, Minhaj al-Siraj, 132

Kalpaklı, Mehmet. *See* Age of Beloveds
*kashf* (Sufi: inner knowledge), 6–7
Kashmir, 14–15, 236–40, 243–44, 246
Kasmani, Omar, 127–28, 137–38, 159
Kaur, Ravinder, 85–86, 91
Keeling, Kara, 140
Keenan, Bernard, 95
*khadra*. *See khwaja sira, khwajasara*
Khaleeli, Bee, 51
Khan, Darakhshan, 149–52
Khan, Faris, 135–36
Khan, Omar Ali, 73–74
Khan, Yasmin, 85
Khawaja Sira Society, 138–39
Khubchandani, Kareem, 230–31, 233n18
*khusra* (Punjabi). *See khwaja sira, khwajasara*
Khusro, Amir, 147–49, 152–53
*khwaja sira, khwajasara* (*khwājasarā'*), 79n1, 142n3, 142n5, 160n1, 160n3, 220; in film, 65–66, 73–74; in history, 125–35, 151–52, 161n7, 161n10; politics and, 8, 135–39, 141, 142n12, 153, 155–56, 160n2, 161n7, 232n5, 241–43; religion and, 13, 18n11, 146–59, 161n6, 253–54; time and, 13, 126–30, 138–39, 141, 253–54. *See also* hijras; trans, transgender
Kidwai, Saleem, 50
Kilito, Abdelfattah, 105
Kim, Claire, 223–24
Kinnar Akhada (Hindu religious order), 159
kinship, 11–13, 51, 55–56, 58–59; *khwaja sira* and, 125–26, 131–32, 146–49, 160nn2–3; translation and, 107–19. *See also* belonging; community
knowledge, knowledge production, 4–5, 16–17, 84; colonialism and, 90, 133; epistephilia, 109–11; religion and, 6–7; unknowing, 29. *See also* translation
Kugle, Scott, 17n5, 50, 167–68
Kumar, Kishore, 169

Lahore Biennale, 181
Lane, Cathy, 89–90
language, 1, 11–12, 121; affect and, 15–16; allusion and, 60–61; belonging and, 28–30; bilingualism, 13; body and,

23–25, 27–29; class and, 23–24, 28–29; desire and, 23–24, 28–29; gender and, 66–70, 73, 75–78, 80n10; geography and, 2–3, 28–29; legibility and, 24–25; nation and, 25; queerness and, 5, 27, 29; time and, 125–26; translation and, 101–2, 105–6, 108, 110–11, 113–14; unmaking and, 5–6

law: colonial, 1, 50, 103–4; criminalizing homosexuality, 1, 50; gender and, 72–73, 137–38, 182n4, 241–43; immigration, 222–23; and LGBTQIA*+ rights, 8, 137–38, 182n4, 241–43; morality and, 40–41; religion and, 40–41, 45n9, 53, 93–94, 97n5; sovereignty and, 103–4

Lebow, Alisa, 109–10

*lehaz* (regard, consideration of social norms), 23–24, 30

Leonard, Karen, 225–26

LGBTQIA*+, 167–68, 253; in Pakistan, 8, 146–47, 159, 171–74, 184–85, 194; as transnational, 8, 13, 196–97. *See also* queer

listening, 4–5, 89–90; counter-listening, 85, 89, 91, 95–96; critical proximity and, 90–91; diasporic, 12; with difference, 84, 92; labor of, 84, 86–88; silence and, 96

local. *See* space

location. *See* space

loneliness, 13–14, 27–28, 171–72, 184–85

love, 46n22, 46n28, 46nn30–31; ethics of, 10–11, 34–36; *Ishq-i Haqiqi* (True Love of the Divine), 39–40, 42–43; *Ishq-i Majazi* (Metaphorical Love), 39–40, 42–43; queer, 2, 5–7, 10–11, 13–14, 33–44, 62n2, 169–71, 181; translation and, 108–13; between women, 18n9, 24–30, 108–13. *See also* affect; desire

Love, Heather, 13, 121

Lowe, Lisa, 135

*maftūn* (disorder), 57

Mahmood, Saba, 149–50, 159

Mahmud of Ghazna, Sultan, 167–68

Mahmud, Shaikh, *Haqiqat al-Fuqara*, 45n2

*majlis* (gathering), 26, 30

*malamati* (Path of the Blameworthy), 32

*Man to Man* (dir. Abir Sengupta), 80n6

Manch, Jana Natya, *Hum Bharat Ke Log* (We the People), 92–93

marginality, 4–5, 8–9, 50, 79n1, 172–73, 222, 245

Masood, Syeda Momina, 1, 73–74

Masud, Muhammad Khalid, 151–52

Mbembe, Achille, 88, 95, 140

Meeno Ji (Meta Messenger application), 136–38

Mehak Malik, 156–59, 161n10

*mehfil* (assembly, celebration, forum), 2–4, 9–10, 16–17, 251–54, 254n1

Melucci, Alberto, 230–31

memory, 13, 121; events and, 95; history and, 84–86; public, 94; time and, 88

Menon, Madhavi, 83–84, 90, 94

Menon, Ritu, 86

Merguerian, Gayane Karen, 53–54

metaphor, 39–40, 93, 103, 111, 113–14, 178–79, 251–52

Metcalf, Barbara D., 149–50

Mikdashi, Maya, 166–67

*milaad* (gathering, collective prayers, recitations), 26, 30

mimesis. *See* realism

minorities, minoritization, 2–3, 8, 15–16, 97n1, 190, 227–29; model minority, 221–24

Mīrābāī, 113–14

miracles, 26, 30, 40–41

Miraji (Sana Ullah Daar), 12, 100–102, 106–14; *Mashriq o Maghrib ke Naghmen* (Songs from the East and the West), 100–102

Mirza, Sultan Mahmud (Timurid prince), 37–38

Mokhtar, Shehram, 75–77

montage, 101. *See also* film

*moorat*. *See* khwaja sira, khwajasara

Morgan, Lynn Marie, 50

Mountbatten, Lord, and Mountbatten Papers, 83, 92, 97n3

Muhammad, Pir Ghulam, 39–40

Muhammad, Pir Qazi, 39–40

Muñoz, José Esteban, 167–68

Murad, Waheed, 77–78

*murid* (spirit), 125–26, 129–30

*musafir* (traveler, guest, visitor, itinerant), 168–69

INDEX 269

*na't* (praise of the Prophet Muhammad), 60–61
Nāgī, Anīs, 107
Naim, C. M., 50, 62n2
Najmabadi, Afsaneh, 53–54
names, naming, 33–36, 38
Nanni, Giordano, 88
Naqvi, Akbar, 175
narrative: culture and, 227–28, 232n12, 232n15; desire and, 2, 65–66; history and, 12, 61, 84–88, 90, 94, 102; nation and, 16–17, 86; queerness and, 2–5, 11–12, 51, 59, 65–66, 78–79, 102, 146–52, 196–97, 217–18, 227–28; religion and, 39–41, 146–52; South Asian storytelling traditions, 175–78
Nasim, Iftikhar (Ifti), 14–15, 217–21, 227–31, 233n16; "Why Children Did Not Knock at My Door on Halloween This Year," 228–29; *Narmaan*, 6–7, 218
nation, nationalism, 14–15, 86; belonging and, 14–17, 135–36; borders and, 84, 97n1, 216–18, 222, 253–54; citizenship and, 135–36, 222–23, 226, 243–44; desire and, 2–4; gender and, 73, 75, 243–44; history and, 16–17; immigration and, 222–23; language and, 25; race and, 222–23, 228–29, 232n10; religion and, 94, 240, 244–45; sovereignty and, 236–37, 240, 243–44; space and, 14–15, 238–40, 245–46, 247n2, 247n7, 253–54; time and, 126–28; violence and, 83. *See also* colonialism
National Register of Citizens (NRC, India), 94, 244
NAZ (NGO), 172–73
Nazir, Musarrat, 66–67
*Neend* (dir. Hassan Tariq), 65–66
neoliberalism, 2, 126–27, 136–38
networks, networking, 8, 13, 39–40, 85–86, 126–27, 131–32; social networking apps, 184–98, 199n3
*nirban* (ritual emasculation), 130
normativity, 216–21, 226–31, 233n18; heteronormativity, 11–14, 44, 50–51, 53–54, 66, 74, 140–41, 151–52, 160n3, 161n6, 190, 196–98, 225–28, 231n4; homonormativity, 219–20, 227–30
Noudelmann, Francois, 107–8

Ong, Jonathan, 189–90
orality, 86–88. *See also* history
order: disorder, 57–58, 90, 94, 149–50, 247n11; gender and, 33, 56–58, 70–73, 149–50, 247n11; moral, 34–36, 41; social and political, 33–39, 56–58, 172–73, 224; time and, 94, 96

*paindu* (Punjabi: someone belonging from a village), 23, 30
Pakistan (Pak*stan), 1–5, 14–17, 216–18, 247nn2–3, 252–54; activism in, 7–8, 17n7, 50–51, 94, 102, 135–39, 142n12, 146–47, 160n1, 174–75, 181, 184–85, 218–19, 229, 244; arts and, 8–9, 174–75, 181; colonialism and, 167–68; desire and, 3–5, 8–9, 13, 17n6; film and, 65–66, 73–74, 78–79, 79n2, 80nn3–4; gender and, 5, 8–9, 13, 17nn6–7, 78–79; history and, 3–4; Kashmir and, 236–40, 243–44, 246; *khwaja sira* and, 125–30, 135–39, 141, 142n5, 142n13, 146–47, 160nn1–2; literary life of, 106–7; as minoritized form, 2–3, 15–16; nation and, 14–15, 244; Partition and, 12, 17n1, 35, 80n4, 83–85, 91–92, 97n1, 101, 236–39, 244–45, 247n7; preserving Hindu temples, 35; queerness and, 2–3, 5, 8–9, 13, 15–16, 17n6, 18n8, 166–69, 171–75, 181, 184–87, 190–91, 193–94, 197–98, 236, 239, 246, 251–54; space and, 14–15; trans movement and transgender rights in, 5, 8–9, 13, 17n6, 142n12, 146–47, 160nn1–2, 172–73, 237–38, 240–46, 247nn10–11
Pamment, Claire, 136–37
Partition, 12, 17n1, 35, 80n4, 83, 97n1, 101, 236–39, 244–45, 247n7; destruction of historical records, 83, 85, 90, 97nn2–3; as event, 85; listening with, 84; memorialization of, 84–92, 94; performative reparation and, 86; queer theory and, 84; as sonic condition, 84, 92–93, 95–96; time-spaces of, 87–90; universalism and, 84, 90
Partitioned Listening (PL001): "You Trust Your Memories?," 84–85, 89–92, 95–96
Partitioned Listening (PL002): "We Shall Witness," 92–96

270 INDEX

Partitioned Listening (PL003): "I Hear (Colonial) Voices," 96
Pashto, 78–79, 80n4, 182n1. *See also* language
Patel, Geeta, 7, 15–16
Penny, Tom, 189
performance, 13, 57–58, 127, 136–37, 148–59, 220. *See also* gender
Persian, 2–3, 9–10, 31–32, 35, 45n2, 49, 57–58, 60–61, 126, 132, 142n2, 160n1, 175–78. *See also* language
Petievich, Carla, 50, 62n2
Phillips, Rasheedah, 88, 95–96
place. *See* space
plurality, 2–4, 8–9, 129–30, 246
poetry, poetics, 13, 32, 60–61, 100–101; Islam and, 103; *necaral shairī* (natural verse), 103; queer history and, 101; realism and, 111; translation and, 102–3, 110
Portelli, Alessandro, 87–88
postcolonialism, 3–4, 42, 85, 90, 127–28, 140–41, 142n6, 237, 239–40. *See also* colonialism
power, 4–5, 8–9; desire and, 37–38; gender and, 52–53, 75–79, 237–38; hierarchies of, 35–38, 224, 233n16; inversion of, 36, 75–77; politics of, 55–56, 91–96, 104, 221, 224, 229–30, 233n16, 237–38
Prashad, Vijay, 223–24
pronouns, 29, 80n10, 157, 188
prophecy, 111–12
Puar, Jasbir K., 166–67, 228–29
Punjab, Punjabi, 11–12, 23–24, 28, 35, 42, 46n3, 66–79, 79n2, 80nn3–4, 102, 167–68, 190. *See also* language

Qalandar, Lal Shahbaz (Red-Ruby Falcon, Usman of Marwand), 32–36, 45n13
Qasim, Muhammad bin, 35
*Qayamat* (Islamic day of reckoning), 93
*qissah* (tale of possibility), 11–12, 49–51, 53–55, 60–62; *barā'at-i istihlāl* (poetic device), 61. See also *Agar's Tale (Qissah-i Agar Gul)*
queer, queerness, 2, 4–6, 8–9, 15–16; affect and, 5, 13, 15–16; agency and, 73–74; archives and, 12, 102, 114; belonging and, 172–73, 184–85, 216–18, 229–31; body and, 26; class and, 23–24; colonialism and, 50, 167–68; deidealizing, 50–51, 59; desire and, 2, 5–7, 12–14, 18n9, 50–53, 59, 62n2, 66, 253; discipline and, 16–17; everyday life and, 3–4, 44; failure and, 10–11; fluidity and, 169, 239–40; foreignness and, 169, 173–75; gender and, 11–12, 18n9, 78–79; history and, 2–5, 7, 11–12, 14–15, 23–24, 42–44, 50, 60, 101–2, 105, 108, 113–14; idealizing, 167–68; Islam and, 5–6, 17n2, 26, 159, 191, 197–98; language and, 5, 23–24, 27, 29; from local perspectives, 65–66, 173–79, 181; normativity and, 216–20; refusal and, 10–11; religion and, 5–7, 13–14, 17n2, 18n11, 159; social networking apps and, 187, 189–98; space and, 2–6, 8–9, 14–17, 166–67, 181, 246, 252, 253–54; thinking, 1, 5, 8, 15–16; time and, 3–4, 7–9, 27–29, 52, 140–41, 252; translation and, 110–11. *See also* trans, transgender
queer studies, queer theory, 4–5, 15–16, 127–28; different contexts for, 166–67; interdisciplinarity and, 16–17; Partition and, 84; South Asian Studies and, 18n8; universalism and, 84
Quran, 26, 29, 31–32, 40, 93, 154–58; *Quran Khawani* (recitation of the Quran), 29–30

race, racialization, 14–15; belonging and, 216–18; body and, 228–29; class and, 221, 223–25, 229–31; culture and, 221, 223–28; desire and, 189–90, 220–21; nation and, 222–23, 228–29, 232n10; normativity and, 216–21, 226–31, 233n18; sexuality and, 216–18, 221, 225–29; transness and, 50; whiteness and, 222–23. *See also* ethnicity
Radhakrishnan, Rajagopalan, 225
Rahi, Sultan, 77–78
Rahman, Tariq, 50, 62n2
Rai, Amit, 228–29
Rajani, Shahana, 91–92
Rana, Bindiya, 126, 128–30, 135–36
Rana, Neeli, 130, 136–39, 141
*Rangeela aur Munawar Zareef* (dir. Nazar Shabab), 73–74
rape, 51, 58–59, 70–71, 76–77, 138–39, 193–94. *See also* violence

Raustiala, Kal, 238
Raza, Ali, 3–4
reading, 4–5; close, 108; fragmentary, 53–54
realism, 109–11, 113
refusal, 10–11, 13–14, 38
Rehman, Hadi, 166–67
Rehman, I. A., 174–75
religion: affect and, 7; citizenship and, 94; conversion and, 34, 36, 44, 45n11, 45n13, 247n1; desire and, 40–41, 44; gender and, 7, 247n1; *khwaja sira* and, 146–49, 151–57; law and, 103–4; miracles and, 40–41; nation and, 240, 244–45; piety and, 146–59; queerness and, 5–7, 13–14, 17n2, 18n11, 159; sexuality and, 169–72, 191; transformation and, 34–35. *See also* Islam; sacred
representation, 60, 92, 137, 239–40; queer, 8–9, 13–14, 65–66, 72–74, 146–47, 166–67, 175, 189, 227, 233n16, 251, 253; speech and, 89; visual, 13–14, 175–78
repression, 8, 14, 96, 146–47, 174–75, 178–79
reproduction, reproductive imperative, 37–38, 42, 51, 54–55, 59, 61–62, 150–51
resistance, 8–9, 13–14, 16–17, 65–66, 87–88, 90–91, 94, 108–9, 134–37, 141, 149–50, 155–56, 159, 167–68, 230–31, 233n18, 236. *See also* activism
respectability, 23–24, 125–29, 136–37, 142n3, 153–55, 192–93, 219–20
*Return of the Native* (exhibition), 169–72
revolution, 27–28, 93, 253
rights, rights movements, 1, 5, 8–9, 13, 17n6, 137–38, 142n12, 146–49, 153, 159, 160nn1–2, 161n7, 172–73, 182n4, 237–38, 240–46, 247nn10–11. *See also* activism; Transgender Persons (Protection of Rights) Act
Rizvi, Fazal, 95–96
Rofel, Lisa, 2
Roy, Raina, 126–27
Rudrappa, Sharmila, 225–26

Saadullah, 31–32, 38. *See also* Hussain, Madho Lal
*Sacha Jhoota* (dir. Zafar Shabab, 1974), 73–74
sacred: body and, 26–30; desire and, 26–30, 39–40; failure and, 27; gender and, 26–27; law and, 40–41; queerness and, 6–7, 10–11, 13–14; transness and, 13, 18n11. *See also* religion
Saeed, Anwar, 13–14, 166–67, 173–78, 181; *Birds Flying against Window*, 178–79; *A Book of Imaginary Companions*, 175; near-death experience, 175; *Other Ways of Love*, 169–72; *Our Lady of the Unfulfilled Desires*, 178; *The Punishment Orders*, 175–78
Saffar in Islamabad (NGO), 153–56
*Saheli* (dir. S. M. Yousaf), 65–66
Said, Ahmad, 66–67, 79n2, 80n3
Sangat (South Asian gay organization in Chicago), 217–21
Sappho, 12, 100–2, 108–14. *See also* Miraji
Saraiva, Santos, 190
Sarmad, 40–41, 44, 46n34, 47n41. *See also* Hussain, Madho Lal
Section 377 (Penal Code, Pakistan), 50, 172–73
Sevea, Iqbal, 72–73
sex work, 129, 134–35
sexuality, 7–10; belonging and, 14–15, 216–18, 251–52; body and, 228–29; class and, 173–74, 220–21, 225–28; colonialism and, 1, 50, 129; cosmopolitan identity and, 194–95, 197–98; culture and, 225–28; desire and, 13–14, 37–38, 169–75; digital intimacy and, 187, 189–98; gender and, 11–14, 53, 55, 65–69, 73–74, 78–79, 127–28, 189, 220; history and, 5; migration and, 196–97; normativity and, 216–18, 221, 226–31, 233n18; race and, 216–18, 221, 225–29; religion and, 10–11, 13–14, 149–51, 169–72; in South Asia, 15–17, 17nn5–6, 62n2, 129, 131–35, 140–41, 141n1, 166–68, 184–86; time and, 140–41; visibility and, 173–74, 194–97, 226–31. *See also* queer, queerness
Shah, Abbas, 175–78
Shaheen Bagh, 94
*sharafat* (respectability), 126–27, 129
Shelley, Mary, *Frankenstein*, 60
Shield, Andrew DJ, 188, 190
Shīrānī, Akhtar, 113
Sid, Kami, 136–37
Sikandar b. Muḥammad, *Mirʾāt-i-Sikandarī*, 131–32

silence, 191; historical, 84; representation and, 89; speakability and, 94, 96; women's, 14, 28–29
Sindh, Sindhi, 35, 39–40, 44, 45n1, 80n4, 182n1, 190, 245. *See also* language
social networking, 13–14, 185–98. *See also* Grindr
sociality, 126–27; digital, 13–14; heterosociality, 55; homosociality, 11–12, 55–56, 65–66; public space and, 14
solidarity, 126–27, 229, 236–37
sound, sound arts, 12, 89–90; archive and, 91–92; fragments and, 92–93, 95–96; Partition and, 84; politics of, 95; time-spaces of, 88–89, 95–96. *See also* listening
sound studies, 89–90
South Asian Lesbian and Gay Association (SALGA), 226, 232n13
sovereignty, 14–15
space: affect and, 15–16; archives and, 84, 87, 89; colonialism and, 12, 88, 107; desire and, 2–4, 9–10; diaspora and, 12; fixity and, 57–59; gender and, 69, 237–38; geography, 4–5, 9–10, 237–40, 245–46, 247n2, 247n7, 253–54; history and, 2–4, 9–10; language and, 28–29; of local, 16–17; location, 15–17; nation and, 14–15; place, 2–6, 8–10, 15–16, 216–18; public, 14; queerness and, 2–3, 5–6, 8–9, 14–17, 246, 252–54; of separation, 10–11; sound and, 84; territory, 2–3, 9–10; time and, 9–10
speech, speaking, 25, 84, 89, 94, 96
spirituality. *See* religion; sacred
Spivak, Gayatri, 106, 109
*stan (Persian: land or dominion), 2–4, 9–10, 15–16
state. *See* nation, nationalism
status, 2–3, 36, 111, 188, 190
*stehen* (German: to stand), 2–3
Stewart, Kathleen, 8–9
Straayer, Chris, 67–69, 78–79
subjects, subjectivity: affect and, 216–18; belonging and, 216–18, 220–21; desire and, 2; gender and, 126–38, 141; imperialism and, 89; neoliberalism and, 15–16; Partition and, 84; sacred and, 6–7; time and, 127–30, 137–41
Subramanium, Ajantha, 223–24

Sufism, 5–7, 10–11, 17nn4–5, 93, 151–52. *See also* Islam; *tazkiras*
*Syed Amjad Hussain Shah v. Ali Akash alias Asima Bibi and Five Others* (Lahore High Court), 241–43

*taʿzīr* (discretionary punishment for sex between males), 50
Tablighi Jamaʿat (Islamic missionary movement), 13, 146–59, 160n1, 161n6
*Taj Mahal* (dir. S. T. Zaidi), 73–74
*tali* (hollow clap), 136–37, 139
*talib* (Sufism), 2
*tauba* (repentance of performance), 148–51, 154–55
*tazkira* (biographical dictionary), 10–11, 31
territory. *See under* space
testimonies, 84–86, 96
Thind, Bhagat Singh, 222–23
thought, thinking, 1, 4–5, 8, 15–16
TikTok, 156–58
time, temporality, 1–2, 38; archives and, 84, 86–90, 95–96; body and, 126–28, 138–41; chrononormativity, 126–27, 136, 139; colonialism and, 87–88, 127–29, 140–41; community and, 126–31; desire and, 9–11, 140–41; distemporalization, 13, 127–28, 135–37, 140–41; future and, 1–4, 7–11, 27–30, 38, 42, 61–62, 95–96, 111–12, 126–28, 140–41, 252; gender nonconformity and, 125–30, 135–37, 140–41, 142nn4–5; history and, 87–89; identity and, 125–27; language and, 125–26; linearity and, 12; listening and, 12; nation-state and, 126–28, 135–36; orality and, 87–88; queerness and, 3–4, 7, 27–29, 52, 252; remembering and, 88; sexuality and, 140–41; sound and, 84, 95–96; space and, 9–10; subjectivity and, 127–30, 137–41; transness and, 13, 140–41; worlding and, 135–36, 140–41
Towle, Evan B., 50
trans, transgender: colonialism and, 127; detransitioning and, 13, 146–49; disability and, 241; gender and, 49–51, 73; gender-affirmation surgeries and, 71–72, 78–79, 80nn5–6; history and, 11–12, 42–44, 60; race and, 50; rights and, 8, 14–15, 17n6, 237, 240–46, 247nn10–11; sacred and, 13, 18n11; in

INDEX 273

trans, transgender (continued)
South Asia, 49–52, 62n3, 79n1, 126–27, 136–38, 151–52, 159, 160n2, 161n7; time and, 13, 125–27, 140–41; "transgender native," 50. See also *khwaja sira, khwajasara*
transformation: mutual, 34–36; religious, 34–35; trans-species, 51, 53
Transgender Persons (Protection of Rights) Act, 8, 142n13, 146–48, 154–56, 160nn1–3, 237, 241–43, 247n10
Transgender Remembrance Day, 155–56
translation, 4–6, 12, 25, 35, 100–101, 115n5; archives and, 114; belonging and, 106–7, 112–14; colonialism and, 102–10; as counter-teleologies, 105; failure and, 106; history and, 101–2, 110–13; kinship and, 107–9; queerness and, 110–11; *tarjumah* and, 105–6, 110, 115n4; untranslatables, 108–9
Trans Pride March, 135–36
trans studies, 127–28
trauma, 85–86
Tripathi, Laxmi Narayan, 159
Trottier, Daniel, 189–90
two-spirit, 50

United Nations (UN), 194, 239
universalism, 84, 86, 90, 126–27
Urdu, 2–3, 5–16, 23–24, 28–29, 45n2, 49, 60–62, 61n1, 66, 69–71, 77–79, 80nn3–4, 91–94, 100–106, 109–14, 167–69, 182n1, 186, 241, 251–53. *See also* language
*Urdu Feminist Writing* (Alvi, Chaudhry, Mehak, Kolb, Patel, and Shahbaz), 5–6

van Nieuwkerk, Karin, 150–51
Vanita, Ruth, 50
violence, 13–14; colonial, 85, 89; gender-based, 76–77; against queer community, 131–33, 136–30, 161n10, 172–73; state and, 83. *See also* rape
visual, 12–14, 67–69, 75, 89–90, 95–96, 173–80, 189
Voegelin, Salomé, 89–90, 92
voice, 5–6, 12, 14, 75–79, 85–86, 89–92, 96, 108, 111–13, 121, 137–38. *See also* listening; sound

wanderer, wandering, 100–101, 106–7. See also *musafir*
War of Independence (1857), 102–4
Waseem, Jawad, 154–55
Weiss, Kevin M., 189–90
wildness, 24–25
Wittgenstein, Ludwig, 104
Women's March. See *Aurat March*
*Words without Borders* (periodical), 5–6
writing, 186; body and, 29; failure and, 29; queerness and, 1, 8–9; translation and, 5–6, 12; unmaking, 5–6. *See also* languages; translation
Wu, Shangwei, 189–90

*Yakkey Wali* (dir. M. J. Rana), 66–69, 77–79, 80n3

Zaidi, Ali Mehdi, 173–74
Zareef, Munawar, 70–71, 73–74, 78–79
Zaynab (the Prophet's granddaughter), 26, 28, 30
Zia ul Haq, Muhammad, 93, 174–75, 178–79
*Zibahkhana* (dir. Omar Ali Khan), 73–74